Locating Translingualism

Encounters involving different cultures and languages are increasingly the norm in the era of globalization. While considerable attention has been paid to how languages and cultures transform in the era of globalization, their characteristic features prior to transformation are frequently taken for granted. This pioneering book argues that globalization offers an unprecedented opportunity to revisit fundamental assumptions about what distinguishes languages and cultures from each other in the first place. It takes the case of global Korea, showing how the notion of "culture" is both represented but also reinvented in public space, with examples from numerous sites across Korea and Koreatowns around the world. It is not merely about locating spaces where translingualism happens but also about exploring the various ways in which linguistic and cultural difference come to be located via translingualism. It will appeal to anyone interested in the globalization of language and culture.

JERRY WON LEE is an Associate Professor at the University of California, Irvine. He is author of *The Politics of Translingualism* (Routledge, 2018), co-editor of *Translinguistics* (Routledge, 2019), and editor of *The Sociolinguistics of Global Asias* (Routledge, 2022).

KEY TOPICS IN APPLIED LINGUISTICS

Series Editors

Claire Kramsch (University of California, Berkeley) and Zhu Hua (Birkbeck College, London)

Books in this series provide critical accounts of the most important topics in applied linguistics, conceptualized as an interdisciplinary field of research and practice dealing with practical problems of language and communication. Some topics have been the subject of applied linguistics for many years and will be re-examined in the light of new developments in the field; others are issues of growing importance that have not so far been given a sustained treatment. The topics of the series are nuanced and specialized, providing an opportunity for further reading around a particular concept. The concept examined may be theoretical or practice oriented. Written by leading experts, the books in the series can be used on courses and in seminars, or as succinct guides to a particular topic for individual students and researchers.

Locating Translingualism

JERRY WON LEE
University of California, Irvine

CAMBRIDGE
UNIVERSITY PRESS

University Printing House, Cambridge CB2 8BS, United Kingdom

One Liberty Plaza, 20th Floor, New York, NY 10006, USA

477 Williamstown Road, Port Melbourne, VIC 3207, Australia

314–321, 3rd Floor, Plot 3, Splendor Forum, Jasola District Centre, New Delhi – 110025, India

103 Penang Road, #05–06/07, Visioncrest Commercial, Singapore 238467

Cambridge University Press is part of the University of Cambridge.

It furthers the University's mission by disseminating knowledge in the pursuit of education, learning, and research at the highest international levels of excellence.

www.cambridge.org
Information on this title: www.cambridge.org/9781009100106
DOI: 10.1017/9781009105361

First published 2022

Printed in the United Kingdom by TJ Books Limited, Padstow Cornwall

A catalogue record for this publication is available from the British Library.

ISBN 978-1-009-10010-6 Hardback
ISBN 978-1-009-10869-0 Paperback

For 엄마 *and* 아빠

Contents

Figures

Acknowledgments

I start by expressing my gratitude to the Cambridge University Press team, including Becky Taylor, Izzie Collins, Chris Harrison, and Ruth Boyes. It has been a dream of mine to one day publish a book with Cambridge, and I am grateful to my editor Becky for believing in this project from the beginning stages and for her patience and guidance in seeing it through the end.

Thank you also to the Key Topics in Applied Linguistics series editors Claire Kramsch and Zhu Hua for their support of this project and for their wisdom and feedback that helped improve it along the way. Thank you also to the three anonymous reviewers who provided not only support but constructive criticism in the earlier stages.

Many conversations with David Gramling, who always pushes me with unmatched kindness and generosity, helped shape the thinking of this book. Daniel N. Silva helped me tremendously in outlining the theoretical stakes of the book – the amount of guidance he provided cannot be overstated. José M. Cortez listened on countless occasions as I talked through this project, and he has read many drafts of various parts of this book. Thinking with Jackie Jia Lou on our separate Chinatown project was also immensely helpful.

At the University of California, Irvine (UCI), I have received tremendous support from the Humanities Center, from the Center for Critical Korean Studies (CCKS), and the Center for Asian Studies (CAS). Having such a community of support makes it quite easy for me to do my research, especially for the kind of work that I do. Judy Tzu-Chun Wu and Amanda Jeanne Swain of the Humanities Center have been so supportive of my work and generous with their guidance. Julia Reinhard Lupton, who directed the Humanities Center when it was called Humanities Commons, deserves infinite gratitude for her support of earlier iterations of this project. The founding director of CCKS, Kyung Hyun Kim, has been unwaveringly supportive of my work and has created many opportunities for me. Also owed thanks are Erica Yun, Joo Hoon Sin, and current CCKS director Joe Jeon. CAS has also been consistently supportive of my work, and for that I owe much thanks to current CAS director Qitao Guo and former CAS director Vinayak Chaturvedi.

Many of my former and current graduate student colleagues at UCI helped me in various ways. I therefore would like to thank Monica Cho, Juan Carlos (JC) Fermin, (now Dr.) Chung-jae Lee, (now Dr.) Jasmine Lee, (now Dr.) Tian Li, Letizia Mariani, (now Dr.) Eun Young Seong, Ann Thuy-Ling Tran, and Jonas Weaver.

My staff colleagues at UCI, both in the Program in Global Languages & Communication and in the Department of English, including Jasmine Diaz, Michelle Hu, Camille Laws, DeeDee Nunez, and Veronica Portal all directly supported the completion of this project in many different ways. A special thank you is owed to Angeline Hernandez, who helped me decide on the cover image.

Also at UCI, Eleana Kim has been a tremendous mentor and supporter of my work. James Kyung-Jin Lee has provided much mentorship as well, along with support for this project in its earlier stages. Chris Fan has always been available as a sounding board for ideas. Long Bui has also been an especially inspiring and generous colleague. Daniel M. Gross and Jim Steintrager both encouraged me to finish this project, which was especially needed at a few moments when I was losing the energy to do so. Serk-Bae Suh has been a great mentor, colleague, interlocutor, and most importantly, friend, and I am thankful to him for keeping me centered.

Jeff Wasserstrom first introduced to me to the intellectual movement known as global Asias. After a conversation on campus in which he asked me what I was working on, the next day he left a copy of the spring 2015 inaugural issue of *Verge: Global Asias* outside my office door, encouraging me to check it out and to try publishing in it. I could not have known how great an impact this small gesture would have on my academic career.

On that note, I owe infinite thanks to Tina Chen Gouldie for taking a chance on my work and publishing it in *Verge* (see permissions below). This early but large vote of confidence in my project was and continues to be so meaningful to me. Beyond this, she continues to open so many doors for me and I am eternally grateful to her for showing far more faith in me and my work than I could on my own.

Julia Lee and Philip Broadbent provided much needed support as I finished this book. Julia kept me on track to finish by setting "hard" deadlines for our respective book projects that we both met (eventually). Philip, who speaks an English very much different from my own, was instrumental in informing me of what "casserole" means in the UK (see Chapter 3).

Finally, I thank my family for providing unending love, support, and patience. My son would periodically look over my shoulder as I was working on this book and declare "that's not a real word." My wife read through drafts of chapters and once remarked "this is actually interesting." I am pretty sure she was just humoring me, but I'll take it.

–

This work was supported by the Core University Program for Korean Studies through the Ministry of Education of the Republic of Korea and the Korean Studies Promotion Service of the Academy of Korean Studies (AKS-2016-OLU-2250005).

Small portions of Chapter 2 and Chapter 5 represent substantially revised portions of an article previously published as Jerry Won Lee (2017), Semioscapes, unbanality, and the reinvention of nationness: Global Korea as nation-space, *Verge: Studies in Global Asias*, 3(1), 107–136. *Verge* is published by the University of Minnesota Press. Copyright 2017 by the Department of Asian Studies, The Pennsylvania State University.

Chapter 3 represents a significantly reframed and revised version of a chapter previously published as Jerry Won Lee (2021), Translation, transliteration, and translingualization: On the possibilities of "Korea" in the linguistic landscape, in Irene Theodoropoulou and Johanna Tovar (eds.), *Research companion to language and country branding* (pp. 259–278), London: Routledge. Reproduced with permission of The Licensor through PLSclear.

Notes on the Text

A note on the transliteration: There exist three main systems of Romanization for Korean, or systems of transliteration into Roman alphabetic letters: McCune-Reischauer, Yale, and Revised Romanization. Of the three, I have found the Revised Romanization system to be the most logical, even though the Yale system is more commonly used within linguistics. Throughout this book, with the exception of the names for people as they are self-presented, places with commonly circulated transliterations, or direct quotations, I rely on a slightly modified version of Revised Romanization, using hyphenation to break up consonant clusters in order to facilitate reading. For instance, a word like *Hangeul* will be presented as *Han-geul* to guide readers who are unfamiliar with Korean (avoiding potentially incorrect renderings such as *Hang-eul*).

A note on the reference style: While there are nearly 300 Korean surnames, the most common are Kim, Lee, and Park. As such, conventional reference practices of denoting just the surname are not particularly useful for citing Korean authors. Therefore, the References list for this book uses full author names. In addition, in-text references make use of full author names for those with common Korean surnames (e.g., "Joseph Sung-Yul Park" instead of simply "Park").

Introduction

I.1 LANGUAGE, CULTURE, AND CATERPILLARS FROM A BIRD'S EYE VIEW

This book is about the wager of studying language as a global phenomenon, from a bird's eye view as it were. While the expression "bird's eye view" is typically used in a figurative sense, it is useful to speak about birds in a more literal sense as well. Birds, for one, are accustomed to seeing the world from a vantage point that humans, at least without the assistance of technology, cannot. The way the bird sees the world offers a way to understand how that which is "global" is contingent on its "local" iterations, but also how a "global" view can help us to make sense of that which is encountered "locally." Consider, for a moment, the fact that in flight birds must avoid predators nearly everywhere they go, even as they locate their own prey. This reality becomes even more complicated if a bird considers eating a caterpillar, because they rely on all defense mechanisms that can be imagined, ranging from bristles that release venom, glands that discharge repugnant odors, or various forms of mimesis (blending into its surroundings) and mimicry (looking like another animal). Among the most unusual defense mechanisms is that seen in caterpillars which have evolved to develop "eyespots" on the anterior (front-end) segments of their bodies that mimic the appearance of snakes, which are of course predators to the birds (Janzen, Hallwachs, & Burns, 2010). On top of all this, some species of caterpillar go beyond static resemblances of snakes, inflating their anterior segments to appear more snake-like (Hossie & Sherratt, 2014). Some can even manually palpitate their "eyespots" in a manner that resembles the blinking of a snake (Hossie, Sherratt, Janzen, & Hallwachs, 2013). While a vast majority of snake species actually pose no real threat to humans, with the exception of those that are venomous or large enough to eat a fully grown adult, there appears to be a seemingly universal fear of snakes,

1

which is of course attributable in large part to Judeo-Christian lore (in the book of Genesis, Satan in the form of a serpent in the Garden of Eden), mythology (Medusa in Greek mythology), or fables (the story of the farmer and the viper in Aesop's fables). Birds, on the other hand, are biologically programmed to be fearful of snakes simply because they in fact do pose a legitimate threat to the bird. It must therefore be quite difficult to be a bird; the moment you think you have identified your prey (a caterpillar), it may in fact turn out to be a predator (a snake), and your very survival in that scenario depends on an "irrational fear," which hopefully compels you to not take the risk (Castellano & Cermelli, 2015, p. 2).

The bird's challenge of identifying its prey serves as a useful analogy for the complexities of locating and understanding cultural difference across global space. To continue with the case of the caterpillar as a potential meal for the bird, there are three important considerations related to identifying features of cultural distinctiveness that are worth exploring further. First, it is significant that only one part of the snake, in this case the "eyespots," is what enables the bird to consider or conclude whether the object in question is a snake or not. In this sense, the "eyespots" operate as something of a synecdoche. A synecdoche typically refers to a part that semiotically represents a whole; for instance, an icon of a palm, rather than a depiction of a person holding up their palm, can be a sign for "do not walk." In this case, the part in question (the "eyespots") is that which indexes the possibility of a snake in a manner that distinguishes the semiotic salience of the part. After all, there are other features, such as the color green or an elongated body, which both the snake and caterpillar can share. In short, one small part of a larger whole can differentiate two things that can otherwise be visually difficult to distinguish.

Second, it is significant that the "eyespots" in question appear not on the caterpillar's head itself but adjacently on its anterior segments. What this means is that the masquerade effect can be achieved most optimally if the caterpillar is approached from above. Indeed, the effectiveness of the caterpillar's attempted serpentine mimicry depends on the specific angle from which the prey is approached (Hossie & Sherratt, 2014). There is, in other words, depending on the vantage point from which it is viewed, potential for something of a semiotic-ontological discombobulation in which its predator confuses not only the caterpillar for a snake but also the caterpillar's anterior segments for its head. This serves as an appropriate metaphor for challenging the expectation that the head must assume a dominant or primary position. For our purposes, what this means is that there might be something additional to be learned about the core semiotic features of a given culture by approaching it not only "head-on," as it were, but from other perspectives: not directly but obliquely as well.

Third, it is significant that, within this scenario of semiotic-ontological instability, there is the possibility that the caterpillar not only can be mistaken for a snake but can indeed *be* a snake. Consider the following four scenarios, which all presume via narrative omniscience that the caterpillar is in fact a caterpillar:

1. The bird believes the caterpillar is a caterpillar and eats it.
2. The bird is not certain whether it is a caterpillar or a snake but takes a chance anyway and eats it.
3. The bird is not certain whether it is a caterpillar or a snake and does not want to take a chance and flies away.
4. The bird believes the caterpillar is a snake and flies away.[1]

In scenario one, there is no uncertainty, for the question of whether the object was indeed a caterpillar is resolved at the moment of consumption. In scenario two, there is momentary uncertainty that is eventually resolved at the moment of consumption. In scenario three, there is sheer uncertainty that will never be resolved (as suggested above, it is actually in the bird's best interest to leave it at that). Finally, in scenario four, there is – in the mind of the bird – ontological certitude, even if it is false from a purely factual point of view. The bird flies away and therefore the caterpillar might as well have been a snake and as such was – in the mind of the bird – a snake.

The aforementioned quandary allows us to consider what might be achieved by approaching cultural imaginaries as entities that are semiotically iterated across global space. Similar to how the bird faces challenges locating food, we invariably run into issues understanding culture. Indeed, I would like to suggest that the wager of the bird in its encounter with the "caterpillar" is in many ways analogous to the wager of studying culture from a global perspective. This perspective is perhaps akin to the epistemological locus of "Apollo's eye," as described by Denis Cosgrove (2003). For Cosgrove, the notion of Apollo's eye is a means to envision things as "forged in one locale across global space" (p. 265). On the more obvious side, Apollo's eye serves as a metaphor for the affordances of acknowledging the ways in

---

[1] These scenarios are inspired by the work of evolutionary biologist Sergio Castellano and mathematician Paolo Cermelli (see Castellano & Cermelli, 2015).

which a given culture might undergo changes in relation to and perhaps in spite of its presumed territorial origins. But in addition, this locus compels us to consider how, when we encounter a global iteration of a particular culture beyond its presumed territorial origins, what kinds of assumptions we had relied on to conceptualize the "original" version of the culture. The perspective of Apollo's eye derives from Apollonian cosmology in an effort to reconcile the "contingencies of empirical geographical knowledge" (p. 38). To return to the case of the bird and the caterpillar, empirical conclusions, or those that are reached by methodologically experiential means, are subject to a series of epistemological contingencies.

At this point it is useful to focus on the aforementioned scenarios three and four, for they are illustrative of the mechanics of locating cultural discreteness in relation to the global. More specifically, the confusion of the head and the anterior segments is analogous to the semiotic phenomenology of culture in global space. Consider how it is taken for granted that authentic culture (i.e., the head) must always come before its transnational, global iterations (i.e., the anterior segments): for instance, there are spaces such as Koreatowns around the world, but they are naturally assumed to be derivative of an original, authentic Korea. While my interest is not limited to troubling the distinction between the "authentic" and the "derivative" per se, I would like to foreground the ways in which we can revisit the assumptions by which the features that differentiate the authentic from the derivative can be semiotically delineated but also, more broadly, how those core semiotic features of a given culture come to be rendered as salient in global space at a certain point in time. Put differently, is it possible that the very idea of culture, at least in terms of its semiotically distinguishing traits, can be understood best through its respective iterations across global space and time?[2] While what is encountered may not be "authentic" per se, if we are able to trouble the very conditions and premises of originality and to approach the problem instead as a spatial and semiotic consideration, then the presumed transposability between the "authentic" and the "derivative" (i.e., the head and the anterior segments) can itself be approached from a continuously evolving vantage point.

It is from this vantage point that I examine global Korea as a case study with particular attention to various global iterations of Korea in

---

[2] As I will discuss in Chapter 2, there has been an overt emphasis on time in the imagination of nationalist eras and national cultures, and as such this focus on space will necessarily be historically contingent.

relation to the complex entanglements among language, semiotic resources, and spatial elements. Through an examination of publicly visible signage and other artifacts of the built environment, I examine how such representational assemblages point to the possibility of national imaginaries and perhaps other cultural forms as existing not as a priori categories of cultural belonging but instead as entities that can be relocated and reinvented across global space. My sites in Korea include, for instance, tourist destinations such as the Gyeongbokgung Palace, where visitors flock to experience an "authentic" Korean spectacle; museums such as the Independence Hall of Korea, where Korean secondary school students are taken on field trips to commemorate Korean independence from Japanese colonial rule in 1945; and the small series of islets in the Pacific Ocean referred to by Koreans as Dokdo, whose ownership has been disputed by Korea and Japan since the conclusion of World War II. I also examine the public space of Koreatowns across Asia (China, Japan, Hong Kong), the Americas (Brazil, Canada, Mexico, the United States), and Europe (the United Kingdom), focusing on how uses and circulations of language and other semiotic resources reinvent varied forms of Koreanness.

By doing so, this book proposes that inquiries in the globalization of language need not limit themselves to those that understand how individuals from "culture A" can communicate with those of "culture B," even in spite of their respective dominant languages being "language X" and "language Y." Indeed, in the race to study and theorize how communication can be achieved across and in spite of cultural differences, we lose sight of what constitutes those differences to begin with, and how in some cases the delineations of difference are produced in the very effort to overcome them. Alternatively, this book proposes that, by exploring various moments and sites of translingual encounter, we find ourselves in a position to revisit many of our foundational assumptions about, and therefore arrive at a fuller understanding of, what might constitute culture to begin with. Simply put, this book is not a catalogue of hybridizations of culture and language as they occur in global contexts; instead, it is an inquiry into what such encounters can illuminate about the varied features of cultural distinctiveness that are otherwise difficult to see by approaching culture in its isolated form, but can be seen anew from a global perspective. In this regard, *Locating Translingualism* is not merely about locating spaces where translingualism happens but also about exploring the various ways in which linguistic and cultural difference can be located via translingualism.

1.2 TRANSLINGUALISM IN/AS SPACE

The radical and ongoing transformations to language practices in the context of the transcultural flows of the late twentieth and early twenty-first centuries continue to be a topic of great interest. Perhaps nowhere is this more evident than in studies on "translingualism" within a wide range of language-oriented academic disciplines. In fact, it could be said that the study of language is undergoing something of a "translingual turn," affording greater attention to the reality that the very notion of "language" inherently limits our understanding of the diverse possibilities for communicative practice across cultural and linguistic difference worldwide. This "turn" can be seen in the introduction of conceptual frameworks ranging from transidioma (Jacquemet, 2005), translanguaging (García, 2009; Li Wei, 2018), polylingual languaging (Jørgensen, 2008), polylingualism (Møller, 2008), truncated multilingualism (Blommaert, 2010), metrolingualism (Pennycook & Otsuji, 2015b), translingual practice (Canagarajah, 2013), transglossia (Sultana, Dovchin, & Pennycook, 2015), or transliteracy (You, 2016), among many others. Sender Dovchin and I (2019), in the introduction to our volume, *Translinguistics: Negotiating Innovation and Ordinariness*, have described the translingual turn, at least within the disciplinary paradigm of sociolinguistics, as reflective of three realities:

1. Boundaries between "languages" are the result of ideological invention and sedimentation;
2. Such boundaries do not unilaterally guide communication in everyday contexts; and
3. Communication itself is not limited to "language" insofar as interlocutors draw on a range of semiotic and spatial repertoires. (p. 1)

The first two points may be worth recapitulating briefly. The first point is that categories we understand today as "languages," frequently conceptualized, treated, and studied as "codes," are relatively recent inventions in human history (Makoni & Pennycook, 2005; Gramling, 2016). For Sinfree Makoni and Alastair Pennycook (2005) dominant epistemologies of "language" today are the legacy of the "ideology of countability that was a cornerstone of European governance and surveillance of the world" (p. 142). On this front, it is important to consider that the very notion of "language" is not based on a universal epistemology of communication, evident especially when considering communities in the Global South, such as in Africa, South

Asia, and Southeast Asia, who had always managed linguistically pluralistic interactions irrespective of demarcations according to "codes," (Canagarajah, 2013; Khubchandani, 1997; Makoni, 1998, 2002), and certainly well before scholars began to devote greater attention to such linguistic plurality (see Sugiharto, 2015). As David Gramling (2016) notes, languages came to be further sedimented as monolingually transposable entities at the service of the translation industry, whether in the realm of global literature or in machine translation programming. Meanwhile, such conceptualizations centered on language-as-code have become sedimented over time and continue to be sustained in various realms of social life where individuals and indeed entire communities face discrimination based on their purported inability to use language proficiently, at least according to dominant norms (Cameron, 2012; Dovchin, 2020; González & Melis, 2000; Lindemann & Moran, 2017; Lippi-Green, 2012; Subtirelu, 2013).[3]

The translingual turn secondly draws attention to the reality that peoples in many communities are able to communicate successfully with little conscious regard to which "languages" they are using. Pennycook and Emi Otsuji (2015b) note that part of the problem stems from dominant frameworks such as "bilingualism" or "multilingualism," which reduce communication to an "enumerative" logic by which only that which can be literally counted as a language counts (p. 16). Monica Heller (1999) similarly problematizes dominant approaches to linguistic plurality by referring to it as "parallel monolingualism" (p. 5). As Jens Normann Jørgensen (2008) argues:

> language users use features more than structures. They know that to some people some of these features belong together in sets which are called specific languages such as Danish and Turkish, but the speakers do not necessarily separate features from these sets in their linguistic behavior. (p. 167)

As Ofelia García (2009) puts it, today speakers of multiple languages do not necessarily view their utterances as falling within discrete "codes" but rather as operating in a cohesive "continuum that is accessed" (p. 47). Indeed, as Dovchin and I (2019) have tried to highlight, for many individuals, such translingual practices are part of everyday

---

[3] Indeed, this is especially pronounced in educational contexts, which could be considered bastions of linguistic discrimination (Dovchin, 2019), premised on the notion of language as code (Eunjeong Lee & Alvarez, 2020; N. Flores & Rosa, 2015; Hinton, 2016; Jenny Lee & Rice, 2007; Matsuda, 2006; Mazak & Carroll, 2017; Paris & Alim, 2017).

communication and there is still a need to minimize the exoticizing tendencies of recent scholarship by foregrounding the "ordinariness" of translinguistics (see also Blommaert, 2019; Bolander & Sultana, 2019; Canagarajah & Dovchin, 2019; Li Wei & Zhu Hua, 2019; Pennycook & Otsuji, 2019).[4]

The third point (which is that communication can rarely be considered as limited to "language" insofar as interlocutors draw on a range of semiotic resources and spatial elements), while arguably the least explored consideration in the translingual turn, may be considered as perhaps the most significant and compelling. Pennycook (2020) has referred to this focus on semiotic and spatial relations of communication, which brings "a range of political, epistemological and ontological questions to the table" as endemic to a "4th wave of sociolinguistics" (p. 223, as opposed to the tail end of a 3rd wave as suggested by Penelope Eckert [2018]). In this sense, it could be said that the theoretical foundations to approaching language beyond language as such can be found in M. A. K. Halliday's (1978) conceptualization of "language as social semiotic." A central premise to systemic functional linguistics, "language as social semiotic" represents a shift away from the Chomskyan conceptualization of competence toward a "sociosemiotic" one in which the social structure, including cultural context, is key to understanding the contingency of linguistic systems on social use. As Halliday (1978) noted, situational features (field, tenor, mode) precede semantic components (ideational, interpersonal, textual). While Halliday's tripartite framework of ideational, interpersonal, and textual structures has been critiqued and revised over the years (see Fairclough, 2003), at the very least it can be seen as a critical precursor to the "practice" turn in sociolinguistics. This turn is analogous to the practice turn in the humanistic social sciences more generally, which understands social activities not as limited to those that merely follow a predetermined script of expected behaviors or rituals but as defining and constituting the purportedly given set of expectations through the act of doing (Butler, 1997).

---

[4] Of course, as I have argued elsewhere, while there has been a considerable surge in scholarly treatment on translingual practice since the 2010s, many works merely appropriate the trans-framework to describe or analyze the simultaneous copresence of multiple languages, without meaningfully troubling extant language boundaries (Jerry Won Lee, 2018; see also Pennycook, 2019). It seems as though languages have been "disinvented," but the challenge has been "reconstituting" them, to borrow the words of Makoni and Pennycook (2005).

Within the study of language, the practice turn moves us away from a paradigm of linguistics in which grammaticality is a fixed system that is merely used. Emblematic of this approach is the Saussurean tradition of *langue-parole*, in which *langue*, or language, is a closed ecosystem in the minds of a homogeneous speech community based on a series of arbitrary relationships between the signifier and the signified. In this conceptualization of language, *parole*, or spoken speech, can only be successful if premised on what Mary Louise Pratt (1987) has termed the "linguistic utopia" (p. 50), reflecting a shared understanding between interlocutors of the signifier–signified relationship. The notion of fixed grammaticality is evident also in the Chomskyan linguistic tradition of competence–performance, in which there is an implied, idealized form of language, taxonomized according to grammatical structures (which are differentiated and studied under the traditional branches of linguistics: phonetics, phonology, morphology, syntax, and semantics), even if in everyday use language is expected to be imperfect. The focus on "language" throughout this book (rather than on linguistics in the conventional sense) is therefore based in part on Pennycook's (2010a) approach to language as a "local practice," in which "the notion of language as a system is challenged in favour of a view of language as doing" (p. 2).

My emphasis on "language" in this text is likewise guided by an interest in underscoring a broader understanding of communication beyond the "linguistic" per se. For one, no academic discipline can claim jurisdiction over the term "language" in the way they can over "linguistic." Therefore, inquiry that prioritizes the conceptual category of "language" is free to pursue a broad inter-, multi-, and trans-disciplinary approach that benefits from insights from a range of bodies of knowledge without being arbitrarily beholden to a specific disciplinary orientation to language. In addition, this orientation to "language" invites consideration of the wide range of communicative resources at work, many of which generally fall beyond the purview of the study of the "linguistic." In this regard, to return to the aforementioned "4th wave," it is productive to note an ongoing effort to emphasize the centrality of space in relation to the translingual turn. This emphasis draws on the long multidisciplinary tradition of approaching space not as an empty void but in terms of its relation to social activity and intervention (Harvey, 1989; Lefebvre, [1974] 1991). Doreen Massey's (1995) influential work, for instance, emphasized the importance of viewing "objects in space," whether physical objects or abstract objects like social identities, "as products of the spatial organization of relations" (p. 317). Meanwhile, Michel de

Certeau's (1984) analogy of "walking in the city" opens the possibility that space does not exist unto itself but comes to be the moment humans make use of it. Illustrative is de Certeau's example of the agentive role of the walker in the production of the city space:

> First, if it is true that a spatial order organizes an ensemble of possibilities (e.g., by a place in which one can move) and interdictions (e.g., by a wall that prevents one from going farther), then the walker actualizes some of these possibilities. In that way, he makes them exist as well. (de Certeau, 1984, p. 98)

In short, the wall cannot in itself prevent the walker from going farther insofar as the walker must first encounter the wall in order to be prevented from going farther in the first place, thus reflecting the codependency of spatial elements and human actors.

Pennycook's (2010a), in his aforementioned conceptualization of language as a "local practice," develops de Certeau's notion of "walking in the city" as a means of spatial production in order to theorize how language specifically, even if somewhat paradoxically, reconstitutes the localities in which it is practiced. For Pennycook, de Certeau's metaphor of walking in the city foregrounds how "movement through the city ... performatively produces meaning" (p. 63). Even though it might seem to be a minor example, it does offer a useful illustration of how space is an entailment of human action; space, from this perspective, is not merely the background to or context in which language is practiced but instead that which is constituted by language practice itself. It is, put differently, that which results from the interactions between people, in tandem with their communicative dispositions and linguistic and semiotic resources, and objects from the material and built environment.

The emphasis on space in the study of language is particularly evident in various frameworks such as those of translanguaging space (Li Wei, 2011; Li Wei & Zhu Hua, 2013), metrolingualism (Pennycook & Otsuji, 2015b), semiotic assemblages (Pennycook, 2017), spatial repertoires (Canagarajah, 2018), and translingual space (Du, Lee, & Sok, 2020). The notion of translanguaging space refers to both "a space for the act of translanguaging as well as a space created through translanguaging" (Li Wei, 2011, p. 1223). As Li Wei further notes, we cannot view such practices of translanguaging in a vacuum but need to attend to the strategic ways in which interlocutors produce spaces that are conducive to translanguaging. Relatedly, Suresh Canagarajah (2018) emphasizes the importance of viewing communicative competence as involving more than "language" but also "spatial repertoires." As Canagarajah (2018) writes:

> Spatial repertoires may not be brought already to the activity by the individual but assembled in situ, and in collaboration with others, in the manner of distributed practice. These repertoires may not be part of one's existing proficiency. I would also expand the repertoires beyond the linguistic to include all possible semioticized resources. I would also spatialize these repertoires more completely by treating them as embedded in the material ecology and facilitated by social networks. Spatial repertoires are an alternative to grammar in analyzing meaning making and communicative success. (p. 37)

This ecological orientation to space is essential to a translingual perspective to language because it enables us to expand our treatment of language beyond extant notions of "codes" to conceptualize communicative practice (in the form of how interlocutor A "switches" between code "X" and code "Y").

However, somewhat relatedly and indeed more importantly, these developments ask us to attend to a range of features beyond language that have tended to be relegated to the mere "background" or "context" of communication. As Pennycook and Otsuji (2015b) write in their description of metrolingualism, which confronts the tendency dating to the foundational variationist paradigm introduced through the work of William Labov (1972) to treat urban space as the mere contextual background that shapes a speaker's discrete linguistic patterns, language and space are rather codependent and co-constitutive of one another: "Language is bound up with all of this – it does not just happen against an urban backdrop, it is part of the city, the barber shop, the market garden, the networks of buying and selling" (p. 33). From this perspective, a translingual orientation to language thus is not merely about accentuating the fluidity and negotiability of linguistic boundaries. Simultaneously, as Pennycook (2017) argues, "we cannot merely add more semiotic items to our translinguistic inventories, but need instead to seek out a way of grasping the relationships among a range of forms of semiosis" (pp. 270–271). Pennycook (2018) thus indicates the importance of viewing sociolinguistic competence not in terms of individual ability but in terms of "spatial distribution, social practices and material embodiment" (p. 47), reflective of what he terms a "posthumanist" applied linguistics, in which seemingly immaterial elements of communication can be treated as having agentive qualities: a table, for instance, is not simply an object that humans can sit at to interact with each other but can be viewed as playing a dynamic role in the act of communication, if anything because the same conversation at a different table might look very different.

And while questions of space have been extensively theorized via translingualism, it needs to be noted, following Claire Kramsch (2018), that considerations of time have tended to be neglected. Kramsch argues that such a neglect is curious given the fact that the translingual emphasis on spatiality is invariably contingent on temporality, particularly in Canagarajah's (2018) theorization of spatial repertoires. Kramsch (2018) uses the metaphor of the pinball machine to emphasize what is at stake when time is not accounted for: "This is the time of the pinball machine, which assumes permanence of the identity of the pinball across trajectories, networks, and flows. Pinballs never get old, never get sick, and never suffer from loss of memory or loss of hope" (p. 113). In the same way that humans are not like immutable pinballs, neither are cultures and their respective semiotic traits, as we will see (temporality is discussed in further detail in Chapter 1).

The role of spatial repertoires in sociolinguistic meaning making has become especially evident in ethnographies of language in public space. One of the earliest such inquiries is the landmark study by Rodrigue Landry and Richard Y. Bourhis (1997) of the linguistic landscape of Canada. As they noted in their study, public language artifacts are not limited to their informational function but serve a range of symbolic functions, ranging from reaffirming the value of a particular language or the vitality of a particular ethnolinguistic group. Though the objective of their study, published in the *Journal of Language and Social Psychology*, was to determine the frequency of the presence of a particular language on public signage in relation to the perceived ethnolinguistic vitality of a community, their study is noted for popularizing the study of public language artifacts among sociolinguists. Indeed, their definition of linguistic landscape remains foundational to much scholarship: "The language of public road signs, advertising billboards, street names, place names, commercial shop signs, and public signs on government buildings combines to form the linguistic landscape of a given territory, region, or urban agglomeration" (Landry & Bourhis, 1997, p. 25). Scholars have since made significant advances in sociolinguistic inquiry through the linguistic landscape framework. It has been used, for instance, to foster greater understandings of the role of language in the "symbolic construction" of public space (Ben-Rafael, Shohamy, Amara, & Trumper-Hecht, 2006), particularly in urban environments (Backhaus, 2006; Shohamy, Ben-Rafael, & Barni,

2010).[5] Indeed, linguistic landscape has emerged as something of an intellectual brand, if not its own independent field of study, with at least two undeniable indicators as such: an annual symposium, the "Linguistic Landscape Workshop," which has been held in sites across the world since 2008, along with a peer-reviewed journal, *Linguistic Landscape: An International Journal*, which was first published in 2015. Of course, linguistic landscape research is not necessarily limited to "linguistic" artifacts alone, and as such Adam Jaworski and Crispin Thurlow (2010) have offered the expression "semiotic landscape" as an alternative to linguistic landscape in order to "emphasize the way written discourse interacts with other discursive modalities: visual images, nonverbal communication, architecture and the built environment" (p. 2). Throughout this book, I aim to be mindful of the increased attention to intersections between the "linguistic" and the "semiotic" and the fact that many theoretical frameworks within social semiotics draw frequently from linguistic frameworks (see Van Leeuwen, 2005). Therefore, throughout this book, unless I am referring to a study that is expressly focused on the "linguistic" landscape, I will rely on the expression "linguistic/semiotic landscape," following the lead of other scholars who are similarly mindful of the intersections between linguistic and semiotic resources in public space (Banda & Jimaima, 2015; Curtin, 2015; Moriarty, 2019; Zabrodskaja & Milani, 2014).

Many scholars have more recently taken up the question of translingualism specifically within the context of linguistic/semiotic landscape research (e.g., Gorter & Cenoz, 2015; Krompák & Meyer, 2018; Pennycook, 2017; Pennycook & Otsuji, 2017; Sharma, 2019; Zhang & Chan, 2015). Of course, some linguistic/semiotic landscape research that predates the popularization of "trans-" frameworks had attended to the fluidity of language boundaries: for instance, the findings from Thomas Huebner's (2006) study of the linguistic landscape of Bangkok "calls into question the boundaries of a speech community ... and even what constitutes a language itself" (p. 50). As Durk Gorter and Jasone Cenoz (2015) note, a translingual approach to linguistic/semiotic landscape research can benefit from relevant developments in multilingualism research, particularly the "focus on multilingualism" (Cenoz & Gorter, 2011) approach, which looks at

---

[5] Admittedly, in linguistic landscape research there is certainly a disproportionate representation of urban contexts compared to that of other environments. As Gorter (2006) argues, "instead of calling it the linguistic landscape it could also be named the linguistic cityscape" (p. 2). Importantly, a handful of scholars have demonstrated the importance of attending to the linguistic landscape of rural areas as well (see Jenks, 2018; Kotze, 2010; Lawrence, 2012; Lu, Li, & Xu, 2020).

languages in terms of repertoire (Blommaert & Backhus, 2011), accounting for how an individual can have competence in multiple languages though at different degrees, ranging from maximal to minimal or even momentary (regarding the latter, Gorter and Cenoz use the example of learning a new word while visiting a foreign country). As Pennycook (2017) notes, a translingual approach to linguistic/semiotic landscape research can facilitate the ongoing move beyond "fairly obvious 'givens' (what constituted a language, a sign, and the public space were seen as easily identifiable entities) towards a much broader range of semiotic potential," by taking stock of the "boundaries between different modes of semiosis" (p. 270).

In sum, these collective developments have been instrumental in exposing how the notion of language as a stable and homogenous code is itself an invention that continues to be sustained by various ideological commitments and to showcase how communicative success can be achieved in spite of conventions premised on the veneration of dominant understandings of linguistic boundaries. Further, more recent inquiries have advocated for a "distributed" perspective to communication, foregrounding the potentially agentive role of spatial elements which had previously been disregarded as immaterial, adjacent, or even inconsequential. Taking all these developments together, we are now in a position to approach the linguistic/semiotic landscape not merely as a space to observe instances of translingualism but also as a space to reconsider the fundamental premises of cultural and linguistic contact more broadly, including the extent to which cultural and linguistic differences can be conceptualized in the first place.

I.3   COSMOPOLITANISM AND CULTURAL DIFFERENCE

In order to proceed, there are remaining considerations that need to be accounted for, namely the fact that one of the primary affordances of the translingual orientation, according to numerous proponents, is the ability to understand how "cosmopolitan relations" (Canagarajah, 2013) can be achieved. I am in this context not referring to observations that peoples of certain communities learn dominant languages such as English in order to support their "cosmopolitan striving" (e.g., So Jin Park & Abelmann, 2004). Instead, I am referring to the fact that translingualism has been frequently promoted as a means of theorizing the ways in which people from different cultural backgrounds can manage to, quite simply, "get along." Translingualism, in other words, is presented as a theory of intercultural interaction that shares the logics and aspirations of cosmopolitanism (see also De Costa, 2014; Lemrow, 2016). Though cosmopolitanism is itself a widely theorized concept, an oft-referenced passage by Kwame Anthony Appiah (2006) could be considered an apt representation of, or at the very least a starting point for understanding, its overarching ethos:

> I am urging that we should learn about people in other places, take an interest in their civilizations, their arguments, their errors, their achievements, not because that will bring us to agreement, but because it will help us get used to one another. If that is the aim, then the fact that we have all these opportunities for disagreement about values need not put us off. Understanding one another may be hard; it can certainly be interesting. But it doesn't require that we come to agreement. (p. 78)

Within the context of sociolinguistics, as Canagarajah (2013) notes, Appiah's position reflects the importance of treating cosmopolitanism as a "process" (p. 194; see also Glissant, [1990]1997). In this way, cosmopolitanism is not reduced to universally deduced or idealized outcomes but derived from actual negotiations that have been "evolving for generations in many multilingual communities and contact zones" (Canagarajah, 2013, p. 194).[6] Further, Canagarajah emphasizes the importance of a "*dialogical* cosmopolitanism" (p. 196, emphasis added). In this framework, "there is no need to abandon one's difference for the sake of harmonious cosmopolitan relationships. Cosmopolitanism is vibrant when one's difference and voice are affirmed" (Canagarajah, 2013, p. 196).

While the effort to understand ways to navigate and overcome difference is certainly commendable and not in and of itself by any means a problematic undertaking, it is important to address the fact that the idealization of cosmopolitanism has been called into question. Ryuko Kubota (2016), in particular, problematizes the contemporary valorization of translingual practice in that it "parallels the underlying ideology of neoliberal multiculturalism – that is, individualism, difference-blindness, and *elitist* cosmopolitanism rather

---

[6] Contact zones are defined by Pratt (1991) as "social spaces where cultures meet, clash, and grapple with each other, often in contexts of highly asymmetrical relations of power, such as colonialism, slavery, or their aftermaths as they live out in many parts of the world today" (p. 34).

than critical acknowledgement of power" (p. 487, emphasis added). Indeed, the idealization of cosmopolitanism is in many ways analogous to the idealization of mobility evident in what Thomas Faist (2013) terms the "mobility paradigm" (p. 1638) in the social sciences. As Faist notes, the unstated premise in the discourse of mobility is *upward* mobility, and as such, we frequently tend to neglect the lateral movements practiced by large swaths of the world's population whose collective plight is largely ignored on the basis of their status as "unskilled" migrants. Likewise, in the discourse of cosmopolitanism, there is the risk of only certain kinds of cosmopolitan practice being privileged, for instance, tautologically celebrating the resourcefulness of those who are well-resourced as they move around the world and learn to get along with peoples from various cultural backgrounds.

In light of these concerns, it is necessary to outline the theoretical premises that guide the ethos of cosmopolitanism that is pursued in this present inquiry. To begin, it is helpful to note that translingualism is frequently framed uncritically as a corrective to "monolingualism," especially in the pejorative sense of the term referring either to an individual's or community's inability to speak more than one language, or in the sense of ideological commitments that idealize one language over others (Jerry Won Lee, 2018). This is significant given that the impossibility of monolingualism has been noted not only more generally, for instance through Michael Holquist's (2014) inquiry into the inherently dialogic nature of language, but also in the theorization of translingualism itself, for instance through Pennycook's (2008) description of English as a language "always in translation" or in Canagarajah (2013) declaration of "English as translingual." What we learn from such accounts is that, whether we are describing English or another language, monolingualism is almost inevitably a fiction (Pratt, 2012). This sentiment is echoed in Jacques Derrida's (1998) influential description of monolingualism as prosthetic based on his relationship to the French language as an Algerian living under French colonial rule: "I only have one language; it is not mine" (p. 1). The notion of monolingualism as ideological fiction in Derrida's account is developed in Gramling's (2016) thesis on the invention of monolingualism. Monolingualism, for Gramling, is best understood in relation to an era in which human communication is organized into transposable units (i.e., named languages). This condition of transposability produces the very possibility of "monolingualism" to be conceptualized to begin with, reflective of an epoch Gramling terms the linguacene. Linguacene, derived from the more familiar expression, anthropocene,[7] is presented as:

> the glossodiverse management of common meanings across languages in industrial design ... [that] has resulted in a coordinated translingual idiom of industry that profoundly changes the planet, regardless of which surface-language those industries are being deployed through. The linguacene is in this sense that latter stage of the anthropocene, in which multilingualism becomes sufficiently organized among global industrial actors such that alternative vernacular meanings are effectively decommissioned amid the pursuit of coordinated transnational oil production, geostationary orbit policy, counter-insurgency, data storage, and the like. (p. 37)

The transposability of languages as an invention is theorized most convincingly by Gramling through the analogy of musical temperament. Temperament refers to the practice of placing all intervals between notes *out of tune* so that one is able to modulate different melodies or harmonies across different keys, whether higher or lower. As Gramling elaborates, the very "problem of temperament stems from a natural gap in harmony that confounds mathematically pure ratios of pitch. This gap is called the Pythagorean Comma and is equal to twelve pure fifths, less seven octaves, or 531441/524288 cents, so roughly a quarter of a semitone" (p. 21). In pairing linguistics with acoustics, Gramling argues that "the wager of monolingualism was also Bach's wager: that the sacrifices one makes in achieving transposability, say from the key of E to the key of A flat on a 'well-tuned' clavier, were negligible when compared to the pragmatic benefits of exchangeability across keys" (pp. 23–24). Put differently, while we lose the purity of the intervals between notes, in exchange we are able to access all keys. Monolingualization was a technological innovation that, similarly, involved its own wager: sacrificing the precision of hitherto untranslatable cross-cultural communicative nuance in exchange for the transposability across newly invented, even if imprecise, language categories. The takeaway from the analogy of temperament is that at the point of assuming difference and thus transposability, one is likely to concede to a recognition that the distinction of 531441/524288 cents is negligible if the return is access to a wider range of keys or, in this case, languages.

---

[7] The Anthropocene is a term introduced in 2000 by Nobel Prize winning atmospheric chemist Paul J. Crutzen to describe the geological epoch characterized by significant and irreversible human impact on the Earth's climate (Crutzen & Stoermer, 2000).

I draw our attention to Gramling's theorization of monolingualism because I believe it serves as an apt analogy for how notions of not only linguistic difference but also cultural difference more generally come to be delineated in semiotically transposable ways through the pursuit of cosmopolitan relations. This is because the very pursuit of cosmopolitan relations, if understood as a paradigm not only of cross-cultural identification but also coexistence in spite of differences (following Appiah), can only stem from a scenario of intercultural contact premised and contingent on the conditions of difference. After all, if there is no difference, what is there to overcome? Consider the fictional scenario presented in M. Night Shyamalan's 2004 film, *The Village*, in which the residents of a small nineteenth-century town have for decades been unable to venture outside of their community in fear of the creatures who reside in the surrounding woods, referred to as "Those We Don't Speak Of." The twist of the plot is this: the film is actually set in the modern day and the village was founded in the 1970s by a group of people who decided to start a community in a remote wildlife preserve in order to protect their families from the influence and dangers of modern society and civilization. It also turns out that the creatures did not actually exist but were invented by the village founders as a means of ensuring that nobody from the village would consider leaving and that their community would remain an isolated utopia cut off from the rest of the world.

The film received mixed reviews, with most of the negative ones focusing on the impossibility of an entire town living in isolation from the rest of the world in the late twentieth-/early twenty-first-century United States. Of course, my point in referencing this film is not to debate the feasibility of the plot but to make the point that only in the world of fiction is it possible to even try to avoid exposure to cultural difference altogether. The residents of the village were able to remain in isolation because they avoided, at all costs, encounters with "Those We Don't Speak Of." In the "real world," encounters with cultural difference are inevitable, even if the degree and scale of such encounters can be mediated to a certain extent. But more importantly, the film is an interesting case study of how cultural difference can be neatly dichotomized: for the villagers, differences between individuals and families within the village are immaterial in relation to the larger issue of difference between them and "Those We Don't Speak Of." In the "real world," not only are encounters with cultural difference inevitable, but the assumptions surrounding what constitutes cultural difference are both taken for granted (peoples of culture X do this, peoples of culture Y do that) and also difficult to pinpoint (peoples of culture X do this but so do peoples of culture Y).

I offer the above observations in an effort to describe what I see as the *imperative* of this book. Even if questions of cultural difference are complicated, they seem to matter more than ever today. In the 1990s, in the wake of nationalism's emergence as the dominant form of political belonging (evident, for instance, in the dissolution of the Soviet Union and the breakup of Yugoslavia), commentators debated the role globalization would have on national identification. Key scholars of cultural studies such as Stuart Hall (1996) signaled the dilution of national identity, while other theorists of nationalism such as Anthony D. Smith (1995) noted a rejuvenation of nationalist sentiment in his *Nations and Nationalism in a Global Era*. Sociologist Craig Calhoun (2007) would go on to argue, in *Nations Matter: Culture, History, and the Cosmopolitan Dream*, that while common sense would have suggested a decline in nationalist thought in response to the realities of globalization, insofar as nations have always been resilient discursive formations, the inverse would remain true: nations would continue to "matter." Indeed, in the early twenty-first century we continue to bear witness to a rise in right-wing populism and ethnocentrism in numerous national contexts, including in Brazil, India, the Philippines, Russia, the United Kingdom, and the United States. In both late twentieth- and early twenty-first-century phases of resurgent nationalist sentiment, the global came to be increasingly framed as an inherent threat to the national. This is evident in the United States in Donald J. Trump's "America First" isolationist foreign policy or in Brazil through Jair Bolsonaro's campaign slogan, "Brasil acima de tudo, Deus acima de todos" or "Brazil above everything, God above everyone," which relied on the semiotic valorization of an authoritarian past and the sanctioned denigration of "non-Brazilians," as described by Daniel N. Silva (2020). These developments make it clear that it is imperative more than ever to understand the ways in which people demarcate themselves as different from one another, and the flexible criteria by which cultural distinctions are made and remade, even if such efforts are not deployed to serve overtly or obviously nefarious agendas. My purpose is to understand the negotiability and reinvention of the salient aspects of cultural difference insofar that these same understandings of difference are themselves impediments to cosmopolitan relations. Exploring the logics of difference, at least as they are deployed in the realm of the semiotic, does not come with the promise of ensuring that we will "all get along with one another" or even that we will "get used to one another," but it can at the very least help us arrive at a better understanding of the ways in which cultural differences are delineated, which is invariably responsible for potential sentiments of ambivalence if not animosity toward those who are conceived of as "different." In other words, it raises the question of what it means to conceive of another cultural entity as "different" if such differences are semiotically produced in ways that are tenuous if not arbitrary.

1.4   SEMIOTIC PRECARITY

Questions of cultural difference are further complicated by the fact that cultural categories are themselves not fixed, even though they are frequently subject to appraisals of authenticity. To return to the arena of sociolinguistics for a moment, in Canagarajah's (2013) ethnography of heritage Tamil speakers, he finds that conceptualizations of Tamil ethnolinguistic identity are reinvented bottom-up within local community contexts, rather than adhering to universal notions of what it means to be Tamil. Further, as Canagarajah argues, "they are able to perform in-group Tamil identities and represent traditional identities for strategic purposes, while having the freedom and resources to adopt other identities" (p. 201; see also He [2010] on the dynamic nature of heritage languages). Monica Heller (2011) makes a similar point about the negotiability of ethnolinguistic identities in her ethnography of francophone communities in Canada and Europe, albeit with a focus on how "authenticity" can be commodified in the context of late capitalism (see also Duchêne & Heller, 2012). Of particular interest is Heller's attention to the complexities of maintaining local heritage while manufacturing authenticity in a manner that appeals to outsiders, particularly tourists, which results in a series of inevitable tensions: "Branding authenticity sometimes involves shaping authentic objects in ways that begin to feel, well, inauthentic" (p. 147). And to return to the question of whether culture can be authentic in its transnational iterations, it is important to acknowledge the point made by R. Radhakrishnan (1996) that such questions are prefigured always on an absoluteness of the point of supposed origin and regard heritage as a credential to be evaluated by an imagined authority of authenticity. Likewise, I am not invested in exposing surrogate forms of authenticity but instead in understanding the logics by which authenticity is pursued or promoted (even in its blatantly inauthentic forms), for it tells us something about what is deemed communicable as a semiotically salient feature of a given culture.

While I will return to the question of authenticity in greater detail later in this book, for now the point is to emphasize that considerations of authenticity and more generally questions of cultural or linguistic essentialism (what the core, defining features of a particular cultural group are) can be understood as they are encountered in moments of what might be called *semiotic precarity*: when the presumed essence of an entity is unable to be taken for granted (whether by an "outsider" or even an "insider") and therefore demands affirmation or reaffirmation via semiotic distinction (semiotic acts that distinguish it from another cultural entity). It is useful to begin by understanding what Asif Agha (2007) describes as a semiotic encounter, which is a moment in which "a particular sign-phenomenon or communicative process connects persons to each other" (p. 10). The notion of a semiotic encounter could be conceived of as a moment in which a given semiotic resource performs meaning (signs, after all, have no meaning unto themselves but acquire meaning when they are intersubjectively activated). Semiotic precarity, then, could be understood as a condition imminent in spaces in which the quotidian and unremarkable specificities of cultural difference are unpresumed (either uncertain or questionable) and, as a result, come to be both remarkable (in the sense of literally being worthy of remark) and as semiotically *distinct*. In some ways, it could be said that my focus on distinction is somewhat related to the way Pierre Bourdieu (1984) popularized it in his thesis of cultural capital, wherein the cultural practices of different classes could be differentiated, even though my focus is not on class distinctions within a given culture per se. As such, another way of thinking about spaces of semiotic precarity is to view them as those where the authenticity or the ontological certitude of culture is not presumed and wherein such certitude can be momentarily represented via semiosis. One might additionally be tempted to draw a connection to Baudrillard's (1994) theorization of the simulacrum, in which objects and phenomena in the so-called real world are subordinate to, if not obviated as a result of, their respective representations.[8] While there are indeed many

---

[8] Baudrillard's paradigmatic case of the simulacrum is Disneyland, which is presumed to be a world of make-believe but is instead, according to Baudrillard, an entity that enables us to commit to the possibility that the world outside of Disneyland is "real" in the first place. As Baudrillard (1994) writes: "Disneyland exists in order to hide that it is the 'real' country, all of 'real' America that *is* Disneyland (a bit like prisons are there to hide that it is the social in its entirety, in its banal omnipresence, that is carcereal). Disneyland is presented as imaginary in

overlapping points of interest, it is important to clarify that my approach to semiotic precarity does not aim to argue that culture simply does not exist except in its representational form. Instead, I aim to foreground how we can make better sense of the logics of cultural distinctiveness through various moments of encounter in contexts of *semiotic precarity*. Instantiations of a given culture that are encountered in spaces of semiotic precarity may be thought of in terms of the near polar opposite of what A. Aneesh (2015) describes as placelessness. Aneesh's ethnography of a call center in India foregrounds how workers are trained to adopt a "neutral accent" that is placeless, "not in the sense that it is from no place, but rather that hearers cannot place it" (p. 4). Training regimens in call centers such as the one studied by Aneesh promote "conscious efforts at deregionalizing and removing place marks from an accent, thus making it unmarked" (p. 59). While placelessness pursues a strategic minimalization of linguistic distinctiveness, semiotic precarity affords an opportunity to understand such distinctiveness. Consider the interesting point made by Seunghan Paek (2016) in his analysis of paintings of the Seoul cityscape by French artist Manoël Pillard: Pillard's meticulous rendition of street signage, which is familiar and ordinary to most Koreans, underscores the "tension between the ordinary and extraordinary" (p. 232) while enabling something mundane such as street signage to be viewed "anew with wonder and curiosity" (p. 234). Of particular interest is how a non-Korean's representation of Korean script on the signage produces an opportunity to retrospectively conceptualize what Korean script is "supposed" to look like.

It therefore might be said that spaces of semiotic precarity are those in which features of cultural distinctiveness can be read anew: not necessarily with wonder and curiosity but at least in ways that enable us to revisit or reaffirm the naturalized associations between a culture and its respective semiotic traits. Similar to how Gramling argues that "monolingualism" depends on the possibility of multiple languages and therefore can only become a preoccupation *following*, not prior to, the precarity of monolingualism, I argue that the semiotic saliency of culture is best approached through

order to make us believe that the rest is real, whereas all of Los Angeles and the America that surrounds it are no longer real, but belong to the hyperreal order and to the order of simulation. It is no longer a question of a false representation of reality (ideology) but of concealing the fact that the real is no longer real, and thus of saving the reality principle" (p. 12–13, emphasis in original).

sites of semiotic precarity. To explain what I mean, I return briefly to the case of the authenticity of Tamil heritage described at the start of this section, in which the question of what constitutes Tamil identity and cultural practice is worthwhile as something to be considered because it is being asked in a diaspora context rather than in, say, Sri Lanka or the Tamil Nadu state of India. If we use the example of Korea's global iterations, sites of semiotic precarity can include, for instance, restaurant signage in the linguistic/semiotic landscape of Koreatowns around the world, where it is imperative to convince passersby or discerning customers that the cuisine is just as "authentic" as what you would find in Korea itself. Yet global iterations can also include sites within the nation-state itself that are designated for the "outsider." Such sites are also frequently characterized by semiotic precarity, for instance those that are reliant on a hyperbolic semiosis of an atavistic Korea in sites across tourist destinations where visitors hope to experience an essentialized version of Korean culture in its "authentic" form. Another way to consider this point would be to acknowledge that, since a Korean restaurant in Korea is simply a restaurant, there can be no "Korean restaurants" in Korea. Meanwhile, the restaurant that becomes semiotically encoded as a "Korean restaurant" in a Koreatown – out of Korea proper – is the result of semiotic precarity.

Therefore, the question of whether a particular restaurant is legitimately Korean or not is more likely to be asked of a Korean restaurant outside of Korea.[9] While there is probably little reason to question the authenticity of a Korean restaurant in Korea, a Korean restaurant in an "unexpected" place, such as, say, in the southwestern United States not widely known for having a longstanding or abundant population of Koreans, may have some persuading to do (see Chapter 3). I believe there is much to be learned by studying the semiotic work by which the persuasion is attempted. I am, to repeat, not aiming to valorize "authenticity" for the sake of authenticity, nor am I trying to legitimize or "defend" that which might be dismissed as inauthentic, diluted, or alternative forms of culture. I am using the question of in/authenticity as but an example to describe semiotic precarity. It is from these spaces of semiotic precarity, whether as sites of cultural contact or other sites where the semiotic traits of a given culture are deemed needing of

---

[9] Of course, nowadays, some diners may feel compelled to differentiate "Korean" restaurants from "Korean American" restaurants, both in the United States and even in Korea, where restaurants owned by Korean American expatriates are increasingly common.

distinction, that we can begin to understand not only how cultures and languages are changing in the era of globalization, but also what their core defining features are in the first place, and thus how, through the continued study of language in globalization, we might be able to distinguish them from one another into the future (or not).

In sum, while there is certainly much value in trying to understand the ways in which cooperative relations can be achieved in spite of cultural and linguistic differences, I propose that further inquiry into the entanglements among language, semiotic resources, and spatial elements may put us in a position to better understand the taken-for-granted criteria by which such difference is conceptualized to begin with. It is, in other words, not only about understanding how individuals are able to transcend cultural and linguistic differences through translingual practice but also about understanding the ways in which cultural and linguistic difference come to be salient and are reinvented in such moments of translingual contact.

I.5   BOOK OVERVIEW

In the remaining pages of this book, I explore the question of culture as it is rendered legible in sites of intercultural contact with an emphasis on spaces of semiotic precarity. I continue in Chapter 1 by offering a framework of *translingual inversion*, which facilitates our effort to make sense of the ways in which a given culture can be rendered visible across global space. "Translingual inversion" describes both a theoretical heuristic by which to inquire into what may be the core semiotic features of a given cultural imaginary, which distinguish it from another cultural imaginary, but also the phenomenon of recognizing such features: of *locating* culture. As implied earlier, the application and understanding of translingual inversion is made possible by adopting a global locus, from a "bird's eye view" or from the vantage point of what Cosgrove describes as "Apollo's eye," but also "obliquely." This is because of the simple fact that a given culture typically need not be expected to differentiate itself from other cultures on an everyday basis, though it frequently will in spaces of semiotic precarity. In this sense, it could be said that translingual inversion is about making sense of the ways in which culture can be *located* across global space. Afterwards, I outline some of the complexities inherent to semiotically representing a particular kind of culture, namely the national imaginary, and then briefly describe how translingual inversion can therefore be instrumental to the task of "locating" national imaginaries across global space.

In Chapter 2, "Locating Global Korea," I describe the importance of a sustained study of the linguistic/semiotic landscape of global Korea not only in obvious ways for scholars of Korean studies but also to readers more generally interested in language and globalization even without a stated interest in Korea per se. Doing so comes with the related task of providing necessary background on Korea as a national imaginary with a particular focus on aspects of its ethnic national heritage that are relevant to its iterations across the linguistic/semiotic landscape of global Korea. In other words, I describe what some of the generalizable characteristics of Korea are (for readers interested in the globalization of culture) while also describing what makes Korea "unique," which is particularly important given the focus of the book, to explore the mechanics by which a given cultural entity can come to be semiotically salient (i.e., distinguishable) across global space. This chapter also serves as the space to provide some background to the study that informs this book, describing the various iterations it has taken since 2012.

The remainder of this book is organized around three case studies exploring how Korea is rendered legible and locatable across global space. Chapter 3, "Encountering the Unfamiliar: Languaging Culture," focuses on the case of language, in particular written language. I focus on written language in part due to the fact that the script of the Korean language, known as Han-geul, is frequently referenced as a distinguishing aspect of Korean national identity. More generally, code choice on signage is perhaps the most obvious and simplest way to see cultural difference in the linguistic/semiotic landscape. However, this chapter is not merely an effort to enumerate or catalog instantiations of Koreanness via written language. Instead, I look at moments of what I describe as "weird language," or instances of translation, transliteration, and translingualization that are "unfamiliar," which through their unfamiliarity render intelligible cultural distinctiveness. Examining "weird language" across spaces in Beijing, Los Angeles, Mexico City, Oakland, São Paulo, Shanghai, and Tokyo, I explore what such encounters tell us about our assumptions about the familiar: the taken-for-granted aspects of culture that in a given moment may be expected to stand in for a culture and differentiate it from another.

Representing the nation both as a problem of scale but also as a contingency of scale is the focus of Chapter 4, "Visible Nation: Scaling Culture." I approach the idea of Korea as a discrete cultural entity as a question of scale, which I define as a discursive framing device that enables us to orient or reorient ourselves toward a given element of our social worlds that is otherwise difficult or impossible to make sense of. Korea, in this sense, is treated both in terms of being able to be scaled and perhaps only ever being subject to scale. I first look at the scaling of Korea via the color red, which emerged as synonymous with the nation following the 2002 FIFA World Cup, and how such a chromatic association, even if highly unstable, has been embraced since. I then look to examples of scaling Korea via historical allusions to the ancient Koryo dynasty, a process which demands a strategic manipulation of historical fact. Finally, I analyze the global allusiveness of a small series of islets whose ownership remains disputed between Korea and Japan, and unpack the implications of the impossibility of representing the territory *to scale*.

While Chapters 3 and 4 focused on "languaging" Korea and "scaling" Korea, respectively, Chapter 5 is about "tracing" Korea. This chapter, "Semiotic Excess: Tracing Culture," considers the excess of signification, or the semiotic "traces" of global Korea. I first explore the question of the trace in relation to conspicuous municipal designations of Korean spaces, whether through Koreatown signage in Los Angeles, Honorary Seoul Drive signage in Chicago, or through entry gates for the Koreatown of Osaka, which are in turn juxtaposed with the Gwanghwamun in Seoul, a gate to the royal Gyeongbokgung Palace that has been destroyed, relocated, and restored over the years. I then examine how cultural meaning emerges through semiotic traces that would normally be dismissed as having any significatory value, focusing on the case of European semiosis, namely the presence of Italian and more so French semiotic tokens, and the role they play in signifying Koreanness. Finally, I turn to the unusual case of signage in bathrooms of restaurants and other establishments advising patrons to not flush paper down the toilet, reflective of a uniquely Korean preoccupation that can be traced to the 1988 Olympics in Seoul. These examples collectively show that Korea can be encountered not only in ways that are decidedly Korean but through semiotic traces that seem to have nothing to do with Korea at all. This in turn not only raises questions about what Korea is but also invites considerations of what to look for when trying to make sense of Korea or another cultural entity.

In the Conclusion, in addition to making the typical gestures of recapitulating the main points of the book while attending to various limitations and lacunae, I attempt to inspire readers to pursue complementary inquiry into considerations of global Korea and analogous research into global iterations of other cultural imaginaries. In so doing, I emphasize that the study of language through a translingual orientation has benefits far beyond celebrations of linguistic and cultural fluidity. The chapter therefore attempts to answer the broader question of why the interdisciplinary study of language remains important in today's global era. On the one hand, contact across cultures and the realities of transculturation are increasingly the norm. However, more importantly, approaching language in this manner enables us to arrive at a more comprehensive understanding of the complex dynamics by which cultures can be rendered distinguishable across global space. It further enables us to attend to the reality that questions of what it means to belong to a given cultural entity to begin with are undergoing radical and unprecedented permutations. Therefore, I suggest that perhaps the question is not so much how today the study of language is more important than ever, but how we can continue to adapt it and be flexible enough so that we can continue to try and make sense of the role of language in relation to the ever-changing contours of cultural belonging today and into the future.

1 Translingualism and the Locations of Culture

1.1 *WHERE IS CULTURE?*

It is no longer controversial, if it ever was, to say that culture is a notoriously difficult concept to pinpoint. Given that the topic has been explored in every humanistic and social scientific discipline conceivable, it is perhaps less than productive to provide a survey of the range of definitions available and how they differ across fields and have changed over time. In general, culture is frequently viewed as an aggregate of practices, customs, rituals, languages, speech patterns, belief systems, and the like that differentiate people of one group from another. From this general understanding of culture, these afore-mentioned differences can overlap across different cultures (e.g., it is quite common for people of different cultural groups to speak the same language) and any given person likely belongs to multiple different cultural groups (a point that will be discussed in fuller detail later in this chapter). In the Introduction, I indicated that the focus of this book is to understand the legibility of culture, or how culture can be seen or *located*, in spaces of semiotic precarity, or those in which the quotidian and unremarkable specificities of cultural difference are either uncertain or called into question and, as a result, come to be both remarkable (in the sense of literally being worthy of remark) and as semiotically *distinct*. As such, for our purposes, I would argue that a definition of culture, even a working definition, could in many ways be counterproductive in that, as we will see, the notion of cultural distinction (the ways in which cultures differentiate themselves from others) is itself not fixed, even though we might arrive at preliminary understandings in spaces of semiotic precarity. In other words, what we will see is that culture is a concept that is best understood retro-actively, in moments in which it can be dialectically delineated as distinct from another culture.

Michael Silverstein (2013), in his effort to put an end to longstanding questions of "what" is culture, proposes that we instead focus on the question of "*where* is culture?" (p. 328, emphasis in original). For Silverstein, culture is to be found in the signification, circulation, and emanation of discourse, a point that I will return to later in this chapter. This book could also be said to be guided by the same question of "where is culture?" However, while Silverstein's inquiry pertains primarily to aspects of language in which culture can be found, I am also guided by the question in a somewhat more literal sense of where in the world culture can be located. While I am of course not suggesting that I can put an end to the question of what culture is, I do believe that approaching culture from a global perspective might be a useful way forward.

Given that our present focus is on the challenges and nuances of locating the distinguishing features of a given culture across global space, a logical starting point might be Homi Bhabha's (1994) classic work, *The Location of Culture*. One of Bhabha's (1994) most enduring arguments situates understanding the particularities of culture within sites of hybridity, defined as places "where the construction of a political object that is new, *neither the one nor the other*, properly alienates our political expectations, and changes, as it must, the very forms of recognition of the moment of politics" (p. 37, emphasis in original). In Bhabha's case, "politics" is a mechanism by which peoples of different cultural origins or groups can be categorized according to predetermined criteria premised on the intention of taxonomizing and ranking different cultures in a vertically stratified manner. Meanwhile, cultural hybridization subverts these existing logics of subordination themselves while facilitating opportunities for alternative, horizontally distributed forms of group identification not bound to the hierarchizing logics of "politics" as such. For Bhabha's purposes, questions of cultural distinction matter not unto themselves but come to be relevant as frames of reference that render unintelligible new forms of cultural hybridity. The point to emphasize here is that this question of unintelligibility likewise becomes an issue only when approached from the assumption that there is such a thing as culture as a pure, unadulterated entity.

Of course, in the context of sociolinguistics, the notion of hybridity has been critiqued for a variety of reasons. Such reasons include its "conceptual ambiguity," its presumption of cultural purity prior to hybridization, its associated negative connotations, and its neglect of questions of power and inequality (Rubdy & Alsagoff, 2014, pp. 8–9). These concerns being noted, I would like to emphasize that I am not treating hybridity as a rubric by which to make sense of translingual practice. In other words, I am not suggesting that a hybridized communicative practice combining aspects of culture X and culture Y is somehow politically subversive. Indeed, scholars have increasingly problematized the uneven and unequal distribution of and access to language in the context of globalization (Blommaert, 2010; Dovchin, Pennycook, & Sultana, 2018; Dovchin, Sultana, & Pennycook, 2016; Kubota, 2016; Lorente & Tupas, 2013; Piller, 2016; Tupas, 2015). Relatedly, by invoking hybridity I am not trying to highlight the benefits of ostensibly "hybrid" cultural practices, including linguistic practices. Put differently, this is not an attempt to ascribe value to translingual practice as inherently superior to "monolingual" practices (see Introduction) but to approach it as a rubric by which to make sense of the certitude of cultures prior to their purported hybridizations.

If we return to Bhabha (1994), cultural hybridity "constitutes the discursive conditions of enunciation that ensure that the meaning and symbols of culture have no primordial unity or fixity; that even the same signs can be appropriated, translated, rehistoricized and read anew" (p. 55). Cultural hybridity, from this perspective, is productive not for understanding how multiple, ostensibly homogeneous and stable cultures and their respective practices (including linguistic practices) transform one another via contact. Instead, quite the opposite might be true if we approach culture from what Bhabha (1994) calls a "contradictory and ambivalent space of enunciation" (p. 55). While cultures can never exist in an isolated vacuum, simultaneously, it is through moments of contact with or juxtaposition to others that the representational discreteness of a given culture can be optimally observed. Put simply, hybridity enables us to see what was presumed to be distinctive about a particular cultural category to begin with. I am, of course, not merely aiming to provide a mere reinstantiation of Bhabha's thesis. Instead, by attending to the wide array of elements within translingual ecologies in which cultural discreteness is reiterated, we can move toward a more comprehensive (though perhaps never entirely complete) understanding of the semiotic attributes that enable categorical assumptions around culture and language. In short, it is not a matter of how a particular "culture" or even "language" is transformed as a result of their relocations across global space; instead, it is a matter of trying to understand the features that are considered to be constitutive of such cultures in the first place.

1.2 *TRANSLINGUAL INVERSION*

In order to arrive at a fuller sense of the various ways in which culture can be "located" across global space, it is necessary to both understand how semiotically salient features of a culture can be subject to change over time but also make sense of the ways in which such emblems can come to be enregistered (Agha, 2007) as representative of a given culture. Of course, this approach to culture, in particular the treatment of culture as "semiotic," is indebted to a longstanding history of ethnographic accounts of cultural distinction (see Geertz, 1973, p. 5). For my purposes, I want to focus on understanding the semiotic emblems as they are encountered across global space, in contexts representative of semiotic precarity. I refer to this phenomenon by which semiotic resources come to be enregistered as emblematic of a given culture as *translingual inversion*. The heuristic of translingual inversion reflects the possibility that what is deemed to be representative of a given culture needs to be understood not only in relation to what are assumed to be the core, distinguishable features of culture but also in relation to how the very phenomenon of representation calls into question our assumptions about what we assume the culture is supposed to look like to begin with. My use of "inversion," thus, draws primarily from Miyako Inoue's (2004) notion of indexical inversion, which enables us to historicize the sedimentation of a given indexical order (e.g., how certain semiotic resources have come to be associated with a given culture) while also understanding their indexical capacities in situ. Meanwhile, my use of "translingual" aims to develop one of the points invoked in the Introduction, which is that a translingual orientation to language understands that communication need not be treated as limited to "language" but as inviting attention to the wide range of semiotic resources and spatial elements that are constitutive of a communicative moment or phenomena.

One of the fundamental premises to my inquiry is the notion that semiotic aspects of cultural distinction, or in other words the ostensibly discrete features of a particular culture by which it can be distinguished from other cultures, are not fixed but rather continually reimagined. In regards to this premise, a useful starting point is perhaps Ludwig Wittgenstein's (1953) theorization of family resemblance. The famous example presented by Wittgenstein is the case of games, including "board-games, card-games, ball-games, Olympic games, and so on" (§66). It is indeed difficult to settle on an all-encompassing and categorical definition of something as expansive as a "game," but according to the notion of family resemblance, we are not able to conclude that "there must be something in common, or they would not be called 'games'." However, the very concept of the "game" exists because instead "we *look* and *see* ... family resemblances," that is, "similarities, relationships, and a whole series" of corresponding features, rather than sufficient criteria in every activity we call a "game" (Wittgenstein, 1953, §66).[1] Certainly, there is an inherently diverse denotative range within the concept of the "game," but the point is that we tend to categorize and taxonomize things according to an imaginary checklist of features, but we hardly ever expect the checklist to be complete.

A similar point might be made about the notion of culture. Approaching the semiotically salient features of a given culture as a family resemblance is productive for understanding how various cultural entities *look* in the context of globalization. I am of course not trying to make the simple point that by comparing different cultures we can locate family resemblances with respect to analogous cultural practices among many (to determine, for instance, that most all cultures have some form of a dumpling in their culinary repertoire and to locate the essential feature in each cuisine that makes it categorically a dumpling). I am referring instead to identifying various semiotic iterations of a given culture and trying to determine if there are any shared corresponding traits among them as a family resemblance (what various semiotic objects are chosen to represent a given culture and what, if anything, do they have in common?). This approach is useful because, on the one hand, it is assumed that any cultural entity will undergo changes as a result of movements across geographic spaces and contact with other cultures. Approaching the semiotics of culture as family resemblance could then potentially enable us to take stock of how such changes can be rendered visible. However, such an approach runs the risk of assuming the semiotic fixity of a given culture prior to the changes it is purportedly expected to undergo in response to the cultural flows of globalization. For instance, to continue with the example of "games," when trying to determine how the Japanese "adapt" the sport of baseball one would need to assume to a certain degree that a) baseball is played according to a uniform set of conventions and guidelines across all prefectures, cities, neighborhoods, leagues, schools, and teams in the entire nation of Japan, and b) it is also played uniformly across all states, counties, cities, neighborhoods, leagues, schools, and teams in the entire United States. Such an inquiry would need to rely on a set of unproductive and

---

[1] See also Rosch (1973) on "natural prototypes."

unjustifiable generalizations for both national contexts and would provide, at best, a snapshot in a given moment in time because the sport, in any context, like any sport or game, will invariably undergo some form of change over the years. There is still work to do, in other words, to understand what we believe cultural entities are supposed to look like prior to their transformations across global space.[2] Rather than simply accepting what they look like as fixed givens, examining their iterations across global contexts affords us a unique opportunity to pursue such a line of investigation: to understand what we expect culture to look like in the first place.

The instability but also malleability of cultural semiosis (i.e., the fact that semiotic features associated with a given culture are not fixed and can undergo change, sometimes logical or predictable, sometimes irrational or unexpected, over time) is of course not a controversial point. Iedema's (2003) notion of resemiotization, for one, serves as a reminder of "how meaning making shifts from context to context, from practice to practice, or from one stage of a practice to the next" (p. 41). Silverstein's (2013) framework of three intersecting dimensions of signification–circulation–emanation is an additionally useful way of making sense of such semiotic change. In this framework the three dimensions are conceptualized as such:

a. a regime of evenemential signification immanent in the very experience of situated social practice,
b. a regime of implied paths or networks of circulation of signifying value across such event-nodes in an intuited socio-spatio-temporal structure, and
c. a regime of multiple centers and peripheries – polar-coordinated geometries – of circulatory emanation of signifying value always, inevitably, in flux. (Silverstein, 2013, p. 328)

Silverstein illustrates the phenomenon of cultural signification through an interaction between two law school students in which a complex network of indexical presuppositions shapes their ability to identify with one another. Even in a short interaction, details such as their regional upbringing (Chicago, Illinois vs. Iowa) or connections between their respective undergraduate alma maters (Loyola

---

[2] Perhaps a notable exception is Wierzbicka (1992), who has written on semantic primitives in various cultures, such as "soul," which can be translated into Russian as "duša," but not the other way around. While the focus of Wierzbicka's work is to provide a "culture-independent analytical framework" through "universal" semantic concepts across cultures (p. 26), it is noted that various primitives decline in given cultures as a result of linguistic contact.

University of Chicago and Georgetown University, which are both Jesuit institutions) are representative of how cultural knowledge can be "made flesh" (Silverstein, 2013, p. 333). The circulation of cultural signification, meanwhile, is made possible by the inherently intertextual nature of communication, whereby "communicative events creatively referenc[e] other communicative events" (p. 334). Circulation here is a reminder of not only how signification in communication depends on reference to prior or subsequent events but also how the semiotically salient features of culture are subject to change across social, spatial, and temporal contexts. Finally, emanation is illustrated through the example of "wine talk," or what Silverstein terms "oinoglossia." Wine talk is a compelling case study in semiotic emanation in part because it is both associated with a particular class standing but also regularly lampooned for its snobbery. The culture of wine talk also has come to be adopted to frame the discourse around other comestibles, "turning them into metaphorical wine" (p. 349), so to speak. In Silverstein's words:

> the institutional world of wine has become a center point of "emanation" of ways of constructing prestige throughout a whole world of construable comestibles, edible and potable commodities that are brought into the stratified precincts in which wine has long had a social life. So today, just as one can be admired/reviled, imitated/shunned for being a "wine snob" (a folk term of opprobriousness from outside the fold), so also can one find a parallel place in the universe of experiencers of coffee, beer, cheese, ice cream, olive oil, vodka, et cetera. (p. 349)

In sum, the framework of signification–circulation–emanation enables us to understand how semiotic features of a given culture come to be salient, how they both index expected features and serve as the foundational point for emergent features of a given culture, and how they can shape semiotic regimes of signification beyond the given culture. Whether we adopt Silverstein's framework or the principle of resemiotization, to borrow Iedema's (2003) term, which facilitates inquiries into "socio-semiotic histories and transitions" (p. 48), acknowledging the inherent flexibility of semiosis is a productive starting point to approach cultural signification as a resemblance concept. This acknowledgment enables us on the one hand to account for what is something of a contradiction: while cultures can be represented semiotically, such semiotic representations are at best a mere snapshot of culture in a given moment of time. But more importantly, it allows us to understand how cultural entities are constituted by a subset of traits akin to what Agha (2007) describes as "enregistered emblems," which come to be iconically representative of culture across a range of global contexts.

In the Introduction, I described how I conceive of the translingual turn in sociolinguistics and how its theoretical affordances (namely, the focus on space as central, rather than peripheral, to communication) are relevant to my inquiry at hand. Stepping now into the question of "inversion," I proceed with Inoue's (2004) notion of indexical inversion, which describes the contingency of indexicality on ideological priorities, developing Silverstein's (1996, 2003) concept of indexical orders and Irvine and Gal's (2000) concept of iconization. As we know, the meanings and values of specific words derive not from their linguistic structure but are attributed to them by social actors and institutions. In this sense, returning to Silverstein's (1996, 2003) notion of indexical order turns out to be particularly instructive. For Silverstein, indexical orders, which can be represented as the nth order, $n+1$st order, etc., can direct us to how meanings afforded to semiotic resources can be on the basis of either "presupposition" or of "entailment." As an example, a word that is determined to be "creative" does not inherently signify creativity but can be determined to do so according to "an already constituted framework of semiotic value" (Silverstein, 2003, p. 194). Nevertheless, the relationship between the nth vs. the $n+1$st orders, or the "presupposition/entailment relationship is not simply linear or one-dimensional, like a temporal 'before' and 'after' to an indexical event," but rather "a complex and mediated one" (p. 196).

Additionally central to the notion of indexical inversion is Irvine and Gal's (2000) concept of iconization, a framework for understanding "linguistic features that index social groups or activities [that] appear to be iconic representations of them, as if a linguistic feature somehow depicted or displayed a social group's inherent nature or essence" (p. 37). A compelling historical case in point is to be found in the linguistic mappings of sub-Saharan Africa during the mid-1800s, coinciding with the early years of European colonization of the continent. As we know, in many regions around the world, the *national* as a cultural category, along with the nation-state as a political entity, simply did not exist prior to colonial occupation by Western powers. The designation of peoples and territories according to national boundaries was facilitated by the consolidation of peoples according to their language. Irvine and Gal (2000) use the example of how Senegalese "languages" (Fula, Wolof, and Sereer) were mapped onto the region in accordance with newly formed territorial boundaries. Along the way, languages and linguistic variations that did not fit this new linguistic–political mapping were simply ignored, reflective of what Irvine and Gal term "erasure." Further, assumptions about these languages were in turn treated as iconic of their speakers: speakers of Fula were considered "delicate," speakers of Wolof "less intelligent," and speakers of Sereer as having "primitive simplicity" (p. 55).[3]

Inoue (2004) develops the premises of indexical order and iconization in her theory of indexical inversion, which is illustrated through the engineered pathologization of Japanese "women's language." As Inoue demonstrates, by locating the origins of such speech in the past, "its primordial existence is permanently deferred" to the extent that subsequently any encounter can only be conceived of in terms of "linguistic corruption" (p. 40). This point is illustrated through the case of "schoolgirl speech," also known as "*teyo-dawa* speech" due its frequency of "*teyo*" and "*dawa*" verb endings, which was deemed "unpleasant to the ears" by male educators at the turn of the twentieth century, a moment which coincided with the opening of new high schools for women (p. 45). Ironically, in the late twentieth century, when larger numbers of women entered the labor force and gained economic independence, men began to complain about women who would speak "like a man." They bemoaned the "corruption" of women's speech and the "source of women's linguistic contamination" was pursued "temporally as the consequence of degeneration from the imagined first-order of indexicality, the archaic existence of pristine feminine speech in the past" (p. 51). In short, the very features of speech (such as "*teyo*" and "*dawa*" verb endings) would be retroactively positioned as indexing ideals such as purity or elegance, even if they were, just decades prior, representative of linguistic corruption. The notion of indexical inversion is not only useful for understanding how meaning making of linguistic variables occurs in accordance with a predictable sequence of indexical orders but also within what Penelope Eckert (2008) describes as the indexical field, or the "constellation of ideologically related meanings, any one of which can be activated in the situated use of the variable" (p. 454).

---

[3] This example also illustrates Irvine and Gal's (2000) notion of fractal recursivity, which "involves the projection of an opposition, salient at some level of relationship, onto some other level" (p. 38). In the case of the linguistic colonization of the Senegalese region: "The multilingualism was supposed to have been introduced, along with religious and political complexity, through a history of conquest and conversion that paralleled the European conquest and the hierarchical relationships thought to obtain between Europeans and Africans – relationships of white to black, complex to simple, and dominant to subordinate. That is, relationships between Europeans and Africans were the implicit model for a history of relationships within Africa itself" (p. 55).

Further, while the notion of indexical inversion is a means to understand the role of "temporality and historicity in the *linguistic* analysis" (Inoue, 2004, p. 52, emphasis added), for my purposes I adopt and apply it in a broader sense to understand indexical signification into the larger domain of the semiotics of a culture's enregistered emblems more generally. While I do focus on language in a more conventional linguistic sense in Chapter 3, overall I treat indexical inversion as a productive way of approaching the dynamics of indexical signification as it occurs and plays out both linguistically and also semiotically and spatially. In short, I adopt a translingual orientation to language that sees the semiotic and the spatial as central to communication, which I hope enables us to attend to the wide range of elements that could potentially play a role in understanding the logics of indexical inversion (see Introduction).

By harnessing the above insights, the concept of translingual inversion treats cultural entities as resemblance concepts whose ability to be semiotically represented hinges on a series of emblems that are deemed to share similarities. However, such emblems, even if they can effectively represent a culture in a given moment of signification, are subject to change or resemiotization. Further, the similarities between and among such emblems are not inherent or a priori givens but enregistered as such in ideologically mediated and socially negotiated contexts of meaning making, understood as such only in a given moment of time. In this sense, this phenomenon can begin to be made sense of when approached through the framework of indexical inversion as offered by Inoue insofar as their cultural emblematization is contingent on the assumption of a temporal regime that is "permanently deferred." However, to clarify, this is not only about the manipulation of indexical orders but also about the complex interplay of linguistic/semiotic resources, and spatial elements that are inevitably at work in the semiosis of culture (i.e., determining what culture "looks like" in global space).

Further, the notion of inversion is applicable in somewhat of a figurative sense that deviates from the usage in Inoue's original conceptualization of indexical inversion. In the Introduction, I noted the importance of approaching culture not only from above but obliquely. My proposed approach to culture is in some senses an inverted one: I am looking to understand cultural semiosis not only from the expected sites of cultural production (e.g., the originary homeland) but also from spaces of semiotic precarity where there is an added imperative to semiotize culture and render it legible.[4] In other words, what can we learn about

---

[4] This point is illustrated in Chapter 4 through an engagement with Billig's (1995) theory of banal nationalism, which argues that in contemporary democratic

the semiotically salient features of a culture such as Korea that in turn render it transposable to other cultural entities not based on what we encounter in Korea but in a "derivative" space such as a Koreatown in a different part of the world?

While translingual inversion as a theoretical heuristic can be applied to a broad range of cultural contexts, in this book I focus on the national imaginary of Korea and its global iterations. Further, while the notion of translingual inversion helps us to identify, and therefore better understand, the particularities of cultural difference, there is a wide range of political, ideological, and historical considerations that we need to attend to in order to understand the shifting contours of national imaginaries in particular (Heller, 2011). The affordances of (and limitations to) focusing on the global Korean context will be described in fuller detail in the following chapter. For now, I will first describe some of the complexities related to understanding the representability not only of cultural entities generally but of *national* imaginaries specifically.

1.3   NATIONAL IMAGINARIES AND REPRESENTATIONAL PRECARITY

The nation continues to be imagined, certainly in the sense of "community" according to Benedict Anderson's (1983) now time-less expression of the "imagined community," but also frequently as the site of departure for scholarly inquiries into the *global*. Such is the case with inquiries framed phenomenologically in terms of globalization or cosmopolitanism or, more explicitly, in terms of trans*national*ism and post*national*ism.[5] In such inquiries, the global, as an outcome, a framing, a process, or as a method, is presumed to be derivative of the national, as something that follows the national (to use the same example again: there is an original Korea and a global iteration such as a Koreatown in Los Angeles that is derivative of the original). While it does indeed seem commonsensical to understand the global as the space across which the national can be reiterated, this premise becomes

---

societies national identification is achieved through innocuous or inconspicuous ways.

[5] Darian-Smith and McCarthy (2017), in their foundational work *The Global Turn*, are correct to frame global imaginaries as discrete from international imaginaries and even transnational imaginaries. I address this question, particularly the one considering the global as distinct from the transnational, in further detail in Chapter 2.

complicated when we attend to the challenges inherent to representing any national imaginary.

Following Anderson's (1983) work, the expression "national imaginary" has come to be employed ubiquitously throughout numerous academic fields and is indeed frequently used synonymously with the term "nation." It derives from Anderson's key argument, which is that nations are "imagined communities" in that, without the establishment and development of "print-capitalism," or "print-as-commodity," and the subsequent stabilization and distribution of vernacular languages in stabilized print form, the very idea of national consciousness would not have been possible (p. 37). Anderson proposes that the capacity of print capitalism to forge national consciousness reflects an epistemic shift away from Messianic time, or "a simultaneity of past and future in an instantaneous present" (B. Anderson, 1991, p. 24), to that of homogeneous, empty time.[6] In homogeneous, empty time, it is possible to conceive of a nonfinite number of events occurring in a given moment through a shared synchronization not only through technologies such as newspapers or history textbooks but also through a temporal epistemic shift toward the "meanwhile" and the subsequent possibility of other events happening "meanwhile" (p. 24). Anderson illustrates this point through the example of a hypothetical timeline of events involving a man (A) who is married to a woman (B) but has a mistress (C) who in turn also has a lover (D):

Time:	I	II	III
Events:	A quarrels with B C and D make love	A telephones C B shops D plays pool	D gets drunk in a bar A dines at home with B C has an ominous dream

---

[6] Walter Benjamin (1968) writes: "Historicism rightly culminates in universal history. Materialistic historiography differs from it as to method more clearly than from any other kind. Universal history has no theoretical armature. Its method is additive; it musters a mass of data to fill the homogeneous, empty time. Materialistic historiography, on the other hand, is based on a constructive principle. Thinking involves not only the flow of thoughts, but their arrest as well ... A historical materialist approaches a historical subject only where he encounters it as a monad. In this structure he recognizes the sign of a Messianic cessation of happening, or, put differently, a revolutionary chance in the fight for the oppressed past. He takes cognizance of it in order to blast a specific era out of the homogeneous course of history – blasting a specific life out of the era or a specific work out of the lifework" (pp. 262–263).

All four people, especially A and D, "can even be described as passing each other on the street, without ever becoming acquainted, and still be connected" (B. Anderson, 1991, p. 26). Further, A's infidelities can occur without the knowledge of B, D, and even of C, assuming, of course, that C is unaware of A's marital status. Time, thus, comes to be understood not only progressing horizontally in linear fashion, but also having a vertical capacity to the extent that, even if we do not meet every single individual within our particular national imaginary, we have "complete confidence in their steady, anonymous, simultaneous activity" (p. 26). As we see in the case of the hypothetical persons A, B, C, and D, the certainty of an event having occurred is possible in spite of our precise knowledge of specific details of or bearing direct witness to others' "simultaneous activity." Certainly, while homogeneous, empty time is a critical precursor to the imaginability of the nation, because it is so ubiquitous today it is difficult to imagine the alternative to Messianic time. The takeaway from this is that the temporal contingency of the nation (i.e., that national consciousness depends on a series of discrete moments of communal synchronization) is closely related to the contingency of the national on semiosis, a point which I will return to shortly.

When we attend to the range of social, ideological, and political considerations that have emerged within the scholarly literature of nations and nationalism, one of the most immediate observations is that the very question of the national has itself always been subject to considerable revision and renegotiation. Much has been written on the origins of nations, considering whether nations are extensions of premodern societies (Geertz, 1973; Smith, 1986), or whether nations are better conceived of as inventions of modernity (B. Anderson, 1983; Gellner, 1983; Hobsbawm, 1990). Geertz (1973), writing specifically about "new" postcolonial states, argued that such societies were constitutive of a "primordial attachment" based on

> the "givens" – or, more precisely, as culture is inevitably involved in such matters, the assumed "givens" – of social existence: immediate contiguity and kin connection mainly, but beyond them the givenness that stems from being born into a particular religious community, speaking a particular language, or even a dialect of a language, and following particular social practices. (p. 259)

Human societies have, according to Geertz, always had the capacity for identification on the basis of various "givens," and as such nationalisms scarcely represent anything different from analogous protonational forms of political belonging and coalition. Similarly, Anthony Smith (1986) has proposed that nations are, at their core, evolved formations of premodern ethnic groups. In short, according to the primordialist perspective, national belonging and identification are merely timeless forms of community with a new "face" or under a new "brand" of the "nation."

According to the modernist perspective, however, the nation, and particularly the political doctrine of nationalism, are relatively new developments. As Ernest Gellner (1983) has argued in his *Nations and Nationalism*, nations do not merely coincide with the advent of Western industrialization but also could not have existed in nonindustrial societies, including agroliterate societies. And while various scholars have attempted to identify specific historical moments from which different nations derive, as Walker Connor (1990) notes in his influential essay "When Is a Nation?":

> A key problem faced by scholars when dating the emergence of nations is that national consciousness is a mass, not an élite phenomenon, and the masses until recently isolated in rural pockets and being semi- or totally illiterate, were quite mute with regard to their sense of group identity(ies). Scholars have been necessarily largely dependent upon written word for their evidence, yet it has been élites who have chronicled history. Seldom have their generalities about national consciousness been applicable to the masses, and very often the élites' conception of the nation did not even extend to the masses. (p. 100)

For Connor, there is a larger problem of relying upon historical evidence as representative of the emergence of a particular thing or phenomenon (i.e., nation or nationalism). While he cautions against the conclusiveness of such inquiry, he nonetheless does align himself with the consensus of the modernist perspective: "In any event, claims that a particular nation existed prior to the late-nineteenth century should be treated cautiously" (Connor 1990, p. 100). As Eric Hobsbawm (1990) argues in his *Nations and Nationalism since 1780*, nations are relatively new entities that have been formalized if not outright invented by nationalism itself. As he notes in his memorable adage: "Nations do not make states and nationalisms but the other way around" (p. 10). To illustrate his point, he offers the anecdote of the manufacture of Italian nationalist sentiment following Il Risorgimento (Resurgence), the political movement that led to the unification of Italy in the nineteenth century: "In the days of the Mazzini it did not matter that, for the great bulk of Italians, the Risorgimento did not exist so that, as Massimo d'Azeglio admitted in the famous phrase: 'We have made Italy, now we have to make Italians'" (p. 44).[7]

Bhabha (1994) argues that the historicism of the nation is compounded by the fact that it exists along two contradictory temporal coordinates:

> the people are the historical "objects" of a nationalist pedagogy, giving the discourse an authority that is based on the pre-given or constituted historical origin *in the past*; the people are also the "subjects" of a process of signification that must erase any prior or originary presence of the nation-people to demonstrate the prodigious, living principles of the people as contemporaneity: as that sign of the *present* through which national life is redeemed and iterated as a reproductive process. (p. 208)

In other words, even if there can be agreement on the historical origins of the nation, in order for the nation to survive, it must be continually resignified and performed, and as such the nation's fixity in historical time is effectively negated. This, then, places an additional layer of strain on the already tenuous grounds of national derivation. There can be an official national history by which a people conceive of themselves as a collective entity, but peoples of the present will either challenge or uphold that history, which is invariably irretrievable in its definitive form, according to the more immediate ways in which people talk about, write about, or "narrate" (Bhabha, 1990) the nation.

Certainly, the problem of derivation is not one limited to the question of nations and nationalism but arguably applicable to politics more generally. Such a problem is alluded to in Kevin Olson's (2016) exploration of the problem of the political revolution writ large:

> Consider the following series of numbers: 1649, 1688, 1776, 1789, 1848, 1871, 1917, 1956, 1968, 1989. We are predisposed to look for a mathematical relationship, yet something else stands out. We parse these numbers as a set of dates representing iconic punctuations in the fabric of "normal" politics. The Eurocentrism of this list is problematic. Yet it also illustrates my broader point, that we select particular, often iconic moments of political exceptionality to represent the political in its purest form. (p. 10)

While certainly not all of the dates above are related to nationalism particularly, Olson's point is nonetheless instructive in foregrounding the lure of the "representative" origins of political thinking which can

---

[7] *Il Risorgimento* (Resurgence) refers to the political unification of the different states of the Italian peninsula in the nineteenth century.

in turn "obscure the longer lines of continuity across eras, societies, and cultures" (p. 11). But it is also important to stress that with national imaginaries the question of derivation (i.e., where a nation comes from, what its origins are) is especially tantamount while also reflective of an added layer of representational uncertainty. Within this question of derivation, we additionally see that the "facts" of derivation are not usually bound to questions of historical accuracy. Admittedly, there is also the very real consideration of historical amnesia or indifference by everyday people. As Benedict Anderson (1991) notes, in his discussion of the origins of nationalism in Southeast Asia, "no one imagines, I presume, that the broad masses of the Chinese people give a fig for what happens along the colonial border between Cambodia and Vietnam. Nor is it all likely that Khmer and Vietnamese peasants wanted wars between their peoples, or were consulted in the matter" (p. 161). When it comes to the nation, it is no secret that historical facts are constantly subject to renegotiation and recirculation, even if they are understood to be, in the back of the minds of even those who are minimally rational, simply false. Indeed, even the aforementioned perennialist and modernist approaches to nationalism more generally are essentially questions of derivation in the sense that they collectively aim to understand what historical factors shaped social and political consciousness in a measurable, impactful way, in turn leading to the possibility of nationalist thinking. Certainly, perennialist and modernist perspectives are not diametrically opposed and it could be said that they "are both right to a degree" (Kerr, 2019, p. 106). Nonetheless, all theories of nationalism, whether perennialist, modernist, or otherwise, appear to be bound to questions of derivation, even if they may fundamentally disagree on the *terms* of derivation.

The preoccupation with the question of derivation, while reflective of a larger problem of historicity more generally, serves as a simple reminder that the category of the national, and its respective specificities, has always been subject to contingency and reconsideration via discourse. It might be useful to turn to Ernest Renan's landmark 1882 lecture "Qu'est-ce qu'une nation?" and to consider how it has shaped the discourse of nationalism more generally. In the lecture, Renan insisted that, beyond linguistic, racial, religious, or geographical factors, central to the nation's existence is historical amnesia, or forgetting: "Forgetting, I would even go so far as to say historical error, is a crucial factor in the creation of a nation, which is why progress in historical studies often constitutes a danger for [the principle of] nationality" (Renan, [1882]1990, p. 11). In Benedict Anderson's earlier iteration of his imagined community thesis, the capacity to "forget" was requisite to the individual's capacity to imagine a communal relationship with a stranger within the political rubric of the nation. Here is Anderson in the first (1983) edition of *Imagined Communities*:

> [The nation] is *imagined* because the members of even the smallest nation will never know most of their fellow-members, meet them, or even hear of them, yet in the minds of each lives the image of their communion. Renan referred to this imagining in his suavely back-handed way when he wrote that "Or l'essence d'une nation est que tous les individus aient beaucoup de choses en commun, et aussi que tous aient oublié bien des choses." (p. 15)[8]

The capacity for imagining community was sustained, it was implied in the 1983 version of the text, in spite of the community's ability to both selectively remember but also forget historically significant moments: Renan uses the examples of "la Saint-Barthélemy" and "les massacres du Midi au XIIIe siècle."

To complicate matters further, in the preface to the second (1991) edition, Anderson would later acknowledge that he had misunderstood Renan:

> The origin of the second "appendix" [the "Memory and Forgetting" chapter] was the humiliating recognition that in 1983 I had quoted Renan without the slightest understanding of what he had actually said: I had taken something easily ironical what was in fact utterly bizarre. (p. xiv)

As Benedict Anderson (1991) explains in the "appendix," the possibility of having forgotten such events is illogical not only because Renan invokes examples of historical events that his readers could not have forgotten (he mentions them as if the readers must or should know what he is referring to) but also because of how Renan frames the "obligation" to forget almost as a "civic duty." In other words, "Renan's readers were being told to 'have already forgotten' what Renan's own words assumed that they naturally remembered!" (p. 200).

There is something not insignificant about the fact that Anderson's self-declared *misreading* of Renan was so central to his thesis of the imagined community, if anything because it remains among the most influential scholarly texts by which we understand what nations are and where they come from. The fact that the very notion of the nation

---

[8] This line in Renan might be translated as "However, the essence of a nation is that all of its individuals have much in common, and also that all have forgotten many things."

as *imagined* is based on a fundamental misreading of Renan points also to a potential problem of intellectual *derivation*: many theses of nationalism specifically and social practice more generally derive from *Imagined Communities*, which itself is derived from dubious origins. Therefore, there are many places where the historical and material contours of the nation remain contested: not only in the minds of Renan's 1882 audience but in the pages of arguably the most influential scholarly treatise on nationalism. As of 2020, Anderson's work has been cited well over 100,000 times, according to Google Scholar metrics. As a point of comparison, Ernest Gellner's *Nations and Nationalism*, which was published in the same year, 1983, and posits its own theory for the origins of nationalist thought though not the beneficiary of serendipitous intellectual uptake and influence (cursed in part, no doubt, from being published in the same year but without as catchy a title), has been cited a "mere" 23,000 times. In sum, the question of derivation that surrounds a foundational text of nationalism is analogous to the multilayered complexities surrounding questions of derivation within the nation itself.

To complicate matters a bit further, while Anderson's work is frequently referenced as the key text on the origins of national consciousness, its unstated assumption of the nation as a "universal" political ideal has been called into question, adding another layer of complexity around the issue of derivation. Partha Chatterjee's (1986) *Nationalist Thought and the Colonial World: A Derivative Discourse?* in particular questions the assumption that nationalisms of the Global South are derivative of a post-Enlightenment European ideal. Certainly, while nationalism initiated a new form of political thinking (what Chatterjee refers to as the "moment of departure"), it evolves in postcolonial contexts to the extent that the end result is no longer derivative of a European original (referred to as the "moment of arrival"). The subject of Chatterjee's ire is Anderson's treatment of nationalism as a consequence of "sociological determinism" (p. 21), in which it is viewed as a merely "modular" political movement and an "anthropological fact" (p. 22). He is especially critical of the implied proposition of Anderson's "modularity" thesis with respect to twentieth century third-world nationalisms. While those familiar with postcolonial theory are certainly aware of Chatterjee's argument, an especially memorable excerpt of his polemic from his follow-up work, *The Nation and Its Fragments*, is worth repeating in full:

> I have one central objection to Anderson's argument. If nationalisms
> in the rest of the world have to choose their imagined community

> from certain "modular" forms already made available to them by Europe and the Americas, what do they have left to imagine? History, it would seem, has decreed that we in the postcolonial world shall only be perpetual consumers of modernity. Europe and the Americas, the only true subjects of history, have thought out on our behalf not only the script of colonial enlightenment and exploitation, but also that of our anticolonial resistance and postcolonial misery. Even our imaginations must remain forever colonized. (Chatterjee, 1993, p. 5)

There is of course little to debate in Chatterjee's argument, and by now concerns over the ubiquitousness and dominance of Eurocentric, or in this case Euroamerican-centric, epistemologies have been well documented and extensively problematized. But there is a very minor detail around Chatterjee's book that I believe is relevant to the conversation at hand: the question mark in the subtitle of the book, *A Derivative Discourse?*, does not appear on the book's cover. The fact that this is an error can be confirmed by the fact that the question mark additionally remained missing on the title page of the book through its initial printing and through numerous reprintings.[9] While it is of course in all likelihood a mere oversight introduced at some stage during the book's production process, I can't help but view it as nonetheless having larger implications, if anything since the question mark is key to the book's central thesis: are you saying that nationalist thought in the colonial world is a derivative discourse? Let me show you how it's not. The absent/present question mark is also, more generally, an apt metaphor, even if incidental, of the sheer uncertainty surrounding the question of the national in relation to derivation that I have been describing.[10]

Further, it is important to note that while Chatterjee criticizes Benedict Anderson for locating the origins of nationalist thought in "Europe *and* the Americas" (emphasis added), Anderson himself made it a point to emphasize that it emerged from the Americas, not Europe. Relative to his contemporaries, Anderson was something of an outlier in

---

[9] It is difficult to determine in which printing the question mark was properly included. My personal copy is a sixth printing from 2008, and I have only been able to see the first and second printings, both of which do not include the all-important question mark.

[10] One could even make the argument that the absent/present question mark is also a metaphor for the inherent uncertainty surrounding the utopian aspirations that undergird Chatterjee's (1986) project, from Mahatma Gandhi's utopian vision of the postcolonial nation-state whose foundation would be the moral investment in the nation, secondary to "*political* practice" (p. 117, emphasis in original) to Jawaharlal Nehru's "utopia, a realist's utopia, a utopia here and now," (p. 160) that "could be realized here and now, in the rational life of the state" (p. 161).

making this point, and he himself would bemoan how his readers and critics would assume that he was locating the origins of nationalism in Europe. He in fact complains that it was part of the "original plan to stress the New World origins of nationalism," but that the chapter in which he discusses this point, "Old Empires, New Nations," was "largely ignored" (B. Anderson, 1983, p. xiii). He thus made the decision to rename the chapter in question to "Creole Pioneers" in the revised 1991 edition (p. xiii). Of course, this does not alleviate Chatterjee's concerns entirely, for the presumption that nationalist thought originated in the Americas nonetheless implies that nationalisms of the postcolonial world were derived elsewhere. But it adds just one more, if not again minor, moment of misreading and misunderstanding to the sequence of inaccuracies in derivation.

In summary, there are numerous complications facing any attempt to locate and represent culture generally and the nation particularly, which is in turn complicated by uncertainty surrounding the question of derivation as it pertains to the national both as object of inquiry and within its respective discourses. As I have attempted to show in this section, it is widely acknowledged that nations are dependent on dubious historical facts. On top of this, even leading accounts of nationalism are not only contradictory to others (this is to be expected in any scholarly debate) or subject to considerable scholarly revision (any respectable scholar should be able to acknowledge misguided thinking in their previous works), but also fraught with uncertainty. In short, it is not a matter of nations as contingent on "historical error" as described by Renan, but on one key scholar, Anderson's, self-acknowledged "error" about this "error," which in turn sets off a chain of events: a widely referenced theory of nationalism whose foundations are based on an "error," which coincidentally generates "errors" in reading (locating the origins of nationalist thought in Europe). Therefore, while the question of derivation (i.e., the origins of nations) is central to the subject of the national, both in terms of the object of study and within its respective discourse, it is also what makes the national so difficult to both conceptualize and represent.

1.4   NATIONAL IMAGINARIES AND THE LOGIC OF SERIALITY

So where do we go from here? As suggested so far in this chapter, I have been stressing the challenges of conceptualizing and representing the national not as an exercise of surrender (i.e., the national is notoriously difficult to pinpoint, even for its leading historians and theorists, so we might as well not try) but instead partly as a disclaimer and as a move toward a solution. If we return briefly to the notion of nation as imagined community, significant is the fact, in spite of the criticisms it has been subject to, it has actually served to be key to understanding how people perform community belonging and identification across global space contrary to the political paradigm of nationalism per se. An influential case in point is Arjun Appadurai's (1996) theory of "scapes" as describing "dimensions of global cultural flow," including ethnoscapes (flows of people), mediascapes (flows of information/media), technoscapes (flows of technologies), financescapes (flows of money), and ideoscapes (flows of ideologies and knowledges) (pp. 33–36). Appadurai's theory was offered as an alternative to the then dominant (and arguably still dominant) area studies paradigm, which privileges research focused on phenomena within a fixed geographic region, oftentimes with minimal regard to various aspects of transcultural flow to and from the region in question. Instead of analyzing "trait" geographies, which assume that certain areas "rely on some sort of trait list – of values, languages, material practices, ecological adaptations, marriage patterns, and the like," Appadurai (2001) argues for area studies "based on process geographies[, which] sees significant areas of human organization as precipitates of various kinds of action, interaction, and motion – trade, travel, pilgrimage, warfare, proselytization, colonization, exile, and the like. These geographies are necessarily large scale and shifting, and their changes highlight variable congeries of language, history, and material life" (pp. 7–8).

Appadurai's description of the game of cricket in India is particularly memorable. He describes cricket as representative of a "hard cultural form," or "those that come with a set of links between value, meaning, and embodied practice that are difficult to break and hard to transform" (p. 90). In the postcolonial Indian context, the game is an interesting case for it is not merely a sport but also because it was intended as a means of proselytizing participants to English moral and cultural values. However, as Appadurai argues, the decolonization of cricket, rather than a mere "dismantling of colonial habits and modes of life," is the "product of collective and spectacular experiments with modernity, and not necessarily of the subsurface affinity of new cultural forms with existing patterns in the cultural repertoire" (p. 90). Significant is Appadurai's argument that in the end cricket becomes effectively localized as Indian, resulting in "the appropriation of agonistic bodily skills that can then further lend passion and purpose to the community so imagined" (p. 112).

Appadurai's theory of "scapes" has had a substantial impact on research on the sociolinguistics of globalization (see Dovchin (2017, 2018) on "linguascapes," Tian Li (2019) on "lingualscapes," Pennycook (2010b) on "graffscapes," and Pennycook and Otsuji (2015a) on "smellscapes").[11] As this research shows, cultural and linguistic practices in the era of globalization need not be viewed only in terms of top-down "cultural homogenization" (Appadurai, 1996, p. 11) but also as capable of occurring in "multiple, simultaneous origins of locality" (Pennycook, 2010a, p. 86).

However, at this juncture, I would like to draw attention to a point made by Appadurai while developing his argument about the decolonization of cricket that has remained largely overlooked. In the 1890s, cricket matches would be played between English and Indian teams, though the latter would be a team whose roster consisted primarily of Englishmen. By the 1930s, the level of skill in cricket among Indians themselves had developed to the point where an Indian team composed entirely of Indian players could be created. As Appadurai (1996) writes:

> This process, whereby Indians increasingly came to represent India in cricket, follows not surprisingly the history of the evolution of Indian nationalism as a mass movement. Cricket in the Indian colonial context thus casts an unexpected light on the relationship between nationhood and empire. Insofar as England was not simply identical with the empire [in the 1890s], there had to be other parallel entities in the colonies against which the English nation-state could play: thus "India" had to be invented, at least for the purposes of colonial cricket. (pp. 98–99)

Appadurai goes on to describe how the independence of an Indian cricket team was not merely an inadvertent metaphor for the possibility of Indian national sovereignty but would go on to make national independence conceived of as within the realm of possibility even

---

[11] In my previous work (Jerry Won Lee, 2017), I attempted to theorize the concept of "semioscape," attempting to move beyond the spatio-material limitations of physical territory prevalent within linguistic/semiotic landscape research, which had and has continued to treat communities as bound to a particular place, while also symbolically merging the "semiotic" and "landscape" in order to emphasize their necessary inextricability. Thurlow and Aiello (2007) also use the expression semioscape, imagined as "falling somewhere between" ideoscapes and mediascapes, to "bring into focus the non-mediatized but globalizing circulation of symbols, sign systems and meaning-making practices" (p. 308). My usage, on the other hand, was an attempt to focus more explicitly on the semiotic production of social identification prefigured in relation to the political apparatuses of the nation-state.

though cricket was at one point, ironically, a colonially introduced enterprise: "nationally organized cricket was an internal demand of the colonial demand and thus required cognate national or protonational enterprises in the colonies" (p. 99). An independent Indian cricket team was therefore in many ways the beginnings of an independent Indian nation.

However, what is additionally intriguing about this historical anecdote for our purposes is not only the inspiration of independence or even the affirmation of the national imaginary as subject to ideological invention, which was alluded to earlier in this chapter, but the implication that the materialization (even if via invention) of the national can be witnessed, crucially, from a global view, so to speak. As we know, in the context of British colonial rule, the colonized subject was constructed as both British but simultaneously different and chronically subordinate: as Bhabha (1994) notes, "almost the same but not quite" (p. 122), or "almost the same but not white" (p. 128). But in an effort to facilitate categorical transposability between nation X and nation Y, "India" needed to become a discrete and independent entity for the moment. Therefore, through a global locus, or a view from above where the category of the national is necessarily smaller and thus able to be seen in relation to other categories of the national, we are not only able to account for the national with regard to its respective global cultural flows but, more importantly, how the category of the national is contingent on its continual manipulation and resedimentation in order to be legible in global space.

The affordances of approaching the question of the national from the vantage point of the global can be further understood through what Benedict Anderson (1998) describes as the "logic of seriality." In *The Spectre of Comparisons*, Anderson describes two contrasting types of seriality by which collective subjectivities are conceptualized:

> Unbound seriality, which has its origins in the print market, especially in newspapers, and in the representations of popular performance, is exemplified by such open-to-the-world plurals as nationalists, anarchists, bureaucrats, and workers. It is, for example, the seriality that makes the United Nations a normal, wholly unparadoxical institution. Bound seriality, which has its origins in governmentality, especially in such institutions as the census and elections, is exemplified by finite series like Asian-Americans, *beurs*, and Tutsis. It is seriality that makes a United Ethnicities or a United Identities unthinkable.

The obvious difference is that bound serialities are tied to forms of race or ethnicity and as such are an either/or or a yes/no consideration.

Continuing with Anderson's example of Asian Americans, it is a panethnic political category that one can either belong to or not. This, of course, does not preclude the possibility of becoming Asian American by, say, migrating to the United States from Asia. Further, it does not preclude the possibility of identifying with other racial or ethnic groups, as in the case of a multiracial individual who could be both an Asian American and, say, an African American. And while many important theorizations of ethnicity as socially performed have been offered, as in John Maher's (2005, 2010) notion of metroethnicity, they are not particularly applicable for the purposes of bound serialities. This is not to deny the almost universally accepted idea of the social constructedness of categories of race and ethnicity, but to acknowledge that a census is not really designed to account for whether you opt to perform belonging in one group or another. This is of course not to ignore the fact that the aforementioned yes/no considerations can change in accordance with various shifts in census categories: in the United States, for instance, the category of Asian was introduced for the 1870 census and remained stable until 2000, when it was expanded to include Hawaiians and Pacific Islanders. Regardless of shifts in census categories, however, the point is that while categories of bound serialities can certainly be flexible in this way, they are different from unbound serialities, which are not restricted to considerations of biology or birthright. Unbound serialities, in this sense, reflect the fact that individuals can belong to certain categories that are subject to a higher degree of change and unpredictability. One can be a "nationalist" or an "anarchist" at a given moment in time but the very next day, whether due to enlightenment or disillusionment, not be. Ultimately, they do not pose a contradiction to the organizing unit of the nation.

The logic of seriality also offers some insight into the imperative to distinguish the national specifically in relation to the global, distinct from other categories of the national. Consider, for instance, Anderson's use of the example of the United Nations: it is only through the scale of the supranational that serialization at the level of the national comes to be meaningful, whether we are talking about the United Nations, other supranational entities including international organizations such as the Arab League, the European Union, or the ASEAN (Association of Southeast Asian Nations). Through the logic of seriality, nation X needs to be distinguished from nation Y only when conceptualized in relation to nation Y. Indeed, insofar as a cricket team composed of a group of players from India becomes an Indian cricket team at the moment it needs to compete with (be categorically transposable to) the English cricket team, we might go so far as to say nation X is simply an unnamed entity (i.e., an entity that need not be named) until it is considered in juxtaposition with nation Y. It is therefore from the vantage point of the global (i.e., from Apollo's eye) that we can make sense of how national categories are subject to reinvention and negotiation for the purposes of becoming transposable to other national categories.

1.5 TRANSLINGUAL INVERSION AND THE LOCATION OF NATIONAL IMAGINARIES

In the previous pages, I outlined a theory of translingual inversion that can function as a heuristic to arrive at a more comprehensive understanding of how culture can be "located" across global space, particularly in sites of semiotic precarity. Translingual inversion (1) adopts a capacious view of language not limited to the "linguistic" as such, acknowledging a wider range of communicative agents including semiotic resources and spatial elements, (2) attends to the inherently flexible nature of cultural semiosis, and (3) treats cultural legibility as an "inverted" phenomenon: subject to continual "deferral" to a prior site of indexicality and rendered legible when approached obliquely. Given that the focal point of this book is a specific subset of a cultural form, a national imaginary, I afterwards delineated some core problems related to the conceptualization and representation of the nation, not only due to their dubious histories but also due to the series of "misreadings" or "errors" in the respective discourse of nations. Finally, I noted that the global represents a vantage point from which the category of national can be visibilized, insofar as from such a view it can be conceptualized as an entity transposable to other nations, a point that I attempted to affirm via the logic of seriality.

Bringing this all together, we are now in a position to try and see what the national looks like in the context of the global, guided by the prospect that there is something new we might learn by approaching the national from this perspective. To clarify, I do not mean to suggest there is anything inherently misguided about presuming the national as having an a priori ontological status. I am merely suggesting that there is still work to be done to understand what the national might look like and what new things we might learn about it when approached in this manner. One way to think about this approach would be in relation to Hobsbawm's memorable declaration: "Nations do not make states and nationalisms but the other way around." While

I would not go so far as to argue that "nations do not make the conditions of representational legibility but the other way around," my inquiry might be described as such: "nations do indeed make the conditions of representational legibility but *also* the other way around." The conceptualization of translingual inversion is premised on the fact that it is not an either/or but maybe a both/and: the nation can both be iterated globally but also the global is what renders legible that which is iterated in the first place. Another way of posing the question might be as an extension of Rey Chow's (2014) question, developing Derrida's ([1996]1998) point about prosthetic monolingualism: "What would coloniality look like if and when it is recast as prosthetic rather than assumed as essentially originary – especially in terms of language politics and practices?" (Chow, 2014, p. 33). My question, on the other hand, might be described as such: what would *the nation*, and perhaps culture more generally, look like if and when it is not merely assumed as essentially originary – especially in terms of *global* politics and practices? Like the wager of the bird who encounters a caterpillar that might be a snake, trying to understand what is the head and what is not, or what is the authentic and what is the derivative, along with trying to figure out what helps guide us to make such determinations, even if such determinations are just momentary, is also the wager of translingual inversion.

2 Locating Global Korea

2.1 KOREA AS ICE HOCKEY TEAM

In the previous chapter, I alluded to the subject of inventing the category of the national for the purposes of *inter*national competition (Appadurai, 1996). As we transition to a focused inquiry into the question of global Korea, it is worth mentioning an interesting case in recent memory that is representative of efforts to reinvent and recalibrate the category of the national in order to be in alignment with the parameters of internationality, in which nation X is and needs to be categorically transposable to nation Y. At the 2018 Pyeongchang Winter Olympics, Korea, as the host nation, was automatically qualified to participate in various events, including the men's ice hockey tournament. The problem was that ice hockey had never been one of Korea's strongest areas of sport competition, and by opting to participate there was an immediate urgency to assemble a respectable team that could compete alongside hockey powerhouses like Canada, the Czech Republic, Sweden, and Russia. Of course, the Russian Olympic Committee was suspended from the Olympics that year due to a widely publicized doping scandal. However, the International Olympic Committee agreed to a compromise so as to not unjustly penalize individual athletes who had no connection to the scandal. Such players were thus allowed to compete independently as an "Olympic Athlete from Russia." While the Russian Olympic Committee – the official organization designated to coordinate Russia's participation in the Olympics – was excluded, the nation of Russia effectively was not, and as such did not represent a disruption to the logic of bound seriality (see Chapter 1) by which the category of the national is conceptually possible.

Korea too found itself in a position where it needed to abide by not only the International Olympic Committee's eligibility rules but also the same logic of bound seriality. Rather than proceeding with a roster of exclusively South Korean nationals, the Korean government, in an effort to remain marginally competitive, was willing to fast-track the path to dual citizenship for foreigners, including several Canadians and one US American who were at the time on work visas as professional hockey players in Korea, so they could compete for the national team. The non-Korean hockey players received both approval and legitimization from various media outlets, rationalized by appeals to patriotism (the importance of Olympic success for national pride), pragmatism (the players would enable the national team to be competitive), and acculturation (the players in question had been readily embracing Korean cultural conventions, with some even adopting Korean names) (NaRi Shin, Park, & Peachey, 2020). In some media reports, these athletes were described as "Taegeuk warriors with blue eyes" (p. 21), blending an allusion to the Korean national flag, the Tae-geuk-gi, and the blue eyes associated with Westerners.

Of course, given that we are on the subject of the manipulation of criteria for Korean national belonging via sport, we might be tempted to draw a connection to the case of Hines Ward, a former National Football League (NFL) player who was born in Korea to an African American father and a Korean mother. Despite the fact that Ward's mother, Kim Young Hee, had been ostracized in Korea for marrying a Black man, and that mixed-race individuals in Korea had been subject to (and continue to be subject to) considerable discrimination, Ward was honored along with his mother in Korea after he won the MVP (Most Valuable Player) distinction for Super Bowl XL (40) in 2006. As Rachael Miyung Joo (2012) notes, it was only *after* achieving such accolades that Ward was "embraced as a Korean American with Korean roots" (p. 89) via a romantic "return-to-homeland" (p. 69) narrative. The case of Korean society's postsuccess embrace of Ward along with the contortion of citizenship criteria for the national hockey team both represent cases of how extant criteria for what constitutes Koreanness can be both resourcefully and momentarily reinvented, especially when doing so serves national interests.[1] However, while the societal embrace of Ward was in many ways a calculated attempt to promote Korea as a multicultural and "post-racial" society, what makes the ice hockey scenario distinct is the agenda

---

[1] In the end, perhaps it did not matter, as the Korean team was eliminated in the first round of the qualification playoffs, losing all three matches while being outscored by their opponents for a combined score of 19–3. It is interesting to consider how much worse the outcome would have been for the Korean team had the US- and Canada-based National Hockey League, the most competitive league in the world, opted to permit its players to participate in the Olympics as it did from 1998 to 2014.

of producing a version of Korea transposable to other nations while also in loose alignment with the logic of bound seriality.

While I will return to the above point regarding the flexibility of Koreanness in fuller detail, what I would like to emphasize for now is how the above example of the Korean men's hockey team points not so much to how the nation matters (Calhoun, 2007), but to how the nation specifically matters – or is materialized – in relation to the global. In other words, it is only part of the issue that the very idea of "Korea" was rendered flexible in the interest of a global sporting event that is designed not so much to foster friendly competition among allied nations but to generate millions in revenue for corporate stakeholders and the host nation, especially since the intensified commercialization of the Olympics since the 1960s (Magdalinski & Nauright, 2004). The commercialization of global sport is often achieved through unsustainable development and construction projects, especially when held in rural towns like Pyeongchang, as noted by Jung Woo Lee (2020). Indeed, Aihwa Ong (1999) has argued that even at the level of the individual, decisions for pursuing citizenship and national belonging have less to do with political or ideological commitments to the nation than they do with immediate financial priorities. And of course, this is not the only time in the history of Korean international sport where citizenship criteria were deemed flexible, though there is reason to believe that exceptions were readily made because all the players in question were white, especially when compared to the case of Kenyan-born marathoner Loyanae Erupe, who was unable to secure a similar exception via special naturalization, as argued by Yeomi Choi (2020). I would like to suggest also that the larger issue at hand is the fact that the flexible reinvention of Korea, specifically in relation to the global, provides an opportunity to rethink what Korea is, how it can be rendered transposable to other national imaginaries as such, and what makes it a thing that can be conceptualized in the first place. Take, for instance, the notation of "Taegeuk warriors with blue eyes," which is interesting not only because it represents a clever hybridization of features associated with Korea (tae-geuk) and the West (blue eyes) but also because it puts into relief the impossibility of being both Korean and having blue eyes. As such, it renders explicit what is presumed to make Korea distinct from other cultural groups: a specific national symbol and eyes that are *not* blue. In other words, the condition of not having blue eyes is what renders Korea as a cultural entity transposable to the non-Korean (even if in this case it is momentarily celebrated), and when deployed as a trope reaffirms Korea as a discrete cultural entity.

Following these considerations, this chapter is meant to serve three primary purposes. First, I aim to provide some background on Korea as a national imaginary with a particular focus on aspects of its ethnic national heritage that are relevant to its iterations across the linguistic/ semiotic landscape of global Korea. Second, analogous to how the physiological feature of blue eyes came to be highlighted as a decidedly non-Korean trait in the context of a global sporting event, I describe the importance of approaching Korea globally: not merely as an a priori entity that undergoes transformations as it spreads across the globe, but as an entity which, when approached globally, its presumably distinguishing features can be seen. Third, I offer an explanation of why I adopt this approach by providing some background to the study that informs this book, describing its various iterations since it began in 2012.

2.2 KOREA AS NATION AS DISCOURSE

In the previous chapter, I addressed the various complexities related to representing the nation more generally. By extension, it would seem that the customary offering of a social, historical, and political portrait of nation X in a book about nation X might run the risk of limiting a project's scope while also reducing nation X to a series of unproductive generalizations. This being noted, it is impossible not to at least address a few important points. To begin, it is important to acknowledge the fact that the Korean context brings with it an added layer of complexity in that it is a specific kind of national imaginary – an ethnic national imaginary – founded on and guided by a myth of ethnic homogeneity (Kyung-Koo Han, 2007; Gi-Wook Shin, 2006). Ethnic nations like Korea are frequently differentiated from *civic* nations (Smith, 1991). While civic nations are typically formed around the basis of shared political goals (e.g., "democracy" in the United States), ethnic nations subscribe more overtly to a narrative premised on a collective heritage based on ethnic unity. The latter is based on a political philosophy known as *ius sanguinis*, or "right of blood," in which the people of a given nation conceive of themselves as sharing a bloodline, as opposed to that of *ius soli* (right of territory), in which citizenship is premised on having been born on the territory, or other forms of naturalization via extended residency. The guiding ideology of ethnic homogeneity in Korea is known as 민족 [min-jok], and it has no translational equivalence in English: it can be translated approximately as "people," "nation," "race," or "ethnicity." Due to this ideology, the path to achieving naturalized citizenship in Korea had always been notoriously stringent, only more recently becoming more feasible through an amendment to the 국적법 [guk-jeok-beop], or Nationality Act, in May 2010 (Seol, 2012). Nonetheless, Korea's reputation of rampant ethnocentrism manifest in ideologies of xenophobia and ambivalence toward "mixed-blood" Koreans is no secret (see Kyung-Koo Han, 2007; Jenks, 2017; Nadia Kim, 2008; Nora Hui-Jung Kim, 2012; Claire Seungeun Lee, 2017; Mary Lee, 2008; Lim, 2009, 2010; Lo & Kim, 2011; Watson, 2010).

Of course, the distinction between an ethnic and a civic national imaginary is not always neat. Indeed, Smith (1991) argues that even though modern civic nations may not explicitly claim a shared bloodline per se, they have nonetheless historically relied on some degree of premodern ethnic base in their founding. In Smith's (1991) words:

> even where a nation-to-be could boast no ethnic antecedents of importance and where any ethnic ties were shadowy or fabricated, the need to forge out of whatever cultural components were available a coherent mythology and symbolism of a community of history and culture became everywhere paramount as a condition of national survival and unity. (p. 42)

Of course, in any national context, ethnic homogeneity is less of a biological reality than it is a discursive phenomenon, a result of state ideologues constructing a people as sharing a common ancestry in order to ensure a collective people's commitment to what Étienne Balibar (1990) calls the "nation form" (see also Connor, 1994; Hobsbawm, 1983; Smith, 1991, 2008). In the words of Brass (1991), "ethnicity and nationalism are not 'givens,' but are social and political constructions" (p. 8). For Brass, modern ethnic nations are the result of the ideological manipulation of political elites, or to put it another way, "an ethnic community politicized" (p. 20). A similar argument is made in the work of Balibar (1990), who claims that "no nation possesses an ethnic base naturally, but as social formations are nationalized," and that the people of a nation are "ethnicized – that is, represented in the past or in the future as if they formed a natural community, possessing of itself an identity of origins, culture and interests which transcends individuals and social conditions" (p. 96).

The possibility of Korea as an ethnicized entity is evident in the discourse of the mythical figure Dangun Wanggeom, the god-king who is said to have founded the first Korean kingdom of Gojoseon nearly 5,000 years ago. While most Koreans today acknowledge the story of Dangun as a mere legend, even in recent memory that was not necessarily the case. As Korean historian Jo Hyeon Seol (2006) notes, the earliest version of the Dangun legend appears in the thirteenth century 삼국 유사 [*Sam-guk Yu-sa*], or *Stories of the Three Kingdoms*, which is the most widely accepted historical evidence of his existence. Jo, along with other Korean historians such as Hong Sunae (2009) and Oh Gangwon (2014), notes that the content of the myth underwent a crucial transformation during the late period of the Korean Empire. In the first modern history textbooks 조선 역사 [*Jo-seon Yeok-sa*], or *Joseon History* (1895), 조선 역대사략 [*Jo-seon Yeok-dae-sa-ryak*], or *Joseon Historical Journal* (1895), and 동국 역사 [*Dong-guk Yeok-sa*], or *Dongguk History* (1899), Dangun was represented as a deity. However, from 1905, Dangun began to be portrayed as a historical figure who actually founded the first kingdom in the Korean peninsula (Jo, 2006). As Jo suggests, this process of de/remythologization might have been an attempt to anchor the unity of "Korean nation" in face of the demands of modernization on one hand, and the dominance of Japanization on the other hand (p. 17). Following national independence in 1945, Dangun has maintained a presence in the national history of Korea, as some contemporary history textbooks continue to portray him as an actual person and founder of the Korean nation.

While Dangun is the mythical entity that represents the genealogical foundation to the doctrine of *ius sanguinis* in the Korean context, it is important to note that discourses of ethnic nationhood are frequently tied to discourses of territoriality. Indeed, this becomes especially evident if we turn to the thought of German philosopher Johann Gottfried Herder, whose speeches and writings are considered foundational to the broader ideology of ethnic nationhood. Herder's notion of a "private-property language" would become especially influential throughout Europe in the nineteenth century and in the subsequent (and ongoing) theoretical debates on the origins of national consciousness (B. Anderson, 1991, p. 68). Though the focus of Herder's philosophy is certainly the centrality of language to the German national character, or *Volk*, implicit is the tie to territory. Take, for instance, this passage from his *Ideen zur Philosophie der Geschichte der Menschheit*, or *Ideas for a Philosophy of History of Mankind*, in which Herder articulates the centrality of language to the German *Volk*, or national character:

> every language bears the stamp of the mind and character of
> a national group. Not only do the organs of speech vary with regions,
> not only are there certain sounds and letters peculiar to almost every
> nationality, but the giving of names, even in denoting audible things,
> nay in the immediate expression of the passions, in interjections,
> varies over the earth. (1787, p. 78, cited in Heater, 1998, p. 68)

Elsewhere, in "Idee zum ersten patriotischen Institut für den Allgemeingeist Deutschlands," or "Ideas for the First Patriotic Institute for the Common Spirit of Germany," Herder ([1788]1967) promotes the superiority of the German language. In doing so, he simultaneously promotes the superiority of the German people:

> Our nationality can boast that since the most ancient times of which we know its language has remained unmixed with others, just as our people were not conquered by any other national group and in their wanderings carried their language into different parts of Europe (pp. 600–601).

As Richard Bauman and Charles L. Briggs (2003) note, Herder's writings and speeches "provided a charter not only for homogenizing national policies of language standardization and the regulation of public discourse, but for theoretical frameworks that normalize and often essentialize one society-one culture-one language conceptions of the relationships among language, culture, and society" (p. 195). Bauman and Briggs add that the "metadiscursive regimes," or the conceptualization of communicative practices serving "ideologically founded ends" (p. 15), including those engineered through thinkers such as Herder, facilitated the "regulating access to the public sphere and other institutional arenas on the basis of resultant discursive capacities" and also "continue to play a significant role in this gate-keeping process down to the present day" (p. 196). Of course, the point here is not to problematize the logic driving the presumptions of ethnonational purity but instead to simply highlight how questions of territory emerge in tandem with the articulation of the importance of language to national character. National language is juxtaposed to those of different "regions," and is acknowledged to be varied "over the earth" (i.e., language in one part of the world is different from that of another). Further, the fact that it can be traced to a specific territory, even if it subsequently undertook a series of "wanderings," offers an additional attempt to locate language to a given territory.

To return briefly to the distinction between ethnic and civic nations above, it is important to acknowledge that one key feature distinguishing the two categories is territoriality. While the ethnic nation, according to Smith (1991), thrives on its constituents' collective subscription to a belief in common descent, the civic nation is the possession of a "historic territory," characterized by "legal-political community, legal-political equality of members, and common civic culture and ideology" (p. 11). Even so, as noted a moment ago, Smith (1991) offers the disclaimer that the distinction is frequently tenuous: "every nationalism contains civic and ethnic elements in varying degrees and different forms" (p. 13). Smith's (1999) notion of ethnoscape, or a territory that "is felt over time to provide the unique and indispensable setting for the events that shaped the community" (p. 150) is particularly useful for understanding an ethnic national peoples' ideological relationship to a given territory.[2] Examples of ethnoscapes provided by Smith include Alsace for the French, Trieste for the Italians, or Epirus for the Greeks, all of which facilitate a given people's ability to claim ancestral ties to a particular territory.

This orientation to territoriality in the Korean context, especially as it emerged in the post-1945 postcolonial context, is best conceptualized, according to historian Im Chong Myong (2007), as "토지 민족주의 [to-ji min-jok-ju-ui]" or "soil nationalism." Unlike more conventional understandings of *ius soli*, which prioritize birthright citizenship irrespective of ethnicity, soil nationalism is a form of ethnic nationalism in which national territory is imagined as a closed ecosystem. Though Herder is frequently referenced as having popularized the algorithm of nation = one people + one language + one territory, one of the most immediate contradictions in this logic is the presumption that a given people can be isolated in a given area over an extended period of time, long enough to warrant exclusive territorial claims to a given land: presumably the Germans and their language had managed to stay put while other peoples and languages did not. Meanwhile, according to Im's theory of soil nationalism, despite the influx and outflux of various ethnicities and cultural interactions in the Korean peninsula, "Korea" remains as "Korea" through a synthesis of different "bloods (pi)" (p. 87) within the ecosystem, which in turn artificially homogenizes a national imaginary. Like any nationalist ideology, soil nationalism is just that: an ideology, and as such is only true to the extent that people remain committed to its truth. The untenability of soil nationalism becomes immediately clear when considering the discourse of the territorial origins of Korea.

Consider, for instance, how this discourse is at play at the Independence Hall of Korea. The hall was established in 1987 to function as a space of what Chandra Mukerji (2012) calls "political pedagogy," as a celebration of independence against Japanese colonial occupation and simultaneously a celebration of Korean exceptionalism (Chungjae Lee & Jerry Won Lee, 2022). In the hall there is a concerted effort to laud, for instance, Korea's centuries of prosperity

---

[2] Smith's (1999) notion of ethnoscape is distinct from Appadurai's (1996) notion of ethnoscapes. The former describes peoples' nationalistic ties to a particular territory, whereas the latter encapsulates the migrations of peoples beyond the nation-state in the context of globalization.

prior to colonial occupation. This is evident in the displays such as the one showcasing "우리 겨레의 찬란한 역사" or "U-ri Gyeo-lei-ui Chal-lan-han Yeok-sa / Our Nation's Brilliant History," which emphasizes the founding of the ancient Gojoseon Kingdom in 2333 BCE (Fig. 2.1). And

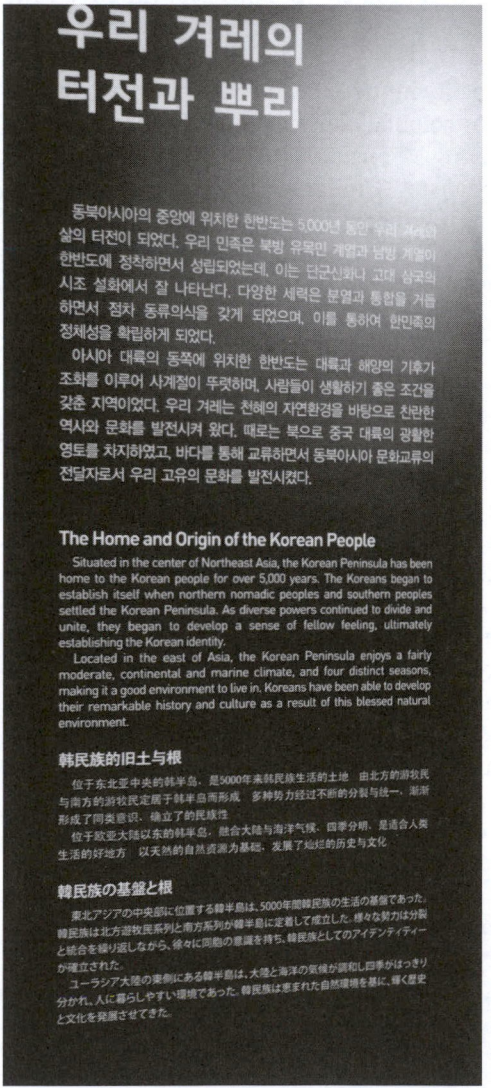

Fig. 2.1   Our People's Home and Origins panel at the Independence Hall of Korea

even in sites such as the Independence Hall, which narrates the time-lessness of the Korean people and their territory, this ideology is readily unraveled. For instance, in one of the first exhibits, the panel on the "우리 겨레의 터전과 뿌리," or "U-ri Gyeo-lei-ui Teo-jeon-gwa Ppu-ri / Our People's Home and Origins," displays the following text:

> 동북아시아의 중앙에 위치한 한반도는 5,000년 동안 우리 겨레의 삶의 터전이 되었다. 우리 민족은 북방 유목민 계열과 남방 계열이 한반도에 정착하면서 성립되었는데, 이는 단군신화나 고대 삼국의 시조 설화에서 잘 나타난다.

The corresponding English translation of the panel text reads as follows:

> Situated in the center of Northeast Asia, the Korean Peninsula has been home to the Korean people for over 5,000 years. The Koreans began to establish itself [*sic*] when northern nomadic peoples and southern peoples settled the Korean Peninsula.[3]

While the objective is to narrate the historical origins of the Korean people in a moment in time over 5,000 years ago, the very act of doing so inadvertently contradicts the foundational assumptions of the ethnic nation as bound to nation-state boundaries. In one panel, for instance, a map is provided for the "Prehistoric Site of the Korean Peninsula," featuring locations of both "구석기시대의 유적," or the "Gu-seok-gi-si-dae-ui yu-jeok / Paleolithic province," and "신 석기시대의 유적," or the "Shin-seok-gi-si-dae-ui yu-jeok / Neolithic province." However, while the sites themselves predate the delineation of the contemporary boundaries of the Korean peninsula, they are presented as if the separation between the northern area of the peninsula and China are prehistoric fact. Indeed, in another panel in the same exhibit hall, on "여러 나라의 등장," or "Yeo-leo Na-ra-ui Deung-jang / Appearance of Several States)," the origins of the Korean peninsula are depicted as inclusive of peoples whose territories extend well into the boundaries of contemporary China (Goguryeo and Buyeo). Therefore, the aforementioned anachronistic rendering of prehistoric Korean peoples as bound to a contemporary Korean peninsular space, while presented in order to facilitate the objective of accentuating Korean independence efforts in the context of Japanese colonization and more importantly to affirm the distinctiveness of Korean heritage, represents a historical impossibility. These narrative strategies of the hall help to affirm that the stability of the nation cannot hinge on

---

[3] For a discussion on the implications of translational decisions at the Independence Hall, see Chungjae Lee and Jerry Won Lee (2022).

historical evidence alone but rather must depend on a commitment to an ideology such as soil nationalism.

In order to unpack this point, a meaningful connection might be drawn to an analogous case study that punctuates how an ideology such as soil nationalism can be not only untenable (as is typically the case with most ideological commitments) but also a useful way of understanding how cultural difference is predicated on the flexible and momentary affirmation of the borders of the nation-state. In Abraham Acosta's (2014) theorization of the United States–Mexico border, he calls attention to the fact that there are segments of the border that are left unenforced and unmonitored as a result of the harsh topography of the Sonoran Desert. While adherents of anti-immigrant sentiment in the United States call for greater enforcement of the border, Acosta (2014) poses a different question: whether "a border left unguarded is failed government policy or its very reason for being" (p. 228). Further, while the discourse of the national border is frequently approached as a question of unconcealing the disconnect between its depiction and its material reality, "it is not a dispute over the relationship between words and things but rather the always already mediated relation between words and referentiality itself" (p. 212). Through Acosta's work, we are able to lay bare the question of who the migrant crossing the United States–Mexico border is and where they are "from," for "the sheer heterogeneity of the figure of the migrant is irreducible" (p. 233). The prototypical migrant is not always Mexican, but frequently from other parts of Central America, and this acknowledgment of the sheer heterogeneity of the migrant in turn destabilizes assumptions of who can lay claim to one nation or the other. More specifically, if parts of the United States–Mexico border have been left unreinforced because of a simple lack of necessity, this is itself an affirmation of the inability to readily delineate the United State from Mexico, which in turn invites broader reconsiderations of assumptions relating territorial claims to national identity. In short: if local territorial jurisdiction is not definitive, to what extent can other foundational assumptions of ethnic national belonging be expected to be?

Of course, scholars today frequently acknowledge that Korean ethnicity is reflective of a continuum, neither biological nor socially constructed (Jeon, 2010; Kang, 2013). And further, this is not to dismiss the material realities of commitments to ideals of ethnic homogeneity: for many contemporary South Koreans, for instance, this is the driving force behind their support of reunification with the North (Paik, 1996; Gi-Wook Shin, 2006). This all being noted, it takes only a bit of common sense to acknowledge that myths of ethnic homogeneity will invariably be in conflict with biological realities, and this is evident in Korean national narratives of shared ancestry and territorial homeland. However, the point in all this is that the manipulation of historical detail is frequently deployed in efforts to establish the legitimacy of the Korean people in light of their ethnonational precarity: Dangun became a real person at the height of colonial rule at a moment of heightened anxiety over the potential dilution if not eradication or erasure of Korean culture; the dubious claims to the Korean peninsula likewise occur in an institutional space designed to reaffirm Korea as a discrete cultural entity. In short, these are examples of how narrative details that are today considered inextricable parts of Korean history have been and continue to be reestablished and solidified in moments of precarity. This lesson invites us to consider how other features of cultural distinctiveness might be made sense of in other moments of precarity – or more specifically semiotic precarity – as I have been suggesting. And it is from the imagined contingency of nation to language within a bound territory, in particular, the premise that the Korean language makes Korea (as ethnicity and as territory) unique, that we are able to take stock of the conditions in which Korea can be encountered across global space.

2.3 GLOBAL KOREA; OR, KOREA GLOBALLY

When exploring the question of Korea as a global entity, it is logical to start by noting the worldwide presence of Korea's diaspora. In fact, Korea's diaspora was described as the "world's widest" in a 2013 article in the *Korea JoongAng Daily*.[4] As noted in the article, while China's is the "largest" diaspora, with over 45 million people across 130 countries, Korea's is the "widest," with over 7.26 million Koreans in 175 countries, based on data from 2011. More recent data from 2019 reflect over 7.49 million Koreans in 193 countries (MOFA, 2019). The largest number of overseas Koreans reside in the United States, and the second largest number of overseas Koreans reside in China, the latter of which are known as 朝鮮族 [Cháoxiānzú] or 조선족 [Joseonjok]. In fact, the Yanbian Korean Autonomous Prefecture in China is sometimes referred to as a "Third Korea" (Enze Han, 2013, p. 65). Another sizable population of overseas Koreans reside in Japan and

---

[4] Special Reporting Team, World's widest diaspora born over 100 years ago, *Korea JoongAng Daily* (October 1, 2013).

are known as 在日 [Zainichi] (see Lie, 2008). Given the scale of the Korean diaspora, it makes sense that overseas Koreans have established a number of large Koreatowns across the world, including those in China, the United States, Japan, and many others. These transnational Korean communities are frequently described as Korean ethnic enclaves. Similar to other ethnic enclaves, Korean transnational communities are characterized by what John Lie (2008) terms an "enclave economy" (p. 8), based on a shared national heritage outside the nation-state. In fact, Korean communities around the world have provided a sense of home for those who had left Korea for various reasons, whether to escape persecution during Japanese colonial occupation, during the turmoil of the Korean War, political oppression during the Park Chung-hee authoritarian regime, or the economic precariousness of the financial crisis in the late twentieth century. Following such migration to a new part of the world, many Koreans have historically made significant efforts to retain ties to their homeland.

At times, it is the very condition of being afar that facilitates the heightening national consciousness for Koreans abroad, as made keenly evident in the response – we may perhaps call it a telescopic response – to the Japanese occupation of the Korean peninsula. According to Richard S. Kim (2011), one of the most significant historical events for Koreans abroad occurred in San Francisco at the turn of the twentieth century: the murder of Durham White Stevens, a US American counselor to the resident-general in Korea, by two Korean men. Stevens's controversial public remarks condoning the Japanese annexation of Korea galvanized San Francisco's Korean community which had hitherto been factioned. When the two men, Chun Myung-won and Chang In-whan, were charged with the murder of Stevens, Koreans from across California and other parts of the world, including Korea, Japan, Siberia, Manchuria, Mexico, and Hawai'i contributed funds to their legal defense. The formation of this diasporic coalition, even if inspired by the advocacy of the justness and expediency of death, or perhaps *necropolitical* in its nature, to adapt Achille Mbembe's (2003) expression, points to the value of not only nebulous collectivities but the desire to engage in the political beyond and irrespective of the political rubric of the nation-state: to participate in a collectivity, as Koreans, in spite of a vexed relation to the Korean nation-state, which, to be sure, during Japanese occupation, was nonexistent, at least in a strictly "legal" sense.

Certainly, numerous scholars have approached the question of global Koreanness, naturally, relative to Korea itself. Indeed, it would seem common sense to want to understand "global Korea" as a "global version of Korea." From this starting point, it is possible to see Korea's transnational iterations as versions of the original Korea, many times in ways that blur the distinction between the origin and the diaspora. Take for instance Nancy Abelmann and John Lie's (1995) description of Los Angeles's Koreatown as "a simulacrum of Seoul in Southern California, a Korea away from Korea" (p. 85). "Cultural certitudes crumble," add Abelmann and Lie, "as we wonder whether this is South Korea or the United States" (p. 85). I will admit that there are no doubt unmistakable sensations of Koreanness within particular establishments, where the interior design choices compel even native Koreans to forget, momentarily, where they are. In some eateries, the taste of the food can deceive even the most experienced connoisseurs of Korean cuisine, a phenomenon complicated no doubt by the fact that conceptualizations of what constitutes "authentic" Korean cuisine is itself always contested, as noted by Robert Ji-Sung Ku (2014).

Building on these developments that problematize the distinction between the authentic and the derivative, I would like to propose that we are now in a position to explore the question of global Korea beyond accounts that are premised on the assumption that Korean diaspora communities represent how peoples migrate to different countries and bring with them their home culture as well as aspirations of producing interstitial and simulacral spaces. In other words, in my approach to the question of global Korea, I am less interested in how Koreans – whether at the level of the individual or the community – establish or maintain ties to an originary homeland. Rather, I am more interested in arriving at a better understanding of what the so-called original is in the first place.

To proceed with this premise, it might be useful to see how the question of homeland is treated in the realm of literature. Especially intriguing is Myung Mi Kim's (1991) poem, "Into Such Assembly:"

> Can you read and write English? Yes____. No____.
> Write down the following sentences in English as I dictate them.
> > There is a dog in the road.
> > It is raining.
> Do you renounce allegiance to any other country but this?
> Now tell me, who is the president of the United States?
> You will all stand now. Raise your right hands.
>
> Cable car rides over swan flecked ponds
> Red lacquer chests in our slateblue house
> Chrysanthemums trailing bloom after bloom
> Ivory, russet, pale yellow petals crushed

> Between fingers, that green smell, if jade would smell
> So-Sah's thatched roofs shading miso hung to dry –
> Sweet potatoes grow on the rock choked side of the mountain
> The other, the pine wet green side of the mountain
> Hides a lush clearing where we picnic and sing:
> > *Sung-Bul-Sah, geep eun bahm ae*
>
> Neither, neither
>
> Who is mother tongue, who is father country?   (p. 29)

The poem begins with a series of questions being asked by a US immigration officer designed to reenact citizenship criteria: proficiency in English, basic political knowledge, and loyalty to the United States. The officer asks the immigrants to raise their right hands, but instead of reciting the oath of allegiance to the United States as expected, the speaker, faced with conflicted loyalties, interrupts with a series of oppositional and sometimes contradictory images: "red" is contrasted with the "slateblue," tactile sensations such as in "crushed / Between fingers" is juxtaposed with olfactory senses such as "green smell." In fact, the crushed "yellow petals" of the chrysanthemum evoke a "green smell" but a smell that is imagined only, and the "rock choked side" of the mountain is juxtaposed with the "pine wet green side." While rain is part of the lines the immigrant must transcribe in accordance with the process of obtaining citizenship, here, rain presents spirituality ("Sung-Bul-Sah" is the name of a Buddhist temple in Korea) and happiness ("geep eun bahm ae" means "in the happy night"). The speaker eventually imagines a return to the "lush clearing where we picnic and sing," performing a momentary escape from the ritualized crucible of citizenship.

The poem reflects the enduring trope of the transmigrant being forever caught between two worlds: the original homeland and the adopted one. However, importantly, in Kim's poem, the speaker, having migrated to the United States and on the verge of obtaining naturalized citizenship, accepts "Neither, neither" of these conflicting options by asking the question, "Who is mother tongue, who is father country?" Kim's poem, as noted by Xiaojing Zhou (2006), represents the "ambivalence of Korean immigrants' national and cultural identities" (p. 239). Further, as Zhou (2006) argues, at the end of the poem "the double negative and the questions refuse the binarized choice of either this or that category of national or cultural identification" (p. 239). While the closing lines might suggest the speaker's miscomprehension of the metaphors, thereby innocently misinterpreting the figures as literal beings, they also compel the reader to reassess the logic of the familiality of the metaphor "mother tongue" through its adaptation and reconfiguration of the metaphor of homeland as "father country." As noted above, nationalistic discourses suture "mother tongue" with "father country," assuming an inextricable tie between one's native language and one's country of origin. Here, the speaker is not simply torn between two categories that are presumed to be mutually exclusive (United States and Korea). Rather, in a poem that thematizes the incongruity and incompatibility of dualisms, "mother tongue" and "father country" are delinked by, as paradoxical as it may be, being paired in this manner through metaphors of maternity and paternity. "Father country" is of course not a common figure of speech, but its usage here compels the reader to interrogate the logic that assumes a link between one's "mother tongue" and one's homeland, along with the logic of US immigration that demands assimilation while simultaneously constructing the immigrant as inassimilable because of their inextricable biological ties to "mother tongue" and "father country." In this regard, Kim's work gestures toward the limitation to viewing questions of global Korea in binarized terms: it is not a matter of either the homeland or not, but "neither, neither." In the case of the subject in Kim's poem, there is a rejection of the very need to feel at home via the nation-state. But most importantly, it enables a momentary view of what "matters" in the momentary attempt to have to choose between two categories of national belonging, even if it is something as minor as a red lacquer chest or the thatched roof of a house.

Consider, then, the significance of these memories being invoked not only in retrospect after no longer being in Korea but the fact that they are materialized in a moment of sheer uncertainty of the difference between Korea and a different national context (the United States). To return to Abelmann and Lie's description of Los Angeles's Koreatown as a "simulacrum of Seoul," what is important to note is how the experience of Koreatown can invoke a realization of what the distinguishing features between Korea and the United States are in the first place. In Los Angeles's Koreatown, Koreanness is enacted and sensed in many ways, including through the dubiousness of the enforcement of and compliance with local laws. Smoking is known to be common in many bars, restaurants, and clubs in spite of California law prohibiting smoking in all enclosed workplaces. Patrons who are under the legal drinking age of 21 are able to enter bars and nightclubs with relative ease. Many establishments stay open into the early hours of the morning, contrary to California law that requires them to close at 2 a.m., and many serve beer and soju in spite of lacking a liquor license in the first place. Employees are commonly paid "under the table." There is even an underground network of taxis, known colloquially as "불법택시 [bul-beop taek-si]," literally translated as "illegal taxi," that, for a nominal fee, will get you and your car home after a long evening of drinking. In the same way that US laws would not be applicable in Korea, they similarly seem to have minimal impact in Los Angeles's Koreatown. Los Angeles's Koreatown, in other words, has come to be a space characterized by the negotiability of law and regulation, which constitutes it as a space of difference within a larger set of regulatory guidelines that construct the state according to criteria of governability. To clarify, I'm not aiming to make any hasty empirical claims about the loose compliance with rules and regulations, and this is of course not to suggest that the refusal to abide by law is what makes a space decidedly Korean. Put differently, I am not trying to make facile points that Koreatowns are lawless, dystopian spaces, nor am I trying to suggest that there is something inherently Korean about lawlessness. It is rather the point that the atmosphere of Koreanness surfaces through the very unregulatabilty of social practice within an ecological network of other social conventions and behaviors along with, of course, semiotic resources and spatial elements. These behaviors, understood as an assemblage of cultural practices, should be approached not as constituting Koreanness per se, but as producing spaces in which the link between law and territory, and thus nation and state, is diluted or otherwise suspended. Los Angeles's Koreatown is therefore not so much an institutionally endorsed exceptional administrative space as it is continually reimagined as such because of the inapplicability, and in many ways unenforceability, of many laws of the nation-state in which the Koreatown ostensibly resides.

In the work of Benedict Anderson (1991), central to his theory of the nation as sovereign, limited, and imagined community is the ability of peoples to occupy a shared territory without physical contact with or recognition of one another. Appadurai (1996) argues that Anderson's concept of "imagined communities" cannot account for the global social imaginaries that people occupy today. "An important fact of the world we live in today," writes Appadurai, "is that many persons on the globe live in such imagined worlds (and not just imagined communities) and thus are able to contest and sometimes even subvert the imagined worlds of the official mind" (p. 33). While both Anderson and Appadurai emphasize the role of the imagination, Anderson's emphasis is on the imagined tie to national territory, a geographically delimited area, while Appadurai's approach is decidedly postnational in its refusal of the very concept of physical territory. It is therefore not so much a rejection of Anderson's theory of national identification but rather through a reimagination of it, across time but also space, that the postnational becomes a possibility insofar as we proceed with the recognition that the territorial substrate of the nation is secondary to these "imagined worlds." What we are able to see, in fact, is not so much social identification around the rubric of the nation-state but a continual reproduction of nationness and, more importantly, a reimagination of what nationness is to begin with, across an undesignated and continually reconfigured space. In other words, in the case of the negotiability of the legal order in Los Angeles's Koreatown, it might be said that the momentary disappearance of law constellates into a symbolic suspension of the state, producing a rupture in which difference – in this case, Koreanness – can not only coexist as a national imaginary within another, so to speak, but can be rendered legible as a differentiating feature of Koreanness. Therefore, on the one hand, we see instances of the sentiment of Koreanness thriving away from Korean territory proper precisely because of the absence of the state (absence, as the cliché goes, makes the heart grow fonder). But more importantly, and as will be seen in the pages that follow, these efforts facilitate our understandings of what Korea "is," at least in terms of what can be semiotically encoded in public space.

2.4 LOCATING THE LOCATIONS OF GLOBAL KOREA

Before proceeding further, it is important to clarify that I am not presuming to offer Korea as anything of a particularly "exceptional" case in point, especially in terms of being "superior" to another cultural or national imaginary. Of course, various historical circumstances, including its prior colonial occupation by the Japanese Empire (see Section 2.2) along with the US military occupation of the peninsula dating to 1945 elicits various kinds of semiotic precarity and thus makes Korea particularly instructive national imaginary to study. Some additional facts of the matter are also undeniable: Korea is the world's "widest" diaspora, as noted in Section 2.2, and the global impact of K-pop, or Korean popular culture, endemic to what is known as *Hallyu*, or the Korean wave, since the early 2000s cannot be ignored (see Kyung Hyun Kim & Choe, 2014). This all being said, it is important to note that my decision to focus on Korea is simultaneously one of coincidence and perhaps convenience. Gayatri Chakravorty Spivak (1999) once famously declared, "I am not a South Asianist. I turn to Indian material because I have some accident-of-birth facility there"

(p. 267). Analogously, the sustained study of Korea that I present is not a semi-nationalistic attempt to celebrate my heritage (readers familiar with the nationalistic undertones of some Korean academics will know what I am referring to). It does, nonetheless, have its genesis in an initial desire to study and understand Korea as such, aided also by "accident-of-birth facility," or at least what I thought would be facility. Both the outcome presented and approach taken in this project required continual, ongoing reconceptualizing of the very notion of Korea from the "bottom-up," even if the view was inherently global and thus "from above," so to speak.

Given that the approach to the question of global Korea in this way is something of an anomaly, its undergirding logics can perhaps be better understood through an explanation of the several iterations that the study that serves as the foundation to this book has undergone. The first phase of this study might be traced to the spring of 2012, when I first revisited the Koreatown in Los Angeles for the beginnings of an ethnographic research project that was guided by an idea that, in retrospect, was half-baked at best. Visiting Los Angeles' Koreatown was by no means an unfamiliar experience for me, as I had spent a considerable portion of my life in the city's suburbs and still have vivid memories of frequent trips to Koreatown on the weekends. I had also spent many years living in Garden Grove, a smaller but still sizable Korean district of Orange County, California. In 2012, when I began this project, I had become interested in the study of linguistic landscapes, because of the range of opportunities it represented for the documentation of a range of issues related to language ideology, stratification, and hybridity (see Chapter 1). Initially, I was primarily interested in analyzing the hybrid Englishes found in the Korean American linguistic landscape, locating usages of both deliberate and unexpected hybridity through English and Korean, aiming to intervene in the popular metadiscourse of Asians as chronically incompetent users of English.[5] The metadiscourse of the purportedly ungraceful and inadvertently humorous English produced by Asians is reflected in books such as Oliver Lutz Radtke's (2007) *Chinglish: Found in Translation* or on websites such as Engrish.com, an allusion to the frequent substitution of /l/ and /r/ phonemes (lallation) by speakers of English whose dominant language is Japanese. And though this feature tends to be unique to Japanese speakers of English, "Engrish" in turn has become a metonym of imperfect English spoken by Asians more generally (inexplicably including some nationalities,

---

[5] This earlier iteration of this project is reflected in Jerry Won Lee (2014). Today, I find many of the ideas within woefully underdeveloped, but so it goes.

such as Chinese speakers, who usually have no difficulties with the /r/ and /l/ phonemes). Instances of "Engrish" include usages that result in moments of unintended humor, due usually to their sheer nonsensicality, at least from a purely "denotative" point of view of language (Blommaert, 2010). Metadiscourses of "Engrish" are reflective of what Theresa Heyd (2014) has called grassroots prescriptivism, which in turn enregister (Agha, 2007), or socially and ideologically sediment as belonging to a specific language typification, certain forms of English as "appropriate" over others. My aim at the time was to offer a counter to this prevalent and covertly racist metadiscourse. However, I started to see arguments I was making on problematizing the racist characterization of such instances as exceedingly predictable (and besides, the curator of the Engrish.com website says he's not trying to be racist, so he must not be!). The more time I spent studying Koreatowns, including those in New York, Chicago, and Dallas, the more I gradually became interested in other, broader questions.

I then found myself trying to understand how people produce nationness outside of the nation-state. This second phase of my project was inspired in part because of recognition that there was far more than "language" constituting transnational Korean environments. I was drawn to the work in linguistic landscape research that insisted on the need to attend to the complex array of meaning making resources in public space beyond "language" alone (see Introduction). In the second phase of my project, I became interested in trying to determine the wide array of ways in which local community actors (such as restaurant owners and managers) could make use of not only linguistic resources (such as on signage and on menus) but also other semiotic resources of the built environment (in terms of architectural choice and interior design) to produce affective ties to Koreanness while being physically displaced from Korea itself. Eventually, the project began to feel like "A User's Guide to Producing Koreanness," and I didn't think it would be interesting or useful. But more importantly, I eventually realized that my project was driven by the fundamental problem of mapping my preconceptions of what "Korea" is onto my findings. This realization led me to the third phase of my project.

The third phase of the research developed from the recognition that Korea can take many shapes and forms, that it is not only a concept that can be easily represented via language or other semiotic resources but also, most importantly, that we come to see Korea, like any other national imaginary I might argue, as it comes into being and as we encounter it globally. Therefore, what I was discovering was the possibility that the category of the national is a potentially spatial and semiotic entailment, and I began to wonder the extent to which it could be said to exist prior to the moment we locate it. This approach was achieved in the process of field research between 2012 and 2017 in 23 sites of "global" Korea. The sites include Korea and Koreatowns across Asia, North America, Europe, and South America. It also includes various sites within Korea itself, particularly "sites of memory," to borrow Pierre Nora's ([1984]1989) expression, along with sites of touristic "ritual places" (Lou, 2016) where it is imperative to perform Koreanness, and where Koreanness operates as a conspicuous commodity (Heller, 2011). Finally, given that my project ultimately concerns the spatial semiotic contingency of the nation, I felt it was appropriate if not necessary to include in my inquiry the islets known to Koreans as Dokdo, which to this day remain disputed between Korea and Japan and are subject to considerable global representation. The following is a list of all sites that were visited for this project:

Sites in Korea (Tourist Destinations)
Gang-nam (Seoul)
Myeong-dong (Seoul)
Itaewon (Seoul)
Insa-dong (Seoul)
Ulleung-do

Sites in Korea (Sites of National Memory)
Gyeongbokgung Palace
Independence Hall
War Memorial
National Hangeul Museum
Soccer Museum
Dok-do

Sites in Asia
Osaka, Japan
Tokyo, Japan
Shanghai, China
Beijing (Wudaokuo), China
Beijing (Wangjing), China
Hong Kong

Sites in North America
Los Angeles, CA
Garden Grove, CA

Chicago, IL
New York, NY
Bergen County, NJ
Washington, DC (Annandale, VA)
Dallas, TX
Oakland, CA
Santa Clara, CA
Mexico City, Mexico
Toronto, Canada

Sites in South America
São Paulo, Brazil

Sites in Europe
London (New Malden), UK

These collective sites do not represent the entirety of global Korea of course. For one, there is undoubtedly a stronger representation of sites within Anglo-American contexts. In addition, my sites studied do not include those in the European Union, Africa, the Middle East, or even Russia, which has both a large population of transnational Koreans and also belongs to the "West." Nevertheless, the sites I present are comprehensive enough in the aggregate to ensure adequate geographic representation across global space and empirical saturation, as it were (i.e., it is not immediately evident that observations from even more sites of global Korea would add more substance to the inquiry at hand, though that remains to be seen).

2.5 CONCLUSION: KOREA VIA THE GLOBE

In the previous pages, I have attempted to offer further considerations of what it means to approach the national imaginary as a discursive form when said form is bound to ideologies of ethnic homogeneity, describing some particularities relevant to the focus on Korea as a case study. I have also described how I am attempting to approach the question of Korea from a global view: not in terms of how Korea as an entity undergoes changes in its various iterations across global space but how Korea as an entity comes to be rendered legible (i.e., encountered) from a view from above.[6] In describing the particularities of the Korean context, I have

---

[6] This view makes Koreanness legible at least in English, that is.

done my best to be mindful of the pitfalls of generalization and have limited myself to merely a few noteworthy points that are necessary for our purposes. To state the obvious, the point was not to try and "debunk" myths of Korean ethnic nationhood. For instance, the mention of the legend of Dangun is not an attempt to expose a baseless ideological commitment to something that is very obviously a myth, nor is it to suggest that your typical Korean today has been proselytized into believing in a fictive origin story. It is merely an illustration of the possibility for that which is immaterial to become material in contexts of political precarity: Dangun is certainly a myth but becomes historical at the moments in which the heritage of the Korean people is threatened or, relatedly, needs to be amplified. Likewise, in moments of representational precarity, the salience of the spatial and semiotic assemblage of Korea can be encountered in its material form. A global orientation can help us to understand what "Korea" looks like as a semiotic materialization in practice. In other words, I am not merely interested in the question of "What is happening in Korea?" or even in "What is happening in the world because of Korea?" While I am obviously interested in the intersection between Korea and the globe, in what follows I will focus on what this intersection can tell us about the legibility of Korea around the globe and indeed via the globe.

3 Encountering the Unfamiliar: Languaging Culture

3.1 UNFAMILIAR LANGUAGE

In my first visit to Hong Kong in 2013, I encountered in the Koreatown on Kimberly Street what was to me then a most unusual sign; it was for a restaurant called *Chowon* (see Fig. 3.1). Of course, the usage of cho-won, or an idyllic grassy meadow, is quite common in restaurant signage across global Korean space, and that is not what makes it unique. Indeed, chowon is reminiscent of Myung Mi Kim's (1991) poem "Into Such Assembly," in which houses with "thatched roofs" are invoked as iconic of the Korean homeland (see Chapter 2). Because the trope of chowon has become encoded in so many sites and forms, one might go so far as to suggest that chowon verges on being a stereotype of Koreanness, somewhat resembling a performance of what Rey Chow (2002) calls coercive mimeticism, a condition in which racialized subjects are compelled "to resemble and replicate the very banal preconceptions that have been appended to them, a process by which they are expected to objectify themselves in accordance with the already seen and thus to authenticate the familiar imagings of them as ethnics" (p. 107).

Yet, what is uncommon about the sign is the manner in which *Chowon*, or 초원, is deconstructed as such: ㅊ ㅗ ㅇ ㅜ ㅓ ㄴ. The sign is curious because it is, quite simply, nonsensical. In the Korean writing system of Han-geul, the individual letters must be clustered into groups of two, three, or four in order to form a coherent syllable. In short, ㅊ ㅗ ㅇ ㅜ ㅓ ㄴ is a morphological impossibility. Admittedly, nowadays, especially in digital communication spaces, isolated usage of Korean letters has in recent years become increasingly common: for instance, ㅋ ㅋ or /k^h k^h/, for a subtle giggle, or ㅇ or /ŋ/ for a simple acknowledgment. Yet, there is still something to be said about the symbolic significance of the fact that the individual letters

Fig. 3.1   Chowon (Hong Kong)

themselves, in their deconstructed form, signify nothing but sounds, at least technically speaking, and that they represent a semantic impossibility: "*broken*" and *designified*. While Korean as "broken" cannot *signify*, the question of language, more generally, as "broken" is nonetheless *significant*, at least when understood in the context of the metadiscourse of language as "broken" as a result of linguistic hybridity. For instance, it is common to refer to a "foreign" usage of language as "broken," as in a nonnative speaker of English being said to speak a "broken English." The popular colloquialism "Konglish," one such iteration of "broken English," is a term used to describe the purportedly undesirable influence of one's first language of Korean on English usage. And simultaneously, it is quite common in Korea to ridicule a person for "imperfect" Korean, as evidenced in numerous popular culture portrayals. The idea of a "broken" usage of language is premised on linguistic hybridity as a defect of an imagined pure monolingual usage. Yet, I'm not here to reiterate the argument to resist the ethnocentric pathologization of a person's language because it does not approximate that of a "monolingual" or "native" speaker.

Instead, I would like to suggest that the strategically aesthetic "breaking" of the Korean text on this signage affords an opportunity for inquiry into what it means to encounter language in unfamiliar ways. The *broken* Korean referenced above was – at least for me in my initial encounter – unfamiliar, and I would like to propose that its perceived unfamiliarity represents an undoing of language that invites us to try and make sense of the identification of culture, not only beyond "familiar" language usage conventions but also outside its "familiar" home: in this case, Koreanness beyond Korea as such. By exploring the implications of the phenomenology of the unfamiliar, this chapter considers what our encounter with the unfamiliar might tell us about our assumptions about the familiar: the taken for granted aspects of culture that in a given moment are frequently expected to "stand in" for a culture and differentiate it from another.

3.2   KOREA AS LANGUAGE?

Language is an important and interesting phenomenon to explore for the simple reason that different cultural groups and national imaginaries in particular frequently center language as an essential facet of their collective history and identity. Language, whether in the form of what Benedict Anderson has described as "print capitalism" or through discourses of the "mother tongue" and "native speaker" (Bonfiglio, 2010), has historically played a central role in the implementation and sustainment of cultural categories via the political ideology of nationalism (see Chapter 1). Of course, history can certainly direct us to instances in which political ideologues did not view linguistic homogeneity as a prerequisite to a consolidated polity. Consider, for example, that the monarchies of Russia and Prussia adopted French as the "cultural language of the ruling class" in the eighteenth century, as noted by Perry Anderson (1974, p. 231). Indeed, according to legend, Catherine II, or Catherine the Great, of Russia was said to have uttered "Je suis un aristocrate, c'est mon métier," in French, not Russian or even in German (her first language); Catherine's statement would become the "epigraph for the age" (P. Anderson, 1974, p. 231). As Paul R. Brass (1991) reminds us, people do not necessarily have an inherent attachment to a particular language, and in some cases people even change languages from their "mother tongues" to identify with other group members or to distinguish themselves from people of other ethnic groups (p. 70). Calhoun (1997) notes that historically, peoples at various moments "flourished in polyglot and more heterogeneous empires and in cosmopolitan trading cities" (p. 19). The desire to "clarify" and to "consolidate" identities through language is rather a construct of modernity (Calhoun, 1997, p. 19). Meanwhile, according to Smith (2008) the idealization of a common language for political unity can be traced as far back as the Middle Ages when early efforts at translating the Bible represented the opportunity for religion to be used as a vessel of nationalization, and by the seventeenth century, translations of the Bible facilitated the "privatization" of religion, and efforts "to impress and seal the distinctive characters of nations" (p. 148). Irrespective of whether the idea of a national language is a construct of modernity or can be traced to protonational roots, the reality is that today there remains a strong ideological link between language and national identity in various contexts. This is especially evident in official state metadiscourses of language, corroborating Pierre Bourdieu's (1991) argument that the idea of an official language is central to the state's capacity to exercise "symbolic violence," which is presumed, unchallenged, and not in need of explicit affirmation.[1] Of course, when it comes to language, it is not so much that the nation-state cannot exist or function without a uniform official language (it is no secret that there are many nation-states today with multiple official languages and even many with no official languages that seem to be doing just fine). It is simply that various state functionaries and other individuals and organizations acting in the name of nationalist ideology are thoroughly convinced that linguistic uniformity is critical to national unity and identification and spend considerable energy attempting to make others believe the same.

   Since the Korean language remains central to imaginations of national identity today (Jinny K. Choi, 2015; Kyung-Koo Han, 2007; Jeong, 2015; Kim Sun Chul, 2009; Gi-Wook Shin, 2006; Song, 2019), Korea is an exemplary case study of a national imaginary guided by an official state ideology of linguistic nationalism. In fact, a key historical moment in Korean history is the legend of the invention of the Korean script, Han-geul, in 1443 by King Sejong the Great

---

[1] According to Bourdieu (1991), symbolic violence is distinct from other types of violence because it is exercised on the basis of the recipient's uncontested understanding of their subordinate position:

> the power of suggestion which is exerted through things and persons and which, instead of telling the child what he must do, tells him what he is, and thus leads him to become durably what he has to be, is the condition for the effectiveness of all kinds of symbolic power that will subsequently be able to operate on a habitus predisposed to respond to them. (p. 52)

As Bourdieu adds, such power is "all the more absolute and undisputed for not having to be stated" (p. 52).

(1397–1450). Of course, whether Sejong actually invented the language is the subject of ongoing debate, with scholars frequently identifying facts that potentially debunk the legend (Park Jae-young, 2013). Nonetheless, Sejong is said to have been driven by his love for the Korean people to invent the new writing system (Kim Yung-Myung, 2013). It is said that Sejong invented Han-geul in an effort to unify the Korean people, who had previously relied on borrowed Chinese characters – also known as Han-mun or Han-ja – for communication (Lee Sang-hyeok, 2008). While the learning of ideographic Chinese characters generally requires years of training and study, another factor that led to the introduction of Han-geul was the lack of a systematic and consistent way of pronouncing the characters, making communication challenging for a majority of users beyond the social elite (Kim Yung-Myung, 2013). Han-geul, on the other hand, is based on a phonetic alphabet and was designed to be easily learned by all, not just the elite who had access to formal education at the time. Indeed, it was the accessibility of Han-geul that caused it in those years to be disparaged as the script of the lower classes while Chinese characters continued to be privileged by the aristocracy and the educated elites (Hong Hyun-bo, 2007). While the Korean language predates the Korean script of Han-geul, it was not until the invention of Han-geul in 1443 that Koreans could claim a comprehensive language that was unique to their national imaginary. Of course, Han-ja characters are still frequently used today in places like legal documents and scholarly literature, and some contemporary Korean linguists such as Choi Yong-gi (2010) argue that the continued use of Han-ja represents something akin to antidemocratic intellectual elitism. Choi in fact offers ways of continuing Sejong's founding intention of promoting Han-geul in the interest of achieving democratic unity, offering, for instance, recommendations for reforming the language's at times illogical orthographic rules and its notoriously inconsistent spacing.

While at first glance it seems as though contemporary narratives of Han-geul portray it as a progressive, democratizing, and unifying script, it is notable that the national metadiscourse around the language also frequently digresses into a narrative of cultural exceptionalism. This is evident in the metadiscourse of the National Hangeul Museum in Seoul (Fig. 3.2). Take for instance a panel at the museum featuring a series of quotes praising Han-geul:

> "The most complete alphabet among those in existence..." John Ross, 1842–1915, A report to the UK Missionary Headquarters (1883)

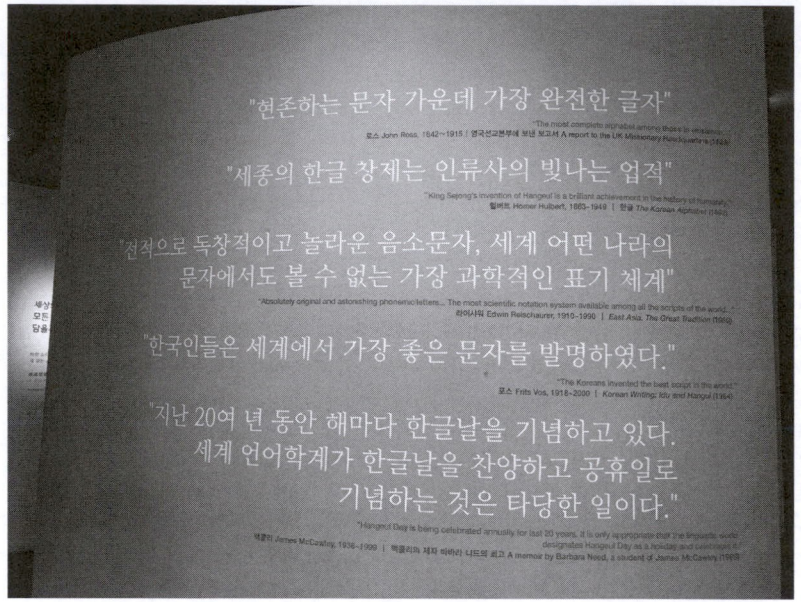

Fig. 3.2   Praise for Han-geul at the National Hangeul Museum

"King Sejong's invention of Hangeul is a brilliant achievement in the history of humanity." Homer Hulbert, 1863–1949, The Korean Alphabet (1892)

"Absolutely original and astonishing phonemic letters ... The most scientific notation system available among all the scripts of the world ..." Edwin Reischauer, 1910–1990, East Asia: The Great Tradition (1960)[2]

"The Koreans invented the best script in the world." Fritts Voss, 1918–2000, Korean Writing: Idu and Hangul (1964)

"Hangeul Day is being celebrated annually for last 20 years [sic]. It is only appropriate that the linguistic world designates Hangeul Day as a holiday and celebrates it." James McCawley, 1938–1999, A memoir by Barbara Need, a student of James McCawley (1999)

As one might have guessed, the National Hangeul Museum is not designed for everyday Koreans who are, in their fervent national

---

[2] Edwin O. Reischauer is, along with George M. McCune, the co-creator of the McCune-Reischauer Romanization system, which was the official method of transliterating Korean into Roman alphabetic letters in South Korea until 2000.

pride, interested in learning about their language per se, and features such as this make it clear that one of the primary targets is foreign visitors interested in learning about different aspects of Korean culture. The display of superlative descriptors such as "best," "most complete," and "most scientific" and other flattering evaluations such as "brilliant achievement" are, on the surface, an innocuous attempt to reaffirm how linguistic luminaries have endorsed the efficacy of Han-geul. Indeed, by providing excerpts from non-Korean "experts," the panel manufactures an understanding of what makes Korea culturally distinct (read: "superior") through a semblance of "scientific" objectivity.

The metadiscourse of Han-geul as a "superior" script is reiterated by contemporary Korean linguists in scholarly publications. Take, for instance, the work of Jang Young-gil (2008), who outlines six features of its supposed excellence:

1. 한글은 지구상의 많은 문자들 중에서 창제자와 창제연대 그리고 창제목적과 창제원리가 신뢰할 수 있는 문헌의 기록으로 남아 있는 유일한 문자이다.
2. 한글은 문자학적인 사치를 다한 음소문자이며 자질문자이다.
3. 한글은 적은 자소로 많은 소리를 표기해 낼 수 있는 매우 경제적이고 실용적인 문자이다.
4. 한글은 자음 자소와 모음 자소의 변별이 용이하며 자소의 꼴이 심미안적으로 디자인된 문자이다.
5. 한글은 음소문자로 창제되었으나 표기상으로는 모아쓰기 함으로써 음절문자인 일본의 '가나문자'와 단어문자인 '한자' 등의 장점을 모두 아우를 수 있었다.
6. 한글은 모아쓰기 함으로써 독서의 능률을 높이고, 좁은 공간에 많은 표기를 담을 수 있는 문자가 되었다.

1. Hangeul is the only writing system in the world for which there exists a reliable historical record of its founder, the date of its founding, along with the purposes and principles for its founding.
2. Hangeul is both a phonological and featural writing system.[3]
3. Hangeul is an economical and practical writing system that can represent a range of sounds with only a few letters.
4. Hangeul is an aesthetically designed writing system in which the vowel and consonant letters can be readily distinguished from one another.

---

[3] A featural writing system is one whose letters approximately represent their respective phonemes (Sampson, 1985).

5. Hangeul was conceived of as a phonological writing system but retains many features of a syllabary and therefore includes benefits of syllabary as in the Japanese kana alphabet and of logography as in the Chinese character system.
6. Hangeul facilitates reading because it is written in clusters, and it is an efficient writing system that can incorporate a high amount of notation in a narrow space.]

(p. 97)

Insofar that it is a given from the perspective of sociolinguistics that no language is functionally superior to another (see Hymes, 1985), it is somewhat unusual to encounter linguistic description with such nationalistic and exceptionalist undercurrents. The point, of course, is not to problematize the (very common) nationalistic tendencies in Korean scholarship. Instead, it is to show how readily the notion of distinction is pervasive in the metadiscourse of Han-geul, which in turn makes it an ideal candidate for indexing the distinctive features of Korean culture.

The ideology of linguistic exceptionalism is also evident at the Independence Hall of Korea, a museum designed to commemorate Korea's anti-colonial resistance efforts and its independence from the Japanese Empire in 1945. Like the National Hangeul Museum, the hall is not frequented by Korean nationalists per se. Most Koreans who do attend are primary or secondary school students who are there as part of a classroom trip, or active duty military personnel whose attendance is incentivized by an extra day of vacation (MBN, 2016). Otherwise, the target audience is foreign tourists, noted by various renovation efforts and translated text throughout the hall that is designed to facilitate accessibility of the material (Chungjae Lee & Jerry Won Lee, 2022). King Sejong is featured in the first exhibit hall, "겨레의뿌리" or "Gyeo-re-ui-ppu-ri / The Origin of the Korean People" (Fig. 3.3). In addition, on the hall's English-language website, designed for potential visitors, under the "Discover Korea" menu there is a tab for "Language," which directs users to a page with the following text:

> Many scholars say,
> "Hangeul is the most scientific writing system in the world" or simply "The best alphabet in the world."
> In the Writing Systems by Professor Geoffrey Sampson, Rice University, it states:
> "Hangeul has the most unique and scientific writing system which cannot be found elsewhere in the world."

Fig. 3.3   King Sejong panel at the Independence Hall of Korea

The late Linguistics Professor Edwin O. Reischauer, of Harvard University stated:

"Hangeul is the simplest, yet most advanced character set in the world."

In The Good Earth by Pearl Buck, she wrote:

"Hangeul is the best alphabet one can dream of."

At first glance, it may seem somewhat strange to encounter such attention to Han-geul in a space that is meant to celebrate Korean national independence. However, it is important to note that during colonial occupation, Japanese was implemented as the official language by the emperor. By the late 1930s, the Japanese policy of cultural assimilation banned Han-geul and aimed to eradicate other Korean cultural practices and institutions. Leaders of the nationalist movement, on the other hand, promoted Han-geul in an effort to preserve Korean national identity. It was not only Japanese colonial occupation that threatened Korean national identity but also the popularization of pan-Asianism, a political ideology that sought to collectivize the peoples of Asian heritage in response to the cultural encroachments of Western imperialism. Han-geul was one means by which Koreans could attempt to maintain and promote their uniqueness in light of these larger geopolitical developments that threatened the very existence of Korean national identity.

Therefore, the appearance of Han-geul, along with its respective metadiscourse of linguistic exceptionalism, in the physical and digital space of the Independence Hall is significant for a few reasons. First, it is important to note that the Korean language was vigorously promoted as a key to national unity primarily following Korea's independence from Japanese colonial rule in 1945. One such effort was the 우리말 도로 찾기 운동 [U-ri-mal do-ro chat-gi un-dong], or Recovery of Our Mother Tongue Campaign.[4] As Jung Jae-hwan (2012) notes, this was primarily a grassroots volunteer-driven campaign led by the now defunct 조선어 학회 [Jo-seon-eo-hag-hoe], or Joseon Language Society, which elevated collective morale and contributed to national unification following independence. As Jung acknowledges, the campaign was not fully successful. No doubt part of the reason for the campaign's lack of success stems from the well-documented difficulties for a populace to rally their collective identification around language, as suggested in Chapter 1. Moreover, in the Korean context, the promotion of Korean was contrary to the ideological and linguistic preferences (or indifferences) of various citizens at the time; as Serk-Bae Suh (2013) notes, following independence from colonial rule, many Koreans – including intellectuals and authors – maintained an allegiance to the Japanese language in part because it was the only language they knew. In addition, following the end of World War II, US Army General Douglas MacArthur, during his oversight of the Pacific region, declared English as the common language, effectively mandating a pan-Asian policy of English as a lingua franca, especially in moments when disparities between Korean and Japanese could not be resolved (Jung Jae-hwan, 2012). On the one hand, we might say that MacArthur's English-language policy implementation might have been the preface to the now nearly ubiquitous reliance on English in Korea and across transnational Korean contexts as reflective of efforts to index a cosmopolitan identity or an alignment with ideals of Western modernity (Jamie Shinhee Lee, 2006, 2016; Mun Woo Lee 2016; Joseph Sung-Yul Park, 2009; So Jin Park & Abelmann 2004; Piller & Cho 2013). Today, English–Korean hybridizations are frequent in

---

[4] Expressions such as "우리 말 [u-ri mal]" present a series of challenges to translation. While "u-ri mal" translates literally as "our language," to Koreans it is common to simply refer to the Korean language as "our language," or Korea as "our country "우리 나라 [u-ri na-ra]." See Chungjae Lee and Jerry Won Lee (2021) on how the discourse of "u-ri" is encoded in the discourse of Koreanness and how it is invoked as a means for Koreans to differentiate themselves from outsiders.

everyday speech and in popular culture (Ahn, 2017; Eun-Young Julia Kim, 2012; Miso Kim, 2017; Jamie Shinhee Lee, 2004, 2014; Jonghyun Park, 2016). This reality has led some language ideologues in Korea to ramp up language purification efforts today, which are both orthographic and lexical preoccupations. There is even an active government-sponsored organization, 국립국어원 [Guk-nip-guk-eo-won], or the National Institute of Korean Language, committed to educating local and foreign users of Korean on correct usage, with the overall objective of purifying the Korean language. For advocates of language purism, the persistence of Chinese characters, along with Japanese and English lexical borrowings, are impediments to the sovereignty of the Korean language and a threat to their ethnolinguistic heritage.

A similar metadiscourse of language purism, though not nearly as explicitly prescriptivist, is promoted by the 한글 학회 [Han-geul hag-hoe], or Hangeul Society. The society was initially established as the Korean Research Institute, or 국어 연구 학회 [Guk-eo Yeon-gu Hag-hoe], in 1908, during the early years of Japanese colonial occupation and would eventually become the Hangeul Society by 1949. The website describes the role of the society in the preservation of both the Korean language and culture as such:

> 말은 생각과 느낌을 전달하는 의사소통의 수단일 뿐만 아니라 이를 사용하는 사람들의 정신세계를 형성하는 구실을 합니다. 그래서 한 국가나 겨레는 공통된 언어 구조에 이끌려 공통된 정신세계를 형성하고, 이를 바탕으로 고유한 문화를 창조합니다. 그러므로 우리 겨레의 생각을 이어 주고 문화를 이끌어 준 것이 바로 우리말입니다.
>
> 우리 한글학회는 지금까지 우리의 정신과 문화를 지켜 온 겨레의 학회입니다. 세종대왕의 한글 창제, 주 시경 스승의 국어 연구, 그리고 일본 제국주의의 탄압에 목숨 걸고 우리말과 우리글을 지켜 온 한글학회 선열들의 투쟁이 없었다면, 우리는 오늘날과 같은 문화와 번영을 누릴 수 없었을 것입니다. 이처럼 한글학회는 평범한 학술단체가 아니라, 우리 겨레 문화를 지켜 온, 그리고 앞으로도 지켜 나갈, 빛나는 큰 별입니다.

[Language is not only a way to communicate thoughts and feelings but shapes the mental worlds of humans who use it. Meanwhile, a nation or a people are guided by a common language to form a collective mental world and can create a common culture based on that world. Therefore, it is our language that has connected the thoughts of our nation and guided our culture.

Our Hangeul Society is an entity that has preserved our spirit and culture. We would not have been able to enjoy the culture and prosperity of the Korean language and writing today without the struggles of the predecessors of the Hangeul Society, who protected King Sejong's creation of Han-geul, along with Master Ju Si-gyeong's contributions to Korean linguistics, which were threatened under

Japanese imperialism. As such, the Hangeul Society is not an ordinary academic organization, but a shining beacon of hope that has protected and will continue to protect our culture.] (Hangeul Society, 2020, n.p.)[5]

There are a few noteworthy points from this description. First, we see once again an ideological chain that links Korea as language to Korea as culture. Furthermore, we see a dedicated emphasis on language as enabling an imagination of Korean as a "unique" culture, almost identical to the Herderian description of *Volk* noted in the previous chapter, which in turn raises the question of what culture is not "unique" while begging the question of whether "unique" is a euphemism for "exceptional" (Spivak, 2010). But most interestingly, the description of the Hangeul Society puts into sharp relief the emphasis on distinction in the context of semiotic precarity: here we see it play out both in historical time (i.e., the emphasis on the Hangeul Society's ensuring of Korean cultural continuity during the threatened erosion of culture during colonial occupation) and in contemporary time (i.e., the emphasis on Han-geul as a feature that can distinguish Korean culture from other cultures today). This, in many ways, is semiotic precarity par excellence: the renarration and amplification (rendering unavoidably salient) of the specificities of culture and constructing a portrait of a given culture as able to be distinguished by a given feature (in this case, language).

In short, what this all shows is that Korea, in a manner not entirely dissimilar to that of other national imaginaries, has defined itself as a discrete nation through the construction and promotion of a national language, particularly in moments of linguistic and cultural precarity. What I have shown is that the metadiscourse, whether in scholarly metadiscourse of Han-geul or in the official metadiscourse at sites of national memory such as the National Hangeul Museum or the Independence Hall, enables us to understand the enthymematic link between Han-geul and the agenda of promoting national identification. The Korean language has historically been promoted and idealized in order to envision Korea as culturally distinct from – for instance – China, Japan, and the English-speaking West. Spaces such as the National Hangeul Museum or the Independence Hall are in this sense spaces of semiotic precarity in that they amplify a token of Korean culture (its language) as that which can be invoked in order to delineate its distinctiveness from other cultures. This link is not

---

[5] The literal translation of "빛나는 큰 별 [bit-na-neun keun byeol]" is "shining big star."

necessarily a given but something that needs to be, as I've shown above, continually renarrated in order to be plausible. This in turn raises an important question: if language operates as a token that is frequently presented as a means of emphasizing the distinctiveness of Korean culture, how reliable is language as a heuristic to "see" culture across global space, and what happens to our understanding of culture when language is encountered in unfamiliar ways? In other words, what can we learn from encounters with language that is unfamiliar or, quite simply, *weird*?

3.3   WEIRD LANGUAGE

The phenomenon that I focus on in the remaining pages of this chapter will enable us to understand the dynamics of locating culture across global space. I term this phenomenon "weird language." By "weird language," I draw initial inspiration from Evelyn Ch'ien's (2004) notion of "weird English." Analyzing the writings of authors such as Vladimir Nabokov, Maxine Hong Kingston, Junot Díaz, Arundhati Roy, and Salman Rushdie, Ch'ien identifies several features of "weird English:"

1. Weirding deprives English of its dominance and allows other languages to enjoy the same status;
2. Weird English expresses aesthetic adventurousness at the price of sacrificing rules;
3. Weird English is derived from nonnative English;
4. The rhythms and structure of orthodox English alone are not enough to express the diasporic cultures that speak it.

(p. 11)

As Ch'ien argues, weird English is a series of purposeful deviations from English, rather than mere "grammatical misdemeanors" (p. 10). For Ch'ien, weird English is not a problem per se but rather a creative alternative for authors to imagine new literary worlds through a subversive appropriation of standardized English.

My conceptualization of weird *language* both intersects with and deviates from Ch'ien's version of weird English in several ways. On the most obvious level, since the subject of my inquiry is global Korea, it does not make sense to limit my analysis to "English." Of course, I have argued elsewhere, along with Christopher Jenks, that

"English" can reasonably be conceived of as a legitimate Korean language (Jenks & Lee, 2017), developing insights from scholars in the field of world Englishes who have extensively documented discrete varietal features of English in Korea (Kaier, 2014; Kyung-Ja Park, 2009; Rüdiger, 2017, 2019, 2021). This being said, if we expand our purview of global Korea to other parts of the world, including Asia and the Americas, it is necessary to attend to a wider range of language resources beyond just English, and indeed beyond Korean. In this sense, I aim to join scholars such as Ngũgĩ wa Thiong'o (2012), Aamir Mufti (2018), and Ruanni Tupas (2020) in decentering English in the scholarly study of language and linguistic phenomena. Within the context of the sociolinguistics of globalization, there is still a need to expand the purview of scholarship beyond the narrow algorithm of "English + another language" (Jerry Won Lee & Canagarajah, 2021), and hopefully the explorations in this chapter contribute to this cause in a useful way.

Additionally, while Ch'ien's conceptualization of weird English focuses on *intentional* "misdeameanors" in English, as I suggested in Chapter 1, I am less interested in the intentions that drive the design and production of different forms of language and other semiotic resources and more on the contextually contingent, indexical, and emblematic characteristics of language and semiotic resources. Ron Scollon and Suzie Wong Scollon (2003) note the importance of distinguishing indexical and symbolic functions of language in the linguistic landscape. As Scollon and Scollon write, starting with the example of code preference:

> A code may be chosen because it indexes the point in the world it is placed – this is an Arabic-speaking community (or business or nation) – or because it symbolizes a social group because of some association with that group – this is a Chinese restaurant because there is Chinese writing in the shop sign. Whether our concern is with code preference based on geopolitical indexing or with symbolization based on sociocultural associations, we must have some evidence from *outside* the signs themselves to make this determination. (p. 119, emphasis in original)

And while my focus is not on code preference (i.e., what does it mean that this sign uses this language as opposed to another), the point that the symbolic value of the sign emerges from the outside is an important reminder if anything because it moves us to think beyond the intentions of the maker of the sign. Jan Blommaert's (2010) distinction between denotative/linguistic signs and semiotic/emblematic signs is additionally useful here. He offers the example of a chocolate shop in

Japan called "Nina's derrière" in order to argue that the sign is not "French," but "Frenchness," serving the semiotic function of "signaling a complex of associative meanings … [to] French chic" (p. 29). While I do not adopt the distinction between "French" and "Frenchness" specifically or "nation" and "nationness" more generally, which in both pairings potentially assumes an inauthenticity to the latter (see Chapter 2), this treatment of meaning-making as symbolic/semiotic is useful is in part because, in the study of public signage in the linguistic/semiotic landscape, the intentions of the individual sign maker are frequently at the mercy of the interpretations of the sign by the public masses who make sense of it on a daily basis. This point is made evident in David Malinowski's (2008) ethnography of the linguistic landscape of the Koreatown in Oakland, California, in which he finds that, even after thorough consideration of multiple options and input from the local community, the names on signs do not always convey what the author intends. Malinowski draws on Judith Butler's (1997) notion of speech as "excitable" insofar as it "is always in some ways out of our control" (p. 15) in order to argue that "the outcome of this process [of users giving voice to an utterance] is, because of the unique context of utterance and embodied production of language, uncertain" (Malinowski, 2008, p. 118).

In other words, the takeaway from this chapter is not something along the lines of "there are lots of Koreans living here, so there is a lot of Korean on the signage," or "this sign uses Korean in order to index authentic Koreanness," or "this Korean restaurant owner is trying to appeal to the local Spanish speaking patrons, so there is Spanish on this sign." In Blommaert's (2013) words, such approaches to language in public space are not exactly "rocket science" (p. 61), but can be treated as the starting point for additional inquiry. The additional inquiry I will pursue focuses on the semiotic/symbolic outcomes of language that is unfamiliar or quite simply "weird." In what follows, I focus on three categories of weird language: translation, transliteration, and translingualization. Translation refers to the representation of language resources in another language (e.g., from English to Korean). Transliteration can be understood as the representation of language resources in the script of another language (e.g., Korean words in the script of Japanese). Translingualization, meanwhile, is what I define as the blending of language resources that results in a condition of untransposability of conventional categories of "languages." Collectively, they represent varying outcomes of cultural salience, with translation and transliteration generally limited to attempts to index or re-present Koreanness to local audiences. Translingualization, meanwhile, would appear to target audiences more specifically with proficiency in multiple linguistic repertoires; however it is significant not in terms of considerations of audience but in that it invites, at times inadvertently, alternative considerations of the presumed discreteness of Korea as both a language and, by extension, a cultural entity.

What I am proposing is in many ways analogous to Naoki Sakai's (1997) argument in *Translation and Subjectivity: On "Japan" and Cultural Nationalism* that the discreteness of cultural difference exists not unto itself but comes to be through the very act of translation. As Sakai argues, a conceptualization of what is "Japanese thought" and even more generally "Japan" can only be achieved intersubjectively, from an outside gaze that presumes what Japan is prior to the inquiry itself. Further, according to Sakai, linguistic and cultural translation provides critical insight into the ways in which the parameters of cultural identity are established:

> "we" as a case of the vocative designation cannot be confused with a group of those who are capable of communicating the same information with each other, for such a group can be posited only imaginarily and in representation. Furthermore, translation is required in order to determine the sameness of the information: what remains the same in information cannot be identified unless it is translated. What is translated and transferred can be recognized as such only after translation. (p. 5)

Sakai offers a series of important meaning-making implications for translation, both as a trope and as a practice. Among them is the dependency on the *outcome* of translation (language Y) as something of a framing device through which the *source* of translation (language/culture X) can be adequately conceptualized.

What I offer in the following pages is guided by a similar imperative, though with a focus on encounters with unfamiliar language. Indeed, it could be argued that translation is in most cases an encounter with the unfamiliar, assuming of course that the reader is not entirely familiar with the source language of the text that has been translated. What is very frequently taken for granted, as Sakai rightly notes, are the linguistic contours of the source language, along with the culture such language purportedly represents or stands in for. And while language that falls into the general category of that which is "weird," especially when found in the linguistic/semiotic landscape, is not regularly treated as warranting analysis or investigation, instances of "weird" language in the linguistic/semiotic landscape have the capacity to enable us to rethink our assumptions not only of what is worthy of scholarly inquiry but also of what constitutes linguistic and cultural discreteness across global space.

3.4 WEIRD TRANSLATIONS

Exploring instances of weird translation, whether they are unintended or intended, is a productive place to start to try and make sense of what we expect a given culture to look like in global space. In the linguistic/semiotic landscape of global Korea, translation is sometimes a direct/literal process. Take for instance a sign from Toronto, Canada: on the sign, "두부마을 [Du-bu ma-eul]" is complemented by its literal translation, which is "Tofu Village" (Fig. 3.4). This is perhaps the simplest way for one to re-present Korean in the linguistic/semiotic landscape, though it is also relatively uncommon. It is instead more common to encounter cases of what might be called minimalist translations. This is evident in a sign for a restaurant in Mexico City: "돈돼지 숯불돼지 갈비전문 [Don-dwae-ji sut-bul dwae-ji

Fig. 3.4 Tofu Village (Toronto)

Fig. 3.5   Money Pig (Mexico City)

gal-bi jeon-mun]" (Fig. 3.5). The sign itself only presents "RESTAURANTE COREANO [KOREAN RESTAURANT]," in the logical target language of Spanish, the dominant language in Mexico. The remainder of the text itself is not translated into Spanish. While the Korean text of "돈돼지 숯불돼지 갈비전문" could be translated into Spanish, hypothetically speaking, as "Cerdo de dinero especialidad de costillas de cerdo a la barbacoa [Money pig speciality barbeque pork rib]," it would not denote what it intends to without including the descriptor of "Coreano." But even this would be an incomplete translation given the fact that "돈 [don]" itself also means pig while also representing the Korean pronunciation of the Han-ja character for pig, "豚," which itself also refers to money, following the historical association of a pig's weight with 1-don (a unit of measurement) of gold.[6] Even so, the name of the restaurant itself, "Cerdo de dinero" would likely be an unusual expression to audiences familiar with Spanish. In other words, it would be an example not of a translation of functional equivalence but of a literal translation of formal equivalence par

---

[6] I thank Monica W. Cho for offering these observations.

excellence: a translation that is word for word, and effectively ineffective (which explains why it is not common to see such translations).

Admittedly, in cases such as those described above, it might very well be tenuous to refer to them as instances of translation in the first place: they are somewhat functional as translations perhaps, but they also deviate considerably from the original language. Consider the following sign in Shanghai, China: "韩国水原王烤肉 [Hánguó shuǐyuán wáng kǎoròu]" (Fig. 3.6). The Korean translation on the sign, "수원 왕 갈비 [Su-won Wang Gal-bi]," includes "Suwon [a city in South Korea]," "Wang [king]," and "Galbi [ribs]," which can be collectively translated as "Suwon-Style king [as in large-cut] beef ribs." Meanwhile, the Chinese characters on the sign, "Hánguó shuǐyuán wáng kǎoròu," represent "Korean Suwon king [as in royalty] barbeque." What is notable is that the Chinese version includes not only the region of Korea (Suwon) but has been supplemented by "Hánguó [Korean]," and thus upscaled from the microlevel of region to the relationally macrolevel of nation.[7] This is not altogether dissimilar from the upscaling strategy represented in the example of "RESTAURANTE COREANO" from Mexico City above. What it specifically signals, however, is that such practices are simultaneously (1) the

Fig. 3.6 Suwon Wang Galbi (Shanghai)

[7] See Agha (2007) on the relational contingency of macro and micro scales. The question of scale is addressed in further detail in Chapter 4 as well.

Fig. 3.7   Seoul Bulgogi (Shanghai)

result of the signs' emplacement (Scollon & Scollon, 2003) outside of the nation proper (as suggested earlier, we can presume that a Korean restaurant in Korea proper is simply a "restaurant"), and (2) reflective of how the emblematic reinvention of Koreanness is achieved through translation, in this case, the practice of translational upscaling, which in turn works to reconstitute the space as Korean.

In this sense, translations are oftentimes shaped by considerations of local audiences, and as such need to be interpreted with respect to their emplacement within a given region. To expand on this point, I turn to another sign from Shanghai: "首尔烤牛肉 [Shǒuěr kǎo-niúròu]" or "Seoul barbequed beef" (Fig. 3.7). The significance of this translation emerges in relation to the Korean text of "서울불고기 [Seoul Bul-go-gi]." Bul-go-gi is a popular Korean dish comprised of grilled beef, though it would be scarcely accurate to refer to it as "barbequed beef," as it is presented in the Chinese text. The Chinese characters for "烤牛肉" are offered as a generic and approximate translation of "bul-go-gi," as there is no Chinese character for "불고기" itself. "烤牛肉" thus achieves its meaning on this sign as a linguistic entailment if read complementary to the Korean text of "불고기" and in relation to its spatial context. At first glance, from a communicative perspective, it would appear that such signage is reflective of a translational rendition that is bordering on the nonsensical. However, such "inaccurate" translations nonetheless are what enable us to locate Korea, as it were.

Fig. 3.8   Jeongol House (Oakland, CA)

This point can be further affirmed by examining a sign for a restaurant in Oakland, California, for "전골하우스 [Jeon-gol Ha-u-seu]" (Fig. 3.8). On the sign, the word "Jeon-gol," a stew with various combinations of vegetables and proteins, has been translated as "Casserole." A casserole is generally understood, according to the Oxford English Dictionary, to be "a dish cooked and served in a casserole," or a "kind of stew-pan." However, it also has varying connotations in different national contexts. In the UK, for instance, it is generally understood as a slow-cooked stew, whereas in the US it more frequently refers to a baked dish. There are thus two points of interest in the translational choice of "Casserole." One potential interpretation is that, like the "Kǎoniúròu" example from Shanghai above, "Casserole" is a linguistic entailment whose meaning emerges through its adjacency to "Jeon-gol." Another possibility is that the sign achieves its intended denotation only when upscaled to the macro, or global, context that renders feasible the indexicality of "casserole" as "stew," beyond the relationally micro contexts of Oakland, California, or even the United States. In other words, it can be suggested that the choice of "Casserole" is not entirely infelicitous if we approach the term as it would be used in the UK context as a slow-cooked stew. Simultaneously, though, it is far from "accurate" in the sense that jeon-gol is not a slow-cooked dish but is rather prepared within a few minutes and is normally served at the table under an open flame. However, it needs to be acknowledged that its usage is nevertheless somewhat unusual given its emplacement in the US context, where casserole, as noted above, refers to a baked dish that is far from a stew, whether slow-cooked or "fast-cooked." I would therefore argue that its emplacement results in a spatial and discursive dissonance from its more common connotation in the US context, producing the conditions in which the seeming mistranslation of "jeon-gol" as "casserole" effectively reconstitutes it as a successful translation of "jeon-gol." Put differently, the point is not that "casserole" represents an incompetent or ungraceful translation of "jeon-gol" but instead that it reflects the very defeasibility (Agha, 2007) of words from languages other than Korean, given their emplacement in a context in which they attempt to achieve Koreanness. Translations, thus, whether "accurate" or "inaccurate," by dint of their defamiliarization of the familiar (e.g., casserole) facilitate the reinvention of "Korea" in such spaces.

This directs us to a larger issue, which centers on the question of untranslatability more generally. The complexities of translation have long been noted by numerous scholars (see Benjamin ([1955]1968) for a foundational text and Venuti (2008) for an overview). More recently, scholars of comparative literature and translation studies, such as Emily Apter (2013), critique the "translatability assumption," or the willful abandonment of cross-cultural and cross-linguistic nuance in the interest of arriving at a re-presentation of a word or concept into another language. David Gramling (2016), more broadly, identifies the Globalization, Internationalization, Localization, and Translation (GILT) industry as the culprit of the contemporary condition of translatability in which communicability across different "languages" is prioritized in a manner "such that alternative vernacular meanings are effectively decommissioned" in the interest of industrial efficiency (p. 37). In other words, the limitations to the very act of translation are widely acknowledged even if they are ultimately deprioritized through the guise that effective translation is possible in the first place. It therefore comes as little surprise that a common strategy for branding an establishment as Korean is achieved not only through translation but through transliteration, which will be discussed in the following section.

3.5   *WEIRD TRANSLITERATIONS*

Like translation, transliteration – or the representation of language resources in the script of another language – is evident throughout the linguistic/semiotic landscape of global Korea. Returning to the afore-mentioned differentiation between denotative/linguistic and semi-otic/emblematic signs as described by Blommaert (2010) or the differentiation between indexical versus symbolic outcomes of language as described by Scollon and Scollon (2003) is instructive for an understanding of the functions of transliteration in the translocal production of Koreanness (in the sense of beyond Korea "proper"). It is useful to examine these two instances simultaneously: the first example is "Bulgogi House" in Los Angeles (Fig. 3.9) and the second example is "WOORIJIP" in New York (Fig. 3.10). In the first instance, "Bulgogi" is the Roman alphabetic transliteration of "불고기." As suggested in the previous section, bul-go-gi is a popular Korean dish and it has become an enregistered term that is familiar to many consumers who are familiar with Korean cuisine. Whether in Los Angeles or São Paulo, "bulgogi" or "bulgôgui" respectively, can frequently function without the assistance of translation. The example in the previous section from Shanghai presented a translated version as "烤牛肉," but this does not mean that a majority of Chinese consumers are unfamiliar with the dish in question. Admittedly, its degree of enregisterment and thus worldwide denotational familiarity is not as ubiquitous as say, 김치 [kimchi], or perhaps the more universally recognized Japanese cuisine, すし [sushi], which itself is polysemous. In the United States, for instance, "sushi" is denotative of "California rolls," whose ingredients include materials such as avocado and

Fig. 3.9   Bulgogi House (Los Angeles)

Fig. 3.10   Woorijip (New York)

mayonnaise, deviating considerably from what would be considered "sushi" in Japan. The point here is that "bul-go-gi" represents an instance of transliteration that serves a legitimate denotative/linguistic function to many "non-Korean" audiences.

On the other hand, instances such as "WOORIJIP," which is a transliteration of "우리집" or "Our House," serve a function that is semiotic/emblematic. There are multiple ways to interpret such transliterated text. It can be argued that such transliteration is gratuitous insofar as "WOORIJIP" signifies nothing outside of the Korean language. A more functional interpretation could be that the transliteration is not gratuitous insofar as it provides the conditions for mutual coordination (Agha, 2007): at the very least, it offers customers who are unable to read and thus refer to the Korean text of "우리집" a shared referent that can be uttered (as in "I walked by a Korean restaurant called 'Woorijip' that looks good," as opposed to "I walked by a Korean restaurant on 42nd Street that looks good"). But it is more interesting to consider that "WOORIJIP," like any other transliteration from Korean whose result is nonsensical, is an enregistered emblem of Koreanness. The point is not merely that certain terms in Korean are simply untranslatable. Instead, instances of semiotic/emblematic transliteration index, more generally, unfamiliarity and "difference." Such transliterations result in conspicuously unfamiliar words that, in the moment of encounter, because of their sheer unfamiliarity, signal to readers that the spatial environment is "different," which is analogous to the geopolitical conditions in which we can begin to conceive of "Korea" within the political boundaries of the "United States." In so doing, they produce a space that is "different" and, as is the case of global Korea, produce a space that is "Korean."

3.6 WEIRD TRANSLINGUALIZATIONS

In the instances of translation and transliteration described in Sections 3.4 and 3.5, the boundaries between Korean and other languages remain largely intact. This is not to suggest that transliteration itself cannot result in a disruption of language boundaries as well. This is illustrated perhaps most aptly by Alastair Pennycook (2010a) in his analysis of a sign in Kuala Lumpur, Malaysia, for "Pub dan karaoke" (p. 68). "Pub" may appear to be an English word, while "dan" appears to be a Bahasa Malaysia word, and "karaoke" would appear to be Japanese. But the fact that we do not need a translation for "karaoke" suggests that it could also be an English word, and we cannot conclusively determine the status of the allegedly English word "pub" in Kuala Lumpur. The sign is not "monolingual," "bilingual," or even "trilingual," but instead "none of the above," in the words of Pennycook (2010a, p. 68). The point of such analysis is to remind us that the reliability or conclusiveness of linguistic categorizations is not significant; instead, the point is to "see how we make our surrounds linguistically" (p. 69). Therefore, having noted the complexities of transliteration, it may be productive to refer to the blending of language resources that results in a condition of untransposability of conventional categories of "languages" as translingualization. The phenomenon of translingualization develops the robust body of literature on translanguaging, which can be defined as an approach to language that recognizes the fluidity of named language boundaries reflective of communication in diverse contexts (see Introduction and Chapter 1). Rather than translanguaging or cognate terms such as those invoked and catalogued in Chapter 1, I present translingualization in part to develop a logical parallelism with comparatively more established concepts such as translation and transliteration (e.g., translating : translation :: translanguaging : translingualization). Yet, more significantly, translingualization foregrounds the socio-discursive outcomes of language fluidization in scenarios such as the Korean context in which language has historically been ideologically engineered to be emblematic of national identity. By considering translingualization, I am less invested in rehistoricizing the sedimentation of language resources within established language boundaries (such as the enregisterment of "sushi" as a Bahasa Malaysia word). Instead, I argue that translingualization points to the fluidization of language boundaries in ways that unsettle the presumed discreteness of "Korea" as a language. This is not to suggest that translingualization detaches signage from a geographically defined Korean national identity and space. Instead, translingualization lays bare the question of whether Korean can be its own national "language" to begin with, and, subsequently, the extent to which Korean can be conceived of as a discrete cultural entity.

Translingualization is not particularly uncommon, as is the case in a sign for a restaurant in Los Angeles's Koreatown, "SS ㅣ ㅇ SS ㅣ ㅇ 회 덮밥" (Fig. 3.11). This sign blends Roman alphabetic letters (SS) with Korean alphabetic letters (ㅣ ㅇ) in a rather unconventional manner. As noted before, in order for Hangeul to work, the individual letters must be clustered into groups of two to four letters to form a coherent syllable. In this particular case, the letters "(ㅇ)" and "(ㅣ)" can be paired as "이" but cannot be paired as "ㅣ ㅇ" except in the syllable end position. Certainly, readers can infer that "SS ㅣ ㅇ SS ㅣ ㅇ" is a creative rendition of "씽씽 [ssing ssing]" or "fresh" not only because "씽씽" is presented elsewhere on the sign but also because the letter "ㅅ" is phonetically similar to /s/. The result of "SS ㅣ ㅇ SS ㅣ ㅇ" is, like "ㅊ ㅗ ㅇ ㅜ ㅓ ㄴ" in Section 3.1, a morphological impossibility that

Fig. 3.11   Ssing Ssing (Los Angeles)

Fig. 3.12   Catch Me (Gangnam)

cannot be rendered except through a deliberate and creative deviation from established orthographical conventions.

Of course, while "SS ㅣ ㅇ SS ㅣ ㅇ" is perhaps an interesting example of translingualization, in order to understand the global reinvention of "Korea" in relation to the complexities of contemporary Korean language ideologies, such an analysis would benefit from a complementary investigation of instances that foreground the untransposability of Korean with other languages that have historically been the focal point of metadiscourses of Korean monolingualism (such as Chinese and Japanese). With this objective in mind, a sign for a restaurant in Gangnam, "Catch Me / 캐치味" is particularly compelling (Fig. 3.12). The "캐치味 [Kae-chi-mi]" portion of the sign featuring a shift from red to white text would appear to signal a shift to a different linguistic resource, from Korean (캐치) to Chinese (味). Yet, "캐치" is merely a transliteration of the English word "catch" and "味" is the Han-ja character for "flavor." Therefore, "캐치味" can merely be transliterated into English as "Catch Me" but has no meaning unto itself. It is ontologically dependent on its adjacency to English in order to be rendered as an approximant of "Catch Me." "캐치味," then, is ultimately untranslatable.

In the Koreatown of the Wangjing district of Beijing, there is a Korean restaurant called "꾸미樂" (Fig. 3.13). The sign, at first glance, appears to be a mere pairing of Korean (꾸미) with Chinese

Fig. 3.13 Zui Wei Le (Beijing)

(樂), which includes both translation (KOREAN RESTAURANT) and transliteration (ZUI WEI LE). However, what makes this particular sign intriguing is the various strategies whereby Korean and Chinese are rendered untransposable. Obviously, "꾸미樂 [Kku mi lak]" is presented in a considerably larger size than the Chinese "最味樂 [zuìwèilè]," and in terms of information value, in the ideal (upper) zone while the Chinese text is relegated to the real (lower) zone, which has the effect of subordinating or complementarizing the text. Yet, what complicates the vertical stratification in this pairing is the parallel shift in color (from white to red) in both expressions, which signals the choice to use "樂" in "꾸미樂" instead of a fully transliterated version (i.e., "꾸미락"). Further, the transposability between Korean and Chinese is further troubled by the manner in which "꾸미樂," a hybridization of Korean and Chinese like "캐치味" in Gangnam, is illegible unto itself. "꾸미樂" represents a partial transliteration of "最味樂," or "most taste happy." However, crucially, "꾸미樂" is accompanied by a Chinese transliteration "最味樂" that is a nonsensical expression in Chinese, thus emphasizing the interdependency of Chinese and Korean text in this sign in order for meaning to occur.

For my final example, I turn to the Koreatown of Osaka, where signage for the restaurant "마니무라 [Ma-ni-mu-ra]" affords an additional layer of complexity to the expectation of linguistic and national transposability in the context of efforts to linguistically

Fig. 3.14 Manimura (Osaka)

reinvent Korea as a discrete entity in global contexts (Fig. 3.14). The sign features Korean text of "마니무라," which is the Gyeongsang provincial dialect variation of "많이 먹어라 [man-i-meok-eo-ra]," or the imperative form of "eat a lot." While the sign features Japanese text that reads "韓国カフェ&ダイニング [Kankoku kafe & dainingu]," or "Korean café and dining," the text of "마니무라" is also transliterated into the Japanese as "まにむら," which has no meaning in Japanese. It is commonly understood that the Gyeongsang variety of Korean is distinct from "middle" or "standardized" Korean in terms of phonetic, morphological, and lexical features (Do, Ito, & Kenstowicz, 2014). Yet the Gyeongsang province is geographically proximate to Japan and the variety is similar, at least intonationally, to the Japanese language. In the context of this inquiry, the point is that the consideration of dialect adds a layer of complexity to the question of translation insofar as it shifts the focus away from questions of translating between language X and language Y to a particular kind of language X and a particular kind of language Y (see Berthele, 2000; Queen, 2004). The significance of the "마니무라/まにむら" signage, then, understood in the context of translational nuance and in the context of potential similarities between Gyeongsang Korean and Japanese, is its being an instance of translingualization. It is not merely an innocuous or frivolous instance of translingualization but instead a disruption of the very expectation of cultural and linguistic transposability more generally through the notation of "national" difference.

If such difference is a prerequisite to be able to locate the national in global space, then we perhaps do not arrive at an understanding of the operational logics of national discreteness through Korean language but are instead compelled to reconsider the presumed interrelationships between Korea as national language and Korea as national imaginary.

3.7   CONCLUSION: NEGOTIABLE LANGUAGE, LOCATABLE LANGUAGE

In this chapter, I examined the role of language in the production of the Korean national imaginary across global space. I have focused on the phenomena of translation, transliteration, and translingualization in the linguistic/semiotic landscape of global Korea, including examples in Korea proper and beyond. In terms of translation, it is not that the Korean language is able to be translated into languages that are in alignment with the national or local linguistic expectations of a given city or region, whether Spanish in Mexico City or Japanese in Osaka. Instead, the point is that the various attempts at and outcomes of translation, whether direct/literal or approximate, whether "good" or "bad," produce the very conditions of unfamiliarity in which local or familiar language resources can be reconstituted. Even if this reconstitution takes place "incorrectly," in a manner in which they can operate as enregistered emblems of "Koreanness," it in turn facilitates the local reinvention of Korea. While a similar point can be made about the strategy of transliteration, the outcomes of translingualization are arguably the most compelling, insofar as they more explicitly put into crisis the very expectation of linguistic and national transposability, which is the very precondition of national distinctiveness. In this sense, the above analysis does not offer a schematic of how Korea can be conceptualized but instead invites us to reconsider the very extent to which it is even possible to conceive of Korea as a discrete entity unto itself. While the above instances are not intended to be an exhaustive survey of linguistic re-presentation across Korean global space, they offer at the very least a tentative understanding of the role of unfamiliarity in the reconstitution of space as "Korean." Linguistic unfamiliarity, as I have aimed to demonstrate in this chapter, signals to readers that the spatial environment is "different," which represents the perceptual substrate by which people can encounter Korea even if not within Korea per se. In this sense, "Korea," as a cultural entity, comes to be simultaneously locatable but also negotiable.

4 Visible Nation: Scaling Culture

4.1 STREET FIGHTER II AS NATIONS AND NATIONALISM

I learned what a nation was in the third grade. However, it was not through formal classroom instruction but through a video game. The year was 1991, I had just turned eight years old, and there was an extended period in my life where every weekend all the kids in the neighborhood would flock to their local arcades or corner markets to play a game called *Street Fighter II*. It was a tournament fighting game with characters each representing a different nation: three from the United States, two from Japan, and one each from China, Brazil, India, Spain, Thailand, along with one of unknown national origin (the main antagonist of the narrative), and one from the USSR (in later versions of the game, after the dissolution of the Soviet Union, the lone Soviet character, Zangief, would represent Russia). The game offered me a lesson in scale through its hasty representations of national culture. In addition to the different "types" of fighters from different parts of the world, whether the Muay Thai master from Thailand, the matador from Spain, or the sumo wrestler from Japan, the nation of Japan would be represented though temples and bathhouses, China would be represented by people riding bicycles and slaughtering chickens in the streets, and Brazil would be represented by thatched-roof houses along the river basin.

I think it is understandable for a child, or anybody for that matter, to reduce their conceptualization of a nation to its stereotype: to a series of commonplace distinguishing associations and features. After all, sumo wrestling is the national sport of Japan and up until recently something unique to Japan and the Japanese diaspora. But this chapter is not an attempt to problematize the reductive portrayal of the nation to the stereotype, whether in video games or anywhere else (e.g., there is more to Japan than sumo wrestling!).[1] Nor is it an effort to insist on pursuing and prioritizing an "authentic" understanding of the nation (e.g., the sumo wrestling in *Street Fighter II* is not authentic sumo wrestling!). Instead, I would like to explore the extent to which the stereotype is that which makes the nation semiotically conceivable in the first place, extending the points made in the previous chapters regarding the nation as materialized in forms or units that render it transposable to other nations. In *Street Fighter II*, transposability via the category of the national occurs in the menu screen where players choose from characters representing different nations, who in turn need to travel to other nations to challenge opponents representing other nations. The national here is not conceived of in terms of the bound serialization of populations (see Chapter 1) but through representative images that are not only scaled (downscaled to the individual and a specific site that is meant to stand in for the nation) but *scalable*.

In this chapter, I focus on how the semiotic aggregate of features that are constitutive of Korea as a national category are strategically deployed across global space toward the reinvention of the nation. Crucially, such features are not inherently Korean but come to be salient indexicals of Koreanness. In addition, features that might be said to be of the semiotic aggregate of Koreanness are in turn regularly encountered in rescaled form, namely in an amplified or saturated manner. In short, this chapter argues that an encounter with the nation in global space cannot occur in its quotidian, ordinary form but rather in its semiotically conspicuous form, which operates at the intersections between the purely "authentic" and the merely "invented," both outcomes of scalar work. Cultural distinction, and indeed national distinction in this case, is thus presented as a question of scale: both in terms of being able to be scaled and perhaps only ever being subject to scale. Re-presenting Korea in global space demands that the very idea of Korea be scaled and the outcomes of this scalar work can lead us toward a better understanding of not only the distinctive features of Korea as a cultural entity but also what is presumed to make "Korea" a "distinctive" cultural entity in the first place.

---

[1] Indeed, Akira Yasuda, the creative designer for *Street Fighter II*, confesses that summoning stereotypes was an important starting point for imagining characters in the game: "Maybe I'm a weird Japanese person, but I *want* to make something stereotyped – something exaggerated. To be perfectly honest, I think it's okay if they're discriminatory – not in an offensive way, but in a way that's easy and fun" (emphasis in original, quoted in Hendershot, 2017, p. 27).

4.2 SCALE AS CULTURE

Scale is a challenging concept to define because of its sheer range of denotations. A scale as an object can refer to the series of small plates that cover the bodies of animals such as snakes, fish, or pangolins. It can also refer to a device used to determine the weight of an object based on a specific unit of measurement, or to compare the weight of two objects or masses, as in a balancing scale. In music, scale refers to a set of notes within a given pitch, ordered according to ascent or descent. In cartography, a scaling refers to the ratio of the represented territory relative to the physical territory. In the business world, scalability refers to the ability to increase a given business model by proportionately building up its existing organizational infrastructural components. Scaling can also refer to the practice of distributing attributes in a quantifiable manner, such as in the use of a Likert scale. And scaling can refer to the practice of describing or portraying objects or phenomena in relation to others in order to make them more comprehensible or relatable.[2] With the exception of the zoological definition, what all these treatments of scale have in common is that they all concern measurement and relationality in some form or another, whether relations between similar objects, between those that are analogous or are framed as analogous, or even those that are completely unrelated but come to have a relationship via the praxis of scaling. Therefore, for our purposes, it is sufficient to define scale as a discursive framing device that enables us to orient or reorient ourselves toward a given element of our social worlds that is otherwise difficult or impossible to make sense of.

As E. Summerson Carr and Michael Lempert (2016) remind us, "there are no ideologically neutral scales" (p. 3). Carr and Lempert thus outline the importance of attending to what they term the *pragmatics* of scale: "to take a critical distance from given scalar distinctions, whether our own or others', and focus instead on the social circumstances, dynamics, and consequences of scale-making as social practice and project" (p. 9). The COVID-19 pandemic offered among the most compelling lessons in the value of attending to the

---

[2] In *Star Wars Episode V: The Empire Strikes Back*, for instance, audiences are introduced to the Galactic Empire's newest space vessel *Executor* by witnessing it cruising adjacent to other, comparatively diminutive Star Destroyers. The point is to visually emphasize that the *Executor* is a *Super* Star Destroyer and not just an "ordinary" Star Destroyer, which had been introduced early in *Episode IV* as itself a devastatingly massive vessel, when scaled to the Rebel Alliance's measly cruiser, *Tantive IV*.

ideological work of scale. In the early months of the pandemic, in late 2019 and early 2020, popular news articles with data comparing COVID-19 deaths to annual influenza (flu) deaths were being widely shared across social media by users in the United States. One of the many examples was Liz Szabo's (2020) "Something far deadlier than the Wuhan coronavirus lurks near you, right here in America" in *USA Today* in January 2020, or an article written by Dan Vergano (2020) published that same month in *BuzzFeed News* titled "Don't worry about the coronavirus. Worry about the flu" (by March, the title would later be adjusted to "Here's what we do and don't know about the deadly coronavirus outbreak"). In early 2020, the strategy of downscaling COVID-19 in relation to the annual flu was used to emphasize that the emergent panic and fear around the novel virus was merely driven by anti-Chinese and anti-Asian sentiment. This was, as the argument went, "yellow peril" (Erika Lee, 2007; Tchen & Yeats, 2014) all over again. Interestingly, within a few months, the norm became upscaling COVID-19 by emphasizing its death *rate* relative to the flu, not just in terms of death *tolls* (e.g., Shawn Radcliffe's [2020] "Here's why COVID-19 is much worse than the flu"). While the initial ideological priority of scaling COVID-19 was to foreground and problematize the anti-Asian sentiment, by the time a virtual consensus had been reached by leading epidemiologists and public health officials around the world, it could no longer be denied that COVID-19 was indeed a disease that needed to be taken seriously (not just something receiving inordinate media attention because it had originated in China). By late 2020, COVID-19 came to be scaled in relation to other tragic events in history, with various infographics comparing the number of deaths to those of other historical moments, including various wars and the 9/11 terrorist attacks of 2001.

Of course, the point in all this is not simply to underscore that people "got it wrong," including those who initially argued that the panic around COVID-19 was based on anti-Chinese fearmongering, or those who continue to maintain that the virus was a hoax. There was and is something inherently unknowable about the pandemic, and therein lies the work of scale: to try and make something unknowable into something knowable. Of course, the process of downscaling is frequently a matter of convenience. This is evident in the "What People Think I Do / What I Really Do" memes, popular in the 2010s. As Limor Shifman (2014) notes, digital memes enable users to perform intertextual imitation in terms of content ("the ideas and the ideologies conveyed" by a cultural text), form ("the physical incarnation of the message," including "both visual/audible dimensions specific to certain texts and the more complex genre-related patterns organizing them"), and stance ("the ways in which addressers position themselves in relation to the text, its linguistic codes, the addressees, and other potential speakers") (p. 40). In the "What People Think I Do / What I Really Do" meme, a profession is accompanied by a series of images, many of which are allusive cultural texts, with various captions: what society thinks I do, what my mom thinks I do, what I think I do, etc. The final image of most versions of the meme is mundane and unglamorous, with the caption of "what I really do," representing a form of stance-taking along the lines of "everybody doesn't really get what I do, and maybe I don't really get it myself."

Take for instance the "Linguist" version of this meme (Fig. 4.1). The first image, "What Society Thinks I Do," is a series of dictionaries for multiple languages, no doubt in response to the question commonly posed to linguists: How many languages do you speak?[3] Meanwhile, the image for "What My Mom Thinks I Do" is a "Grammar Police" badge, reflecting the assumption that a linguist's occupation revolves around prescriptivism: "policing" vernacular language to ensure its

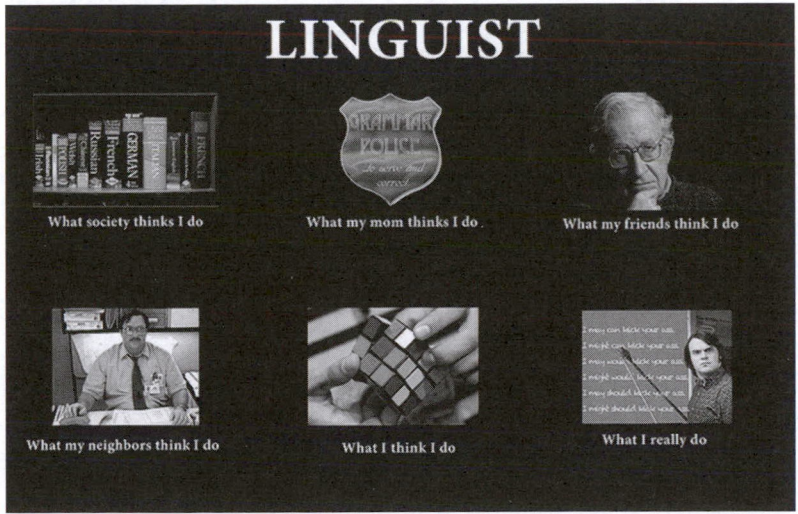

Fig 4.1 Linguist meme

---

[3] Of course, as they say, asking a linguist how many languages they speak is like asking a medical doctor how many diseases they have.

correct usage. The "What People Think I Do / What I Really Do" meme points not only to the ubiquitousness of scalar work but also to its inevitability. I am referring here not to the "pragmatics of scale" as described by Carr and Lempert but perhaps to scale as pragmatics: it is quite simply impossible for one individual to have working knowledge of all available professions and therefore one is bound to deploy scalar work to make sense of certain ones. And the example of "linguist" adds, as I'm sure many professions do, a layer of complexity given the sheer range of subfields within the study of linguistics (applied linguistics, computational linguistics, linguistic anthropology, neurolinguistics, psycholinguistics, sociolinguistics, etc.) and the sheer number of different professions that meet the criteria for a linguist (forensic linguist, lexicographer, speech pathologist, teacher, etc.). In short, the point is that scaling is at work all around us, which punctuates the need to "track and narrate, rather than capture and catalogue, the many ways that social life is scaled" (Carr & Lempert, 2016, p. 21).

The element of social life that I want to focus on is cultural distinction, in particular distinction via the register of the national, and how it operates as an entailment of scalar work. As I've noted throughout this book, representing nationness comes with a series of challenges in part because the nation is simultaneously bound to a historicity that is inherently flexible. Indeed, the representability of nationness is a problem not only due to its contingency on ever-changing historical facts but also due to the disconnect between the unremarkability of everyday life for typical national subjects and the frequently remarkable ways in which we learn and think about life in other nations. Consider, for instance, how "world" or "global" news is reported: we would not regularly hear about what is going on in nation X unless the object were newsworthy enough to warrant the attention of an audience outside a given nation. I am not trying to point out the obvious fact that our understanding of nation X is always going to be inherently limited but trying to make sense of the implications of representation via scalar work. More specifically, what does it mean when – in the same way that we scale different peoples' occupations as a matter of sheer necessity – ideas of the nation are frequently circulated via visualizations that are almost invariably scaled?

In order to make sense of the scalar contingencies of visualizations of the nation, it would be productive to engage Michael Billig's (1995) theory of banal nationalism. Billig challenges the view of nations as constitutive of "collective acts of imagination" (p. 95) à la Benedict Anderson (1991), and contends that the performance of national identification is not a conscious, conspicuous, or concentrated practice. As Billig (1995) writes:

> The citizens of an established nation do not, day by day, consciously decide that their nation should continue. On the other hand, the reproduction of a nation does not occur magically. Banal practices, rather than conscious choice or collective acts of imagination, are required. Just as a language will die rather for want of regular users, so a nation must be put to daily use. (p. 95)

As Billig argues, "the metonymic image of banal nationalism is not a flag which is being consciously waved with fervent passion; it is the flag hanging unnoticed on the public building" (p. 8). Billig's work is especially useful in that it theorizes not the historical formation of the nation-state (which, as we saw in Chapter 2, is a particularly challenging endeavor) but the maintenance of national identification in contemporary democratic societies. Of central importance is the point that, even if nationness is not legible as such, it nonetheless exists, "hanging unnoticed," as it were. However, if the metonymic image of nation X is the flag hanging unnoticed on the public building, the image of the nation from the perspective of the global may not always be nationalistic per se (i.e., the flag being consciously waved with fervent passion). If we return to the metaphor of world news mentioned a moment ago, the image of the nation from the perspective of the global will nevertheless be conspicuous (i.e., newsworthy) enough to warrant the attention of audiences outside of nation X. Images of the nation, in other words, do not necessarily need to center on the flag (whether they are being fervently waved or hanging listlessly), but if they are to be representative of the nation, they have to be scaled. Therefore, there is much that we can learn by studying the ways in which national imaginaries are re-presented across global space via scalar work. In particular, as I will show in the pages that follow, the notion of Korea scaled in accordance with various representational traits offers an important lesson on what "Korea" is, or at least what it is believed to be in a given moment of encounter.

4.3 CULTURE AS COLOR: HOW RED BECAME KOREAN

The first example of cultural scaling centers on the color red. I look to how at the turn of the millennium red came to be synonymous with Korea, largely by chance, and how such fortuitous semiotic chromatism has since been embraced and deployed in a range of contexts to represent Koreanness. As many may remember, arguably among the most prominent instances of global Koreanness in recent memory occurred during the 2002 FIFA World Cup, co-hosted by Korea and Japan. In Los Angeles, home of one of the largest Koreatowns in the world, thousands of fans gathered at odd hours of the morning – owing to the 16-hour time difference between Los Angeles and the host countries – to cheer for the Korean football team, which made a historic run to the semi-finals, far exceeding even the most idealistic of expectations. Dressed in red, the supporters of the Korean football team, known affectionately as the "Red Devils," swarmed in the streets to the point that it could be said that Los Angeles approached a supersaturation of Koreanness, as it were. Significantly, many supporters were not of Korean heritage, but by wearing red were able to momentarily "blend in" and be effectively indistinguishable from an "actual" Korean, especially from an aerial, or bird's-eye, view. Images of massive crowds of Red Devils, not only in Los Angeles's Koreatown but from the actual stadiums in which the events took place, were widely circulated during the World Cup and have since come to be synonymous with Korean national pride. This can be confirmed via a quick Google Images search using the search terms "Korean nationalism."[4] The Red Devils are also featured on the cover image of Rachael Miyung Joo's (2012) *Transnational Sport: Gender, Media, and Global Korea* and on the cover of Gi-Wook Shin's (2006) landmark book, *Ethnic Nationalism in Korea: Genealogy, Politics, and Legacy*. Finally, and perhaps most notably, they are featured on the Korean language translation of Benedict Anderson's (1991) enduring work, *Imagined Communities*, translated by Yoon Hyung Suk and published in 2002 as 상상의 공동체: 민족주의의 기원과 전파에 대한 성찰 [*Sang-sang-ui Gong-dong-chei: Min-jok-ju-ui-ui gi-won-gwa jeon-pa-ei dae-han seong-chal*].[5] They also comprise a major component of the imagery at the Independence Hall of Korea, alongside other visuals of key moments in Korean history (Fig. 4.2).

One of the obvious reasons why the notion of Korea as red is so interesting is that red is not an exclusively Korean color. The color red, in fact, has been noted to serve a series of seemingly universal functions. Ron Scollon and Suzie Wong Scollon (2003) describe the

---

[4] "Nationalism" is a widely misused term, frequently conflated with patriotism, jingoism, national identification, and nationalist sentiment (Connor, 1994). Nonetheless, since the term is frequently used in a more capacious sense, the expression "Korean nationalism" is an apt candidate for informally visualizing "Korea" through the convenience of an online search engine.

[5] See Chapter 2 on the challenges of translating min-jok.

Fig. 4.2   The Red Devils at the Independence Hall of Korea

functions of a prohibitory red circle with a diagonal line, and that of a stop sign in the form of a red hexagon, or a red cross to denote medical support. Color plays an important role in Norma Mendoza-Denton's (2008) ethnography of Northern California Latina youth gangs. Focusing on the inextricability of spoken linguistic features and other embodied cultural practices, Mendoza-Denton shows how red, along with blue, is described as indexical of different kinds of gang affiliations and social positionings. The intensity of the semiotic salience of these colors, along with potential ramifications of wearing the wrong colors in the wrong neighborhood, impacted Mendoza-Denton to such a degree that she reported practicing "bright red and blue avoidance" (p. 53) even a decade after completing her field research. And, of course, global brands ranging from Coca-Cola to Nintendo to YouTube use a variant of red as central to their trademark, each with its own specific color code (Coca-Cola's hexadecimal code is #F40009, its RGB 244 0 0, and its CMYK 4 100 95 0).[6] Among the most intriguing instances of branding involving the color red is women's shoe designer Christian Louboutin's unsuccessful attempt in 2011 to litigate against competing designer Yves Saint Laurent, who had produced products that Louboutin claimed were constitutive of intellectual property theft. Constantine Nakassis (2016) notes that, though Louboutin's shoes are known for their distinctive lacquered red sole – a feature which had indeed been filed in 2008 with the US Patent and

---

[6] These details are derived from BrandPalettes.com.

Trademark Office, when the brand tried to claim that a competitor could not produce a shoe using the color red (even though the Saint Laurent product in question had used red on the entire shoe, not exclusively on the sole) – the essential question being posed was "can the color red be trademarked?" (p. 162). As Nakassis argues, the stakes of the legal battle of *CL* v. *YSL* was centrally a battle of *scale*:

> Two sides, two scalar arguments: on the one hand, not protecting Louboutin would wipe them off the fashion map by unleashing unbridled copying, by the proliferation of the qualities they claimed as their brand dominion; on the other hand, protecting Louboutin would create an unfair monopoly, allowing Louboutin to unfairly expand their control of the commons, thereby contracting the space for legitimate competition. (p. 170)

In the end, the US District Court for the Southern District of New York ruled in Saint Laurent's favor, though Louboutin would appeal the decision through the Court of Appeals for the Second Circuit, which in turn rejected the district court's decision, ultimately ruling that Louboutin owned the rights to producing shoes with red soles and non-red uppers but not shoes with red itself and certainly not the color red more generally. As Nakassis's (2016) analysis demonstrates, *CL* v. *YSL* reminds us that semiosis is invariably an ideological issue, evident in the very attempt to claim something as universal as the color red as distinctive to a particular entity. However, if what makes a brand distinctive needs to be resolved through the nuances of litigation, there is legitimate reason to question the extent to which the trait or feature in question can be considered distinctive to begin with. It is through the framework of scale that we can begin to assess the range of contradictions that emerge when attempting to maintain differentiation on semiotic grounds of something like a color that, when rescaled, loses its distinctiveness.

To return to red in relation to the Korean national football team and the symbolic production of global Koreanness, there are a few significant – though frequently underexplored – points that are worth considering. The first is the symbolic association with global success and appeal within the sport of football that red signified in the early 2000s during Korea's improbable run in the World Cup. In the late 1990s and early 2000s the most popular football club in the world was Manchester United (English Premier League), also known for their iconic red uniforms. This time period was the heyday of megastars such as Ryan Giggs, Roy Keane, Gary Neville, Peter Schmeichal, Paul

Scholes, and of course, most notably, David Beckham. Led by legendary coach Alex Ferguson, the 1999 Man U team – which won the English Premier League title, the FA Cup (Football Association Challenge Cup), and the UEFA (Union of European Football Associations) Champions League – is considered to be one of the greatest football teams of all time. Part of the club's success off the pitch was fostered by global marketing endeavors, most notably in the adjustments to the club's iconic crest. While the crest that was used on the club's kits from 1970 included text of the club's full official name, "Manchester United Football Club," for the 1998 season, it adopted a new crest with simply "Manchester United." According to Leonard Jägerskiöld Nilsson (2018), the new text represented an effort to "make the brand more internationally viable and simpler to print" (p. 40). In other words, in 2002 red was indexical of global success in the world of football in a way that it hadn't been in previous years and is not today and the Korean national team no doubt benefited from the semiotic salience of red at the time. And of course, the nickname of fans of the Korean national team, the Red Devils, is coincidentally identical to Man U's unofficial moniker.

It is also interesting to approach the significance of red in relation to a few other points. The first is the fact that the South Korean national flag, the Tae-geuk-gi, features three colors: red, blue, and black, on a white background. The centerpiece of the flag is a two-toned Tae-geuk, in red and blue, symbolic of positive and negative energy, respectively. Meanwhile, the symbolism of the red on the football uniform is not clear. According to historians Son Hwan and Choi Ji-Man (2009), while the dominant claim is that it is an adoption of the red from the Tae-geuk-gi, it has also been speculated that is symbolizes strength (힘 [him]) and passion (정열 [jeong-yeol]), or that it is representative of the clothing of a king (임금 [im-geum]) (p. 137). In either case, Son and Choi note that when Nike became the official uniform supplier in 1996, red began to be used more prominently and deliberately both to sustain the passion of players and spectators alike while also psychologically intimidating opponents. Regardless of the original symbolic intentionality of red, there is no doubt that the color has been fully embraced since, even deviating from the coloring scheme of the national flag. More specifically, while blue was always featured on each of the Nike uniforms as an accent color and on the crest itself, by the 2018 World Cup, blue was used only on the white away kit and removed entirely from the red home kit. In addition, while the national team emblem had been blue, white, and black since its introduction for the 2002 World Cup, the team went with an

Fig. 4.3   2018 Korean National Football Team home kit

exclusively black and white crest in 2018 (Fig. 4.3). Finally, the latest kit and crest unveiled in 2020 had removed blue in its entirety, semiotically anchoring the national team's brand identity within the color red.

The emergence and embrace of red as symbolic of Korea is particularly curious when considered in relation to the significance of red to other "adjacent" national imaginaries. Red, for one, is

Fig. 4.4 Chinatown, San Francisco

frequently associated with Chineseness (Scollon & Scollon, 2003) and is readily visible in Chinatowns, as seen in Jackie Jia Lou's (2016) ethnography of the Chinatown in Washington, DC.[7] In China, red is associated with happiness and fortune and becomes associated with Chineseness outside of China.[8] It is by far the most chromatically salient feature of San Francisco's storied Chinatown as well (Fig. 4.4). Further, I have noted elsewhere, alongside Lou (Jerry Won Lee & Lou, 2019), the deliberate and extensive use of red in the Chinatown of Incheon, Korea, in an effort to commemorate cultural influences of Chinese–Korean exchange (such as in Korean–Chinese food) while simultaneously attempting to draw conspicuous lines of distinction between Korea and China and thereby resemiotizing the space as "traditionally" and "authentically" Chinese. In Westminster, California, which borders the Korean district of Garden Grove, the epicenter of Little Saigon is the Asian

---

[7] Scollon and Scollon (2003) offer an interesting observation regarding color and modality (i.e., its truth value) with respect to China and Korea: "high modality tends to be associated with reds in Hong Kong, China, and Taiwan but in Korea high modality tends to be associated with darker greens and browns" (p. 91).

[8] I thank Zhu Hua for offering this insight.

Fig. 4.5   Asian Garden Mall in Little Saigon (Westminster, CA).

Garden Mall, which features liberal use of red, though with substantial use of green (Fig. 4.5). In the context of football, Choi Ji-Man (2007) has noted the contradiction of the now naturalized association of the national football team with red, given that for most Koreans red is associated with the Communist Party (공산당 [gongsan-dang]) of North Korea following the semiotic legacies of the Korean War and the Cold War. Indeed, when comparing the national flags of North Korea and South Korea, the former features red much more prominently than the latter does, and the North Korean national football team also has a predominantly red uniform, though it has not enjoyed nearly as much international success as the South Korean team. Finally, to return to the image of the Red Devils at the Independence Hall in Figure 4.2, the use of red in the context of commemorating *independence from* Japan produces what might be called a semiotic dependency on Japan. On the one hand, while Japan's national team has tended to use (somewhat inexplicably) a dark blue uniform, its current national flag and the flag flown during its Imperial days have used only red and white. Further, as I note elsewhere with Chungjae Lee (Chungjae Lee & Jerry Won Lee, 2022), the presence of such imagery also signals the reality of

Fig. 4.6   Liberdade district of São Paulo

unprecedented bilateral cooperation among not only Korea and Japan but of two nations more generally, as the 2002 World Cup was the first in the tournament's storied history to be co-hosted. And not surprisingly, red is also used to index Japaneseness in various communities around the world, as can be seen in the example from the São Paulo district of Liberdade, known as the home of the largest Japanese ethnic community outside of Japan (see Fig. 4.6). This is further indication of the indexical flexibility of red and the contradictions that emerge in the attempt to scale the Korean national imaginary through chromatic signification.

In sum, the semiotic association of Korea with the color red affords a compelling lesson in the pragmatics of scale. Whether by chance or by design, since the turn of the millennium Korea has become red, as it were, and not only in the realm of global sport, but also in other spaces of national identity branding. However, as I have demonstrated, there is nothing inherently Korean about red, though Korea serendipitously became associated with red in the early 2000s, due in obvious part to the Korean national team's unexpected success in the 2002 FIFA World Cup but also due to preexisting indexicality of red within the world of football. This is important because red is something that cannot be "trademarked," and the embrace of red as Korean is curious given the fact that red is in many ways more semiotically proximate to adjacent national imaginaries such as China, North Korea, and Japan. In the end, the semiotic outcomes of scalar work cannot be and are not meant to be 1:1 representations of the nation anyway, but in spite of their representational limitations they are readily deployed in spaces of semiotic precarity while also revealing the paradoxes of attempts to achieve semiotic distinctiveness as well.

4.4   KORYO AS CHRONOTOPE OF KOREA

"Koryo" can be found in numerous sites of semiotic precarity, ranging from the popular tourist destination of Itaewon (Fig. 4.7); to New York (Fig. 4.8); to Fort Lee, New Jersey (Fig. 4.9); to Dallas, Texas (Fig. 4.10). In these spaces Koryo is perhaps best understood as a semiotic chronotope, to adopt Mikhail Bakhtin's (1981) expression, as symbols that bridge relations between time (chronos) and space (topos). The chronotope, in Bakhtin's (1981) formulation, was originally a concept

Fig. 4.7   Koryo Ceramics (Itaewon)

Fig. 4.8   Koryo Books (New York)

Fig. 4.9   Koryodang Bakery and Café (Fort Lee, NJ)

introduced to foreground the "intrinsic connectedness of temporal and spatial relationships in literature" (p. 84) in the context of literary genre analysis but has since been applied more broadly by scholars across the humanities and social sciences. Here, I adopt it in a manner similar to that of other sociolinguists including Manuel Guissemo

Fig. 4.10   Koryo Kalbi (Dallas, TX)

(2019) to underscore the value of attending to how time–space relations are mapped onto the semiotic artifacts of the built environment.

This chronotope in question evokes the name of the Koryo dynasty,
which ruled the Korean peninsula from 936 to 1392 CE. While there is
a clear attempt to signify the timeless and protonational heritage of
Korea, if signifying tradition is the objective in selecting Koryo instead
of the more obvious choice of Korea, one might wonder why Silla, as in
the Silla dynasty, which predates even the Koryo dynasty, is not the
default choice. Of course, the usage of Silla is quite common in global
Korean signage, such as in New York's "Shilla Korean Barbeque"
(Fig. 4.11) or "Shilla Bakery" in Annandale, Virginia (see Fig. 4.12).[9]
One explanation for the preference of one dynastic appellative over
the other is the aural proximity of "Koryo" to "Korea," facilitating
a causal link for many consumers unfamiliar with the history of the
Korean peninsula – it is similar enough that many can infer that there
is some cognate denotative or etymological relationship between
Koryo and Korea. There is, undoubtedly, a degree of uncertainty in
its signification, and by being only partially legible as having relationality to Korea, Koryo can be especially effective in that it encapsulates
the unknowingness that makes the "foreign" alluring. At the very
least, consumers can infer that Koryo is perhaps an alternative spelling of Korea, which is not altogether inaccurate; the etymological

---

[9] "Silla" and "Shilla" are alternate transliterations for 신라.

Fig. 4.11   Shilla Korean Barbeque (New York)

Fig. 4.12   Shilla Bakery and Café (Annandale, VA)

derivative of the Western labels such as Korea, Corea (Spanish), or la Corée (French) is indeed Koryo.[10] The semiotic versatility of Koryo in this sense lies not only in its ability to bridge a temporal link to the distant and unknowable past but also in its ability to traverse the very boundaries of language.

"Koryo," as an exaggerated and protonationalistic symbol of Koreanness, is encountered as an index of national authenticity that raises questions about the very possibility of authenticity. In the space of Itaewon, the authenticity of Koreanness produced by the Koryo Ceramics store is compromised by the adjacency of a sign for "Money Exchange," a clear indication that locals do not frequent this region. The conspicuousness of Koreanness suggests that spaces like Itaewon are not so much Korean as they are spaces for visitors to experience and even consume and purchase Koreanness. The semiotic aggregate of this space, including the "Koryo" label and the abundance of traditional ceramics on display, are in many ways an instantiation of the commodification of authenticity as described by Heller (2011). However, what is additionally note-worthy are the mechanics of scaling culture in spaces of semiotic precarity, in this case, specifically in places that are simultaneously foreign and local. The case of Koryo Ceramics is intriguing for the reason that, for a Korean person who resides in Itaewon or another tourist destination "authentic" Korean commodities are likely everyday and uninteresting objects. Meanwhile, the encounter with Koryo Kalbi in Dallas, Texas, is noteworthy because of an almost identical effort to index authenticity. The sign for Koryo Kalbi, with its brush script stylization, along with the ancient aes-thetic of the lamps, creates a mythic timelessness of Koreanness but also calls attention to an anachronistic irony that the Korean BBQ served inside likely did not exist during the days of the Koryo dynasty. This irony is exacerbated by the production of the sign on a plastic sheet with vinyl decals backlit by fluorescent bulbs, along with the adjacent blue and red neon sign and the notification man-dated by the fire marshal: "This door remains open during business hours." It serves as a stark reminder that any attempt at the

[10] Interestingly, in the early 2000s, many Koreans had become convinced that the current English spelling of "Korea" had been changed from "Corea" by the Japanese so that "Japan" would alphabetically precede "Korea." While it is diffi-cult to "prove" whether the spelling change was deliberately engineered, research by Korean historian Jung Yong Wook (2004) provides an abundance of historical evidence that "Corea" was indeed more prevalent up to the early years of Japanese colonial occupation of the peninsula.

Fig. 4.13 Koryo Korean BBQ (Oakland, CA)

reinvention of nationness, whether via scalar work or any other means, is always contending with the rules and regulatory guidelines of modernity, in this case, literally the rules and regulatory guidelines of local municipal apparatuses.

The Koyro chronotope within the space of Dallas becomes even more interesting when read in relation to nearly identical signage for Koryo Korean BBQ in Oakland's Koreatown (Fig. 4.13). In a culturally diverse place like Northern California's Bay Area, comprised of demographically diverse cities such as San Francisco, San Jose, and Oakland, it is perhaps by no means unexpected to find a thriving transnational Korean community. Yet it becomes somewhat more unexpected to find such a phenomenon in the heart of the US Southwest. This is, of course, not to suggest that cities such as Dallas are not ethnically diverse. I am simply making the point that cities of the US Southwest, unlike those in coastal regions, have not experienced the same demographic shifts resulting from large-scale transpacific migrations between the United States and Asia. So, upon encountering the sign for Koryo Kalbi in Dallas, one is struck by finding a sign evocative of a 700-year-old Korean heritage in Texas. The strangeness of the encounter reflects the discursive and semiotic climate in which the reinvention of Koreanness is tasked with. The production of Koreanness is at odds with – and thus must contend with – a strong local, regional semiosis, which, although by no means homogeneous, is nonetheless characterized by a constellation of symbolic associations with this particular place. When one thinks of Texas, the possibility of a thriving Koreatown is not what one will instantly imagine because of the immediacy of other stereotypical cultural iconography (such as longhorn cattle and cowboy boots) through which non-Texans hastily imagine and construct the region. These are, to state the obvious, not representative of how "people in Texas are" but operate as caricatural symbols that accompany imaginations of the region. In short, Koryo is a scalar rendition of Korea in a semiotic ecology in which there is a wide repertoire of highly salient scalar tokens already at play. But more generally, outside of the Korean nation-state, and outside designated tourist traps within the Korean nation-state, there is always already an assumed lack of Koreanness that precedes the semiotic production of Koreanness: this is semiotic precarity, and it allows us to learn how the notion of an authentic and traditional Korea can be subject to reinvention via scalar work.

The outcomes of chronotopic scaling described here are in many ways reminiscent of a point made by Frederic Jameson (1998) regarding the limitations to accessing the past in its actuality in an era when cultural production in the form of "pastiche" is the norm:

> Cultural production has been driven back inside the mind, within the monadic subject: it can no longer look directly out of its eyes at the real world for a referent but must, as in Plato's cave, trace its mental images of the world on its confining walls. If there is any realism left here, it is a "realism" which springs from the shock of grasping that confinement and of realizing that, for whatever particular reasons, we seem condemned to seek the historical past through our own pop images and stereotypes about that past, which itself remains forever out of reach. (p. 10)

However, even if the past is forever out of reach, the point is not simply to "expose" the anachronism undergirding these instances of semiosis. Patrons of Koryo Kalbi in Dallas do not go there thinking they are getting authentic ancient Korean barbeque. They are therefore effective – and not only engineered but arguably ingenious – scalings of Korea. If anything, they remind us of the role of temporal links that are attempted and emerge in the effort to semiotically scale a given cultural entity. In short, it doesn't matter whether they are "authentic" or not; what matters is the extent to which we accept and enable them to stand in for the nation in a given space of semiotic precarity.

4.5 CULTURE AS SAMPLE IMAGE: DISPUTED TERRITORY AS CARICATURAL GEOGRAPHY

Packaged food items in Korea are sometimes accompanied by a notation on the package, "이미지 예 [i-mi-ji ye]" or "sample image." In the United States, similar disclaimers such as "ENLARGED TO SHOW TEXTURE" can be found on packaging. In both cases, the function of the message is to explain something that is hopefully obvious: the image on the package is designed to optimize the item's appearance, enhancing the color and removing any imperfections, to make it as appetizing as possible. As obvious as such disclaimers may seem to be, they have offered important legal protections to manufacturers facing litigation. For instance, in 2009, the US District Court Eastern District of California dismissed a suit filed against Pepsico in which the plaintiff alleged that one of its breakfast cereal brands, *Cap'n Crunch with Crunchberries*, produced by one of Pepsico's subsidiaries, Quaker, had deceived her into believing that the "Crunchberries" were actual berries. As part of the ruling the judge noted the following:

> the PDP [principal display panel] clearly states both that the Product contains "sweetened corn & oat cereal" and that the cereal is "enlarged to show texture." Thus, a reasonable consumer would not be deceived into believing that the Product in the instant case contained a fruit that does not exist. (p. 7)

On the one hand, such messaging might be more effectively translated along the lines of "please purchase this product based on the image we are providing and please be aware that you should not expect to get what is pictured." On the other hand, it is not merely a frivolous formality but an important reminder that we readily accept that our realities will be scaled for us, even if not necessarily *to* scale.

I have added this brief discussion of food products' dependency on their respective image in order to continue with the question of how culture can be rendered visible across global space. I propose that it would be productive to explore this question through a case study of the visibilization of Korean territory: in this case, how a given territory is made visible through conscious scalar mediation. Critically, the territory in question is Korean but only *disputedly* so, being a small series of islets in the Pacific Ocean that are presently disputed between Korea and Japan, long after the Korean peninsula was liberated from Japanese colonial rule following the conclusion of World War II in 1945. While the islets are referred to as Dokdo in Korean, they are typically known as Takeshima in Japanese. Given their disputed status, any reference to the islets is inevitably bound to a complicated and tense politics of *naming* qua performative *claiming*. Of course, a potentially more neutral label might be the Liancourt Rocks (which the US version of Google Maps uses). However, since this name derives from the French whaling ship whose crew ostensibly "discovered" the islets, privileging this name leaves us reaffirming the colonial logic in which a given territory is open to claiming/naming until it is founded and chronicled by European surveyors. In order to recognize the disputed and undecided status of the islets and to deliberately refrain from participating in an appellative politics that may prioritize one label and thus a particular national claim, I will refer to them simply as the islets.

Given the islets' disputed status, they represent an ideal case study in semiotic precarity in a more literal sense: the legitimacy of the islets is contested between two sovereign states, and as such represent a threat to each state's sovereignty, assuming we accept one of the central premises of nationalism, which is that a state cannot confirm absolute territorial sovereignty if its governability of jurisdictional space remains in a condition of contestation. Some scholars, acknowledging the virtual nonexistence of any strategic or economic value of the islets, point to residual postcolonial tension between the two countries as the reason for such political and cultural investment in the question of sovereignty (Bong, 2013; Sung-jae Choi, 2005). Certainly, some scholars do note that legitimacy over the islets has direct pragmatic implications regarding each country's respective maritime boundaries and horizontal airspace boundaries (e.g., Heo & Roehrig, 2014; Van Dyke, 2007). It has also been argued that while Japan's interest in the islets is merely for commercial purposes, for Koreans the islets hold greater historical and ideological significance and therefore should be left to Korean ownership (Choi Jang Gun, 2012). From the Korean perspective, Japan's continued insistence on its rightful ownership of the islets represents a prolongation of its colonial-era political aggression, territorial expansionism, and cultural hegemony into the twenty-first century. As is commonly the case in territorial disputes, both sides remain steadfast in their conviction, and both sides claim to present irrefutable evidence confirming their rightful ownership of the territory. Those sympathetic to the Japanese narrative will point to historical evidence that Japan recognized the territory as early as 1618.[11] It might also be argued that, although Japan was ordered through the Potsdam Declaration in 1945 to return all territories acquired through imperial seizure, the islets were Japanese territory *prior to* its imperial period and thus Korea's contemporary claims have no legal basis in international law (Masahiro, 2014). Those sympathetic to the Korean cause will point to a 1145 CE document that describes how the Silla dynasty came to acquire the territory in 512 CE (MOFA, 2013), which, of course, endorses a protonationalistic forcible seizure *prior to* the Korean nation as such in order to reject the legitimacy of a colonialist forcible seizure in the time of the nation-state.

The islets are something of a "global" phenomenon: in cities around the world such as Seoul, South Korea; Santa Clara, California; Houston, Texas; and Auckland, New Zealand; one is able to find restaurants whose name incorporates some variation of "Dokdo." In Houston, for instance, there is Dokdo Sushi. In Santa Clara and Auckland, respectively, one will find Shindokdo Sushi Bar (New Dokdo Sushi Bar) and Dokdo Korea. Throughout Seoul, there are six locations of the restaurant Dokdo Chamchi (Dokdo Tuna). "Dokdo" has been used to brand Korean American kimchi from New York: Dok-do Corporation Kimchi (Ku, 2014). The islets have also made an appearance on dry cleaning garment bags in New York, in the form of the geopolitical declaration "Dokdo Island is Korean Territory" (Fahim, 2009). Messages proclaiming Korean ownership of the islets have also appeared in billboards across the United States. Further, controversy over the rightful ownership of the islets has resulted in numerous protests that have received global news coverage, including, perhaps most memorably, a public demonstration in Korea in 2005 following the Shimane Prefecture government's inauguration of "Takeshima Day." During the protest outside the Japanese embassy building in South Korea, Japanese flags were burned as two demonstrators severed their own fingers in an act of self-mutilation symbolic, perhaps, of the appropriation of a small, though not insignificant, appendage of the Korean nation-body.

---

[11] According to the Ministry of Foreign Affairs of Japan, in 1618, two merchants were granted permission for passage to the islets from the shogunate of the Tottori Domain. It is argued that this is the earliest evidence that the islets were part of Japanese territory: the shogunate would not have granted permission had he not recognized the islets as part of Tottori territory.

In order to visit the islets one must first take a ferry from mainland Korea to Ulleung-do, a rural island 120 km east of the peninsula with a surface area of 73 km^2. Ulleung-do is only accessible via the South Korean port cities of Pohang, Gangneung, or Mukho, located on the eastern coast of the peninsula. The ferry ride from mainland Korea to Ulleung-do itself takes 2.5 to 3 hours, depending on the port. Because the only way to access the disputed islets in question is by ferry from Ulleung-do, Ulleung-do itself has emerged since the mid-2000s as a popular tourist attraction. On Ulleung-do, shopkeepers use the modifier Dokdo for multiple establishments, to strategically appeal to tourists who travel there specifically for the purposes of participating in the nationalistic pilgrimage of visiting the nearby islets, including *Dokdo Shikdang* (Dokdo Restaurant) and *Dokdo Banjeom* (Dokdo Chinese Food), along with a *Dokdo Motel*, a *Dokdo Naksi & Deungsan* (Dokdo Fishing & Mountain Climbing), among others. One of the primary attractions on Ulleung-do is the *Dokdo Museum*. The museum features a series of historical documents that are meant to provide affirmation of Korea's rightful ownership of the territory while attempting to delegitimize Japan's historical and contemporary claims. Among the documents are a series of facsimiles and originals of travel logs and maps, including an original 1946 Japanese map that fails to include the islets as Japanese territory, as if to say that, if the islets were considered Japanese territory at the time, then surely the cartographers would have included them in their map. This strategy is mirrored in scholarly works that investigate historical maps in order to devalidate Japan's claims to the islets (e.g., Lee Sang Tae, 2009). The paradox is that while both Korea and Japan understand that these historical maps have no contemporary legal value, they are nonetheless actively relied on to serve each country's respective claims (Medzini, 2017). In the museum, the various documents are complemented by a diorama depicting Korean men "expelling illegally landed Japanese fisherman [sic] from Dokdo," which perhaps implies that a three-dimensional depiction is a degree closer to fact than a two-dimensional image (Fig. 4.14). In the nearby hall, a 150-cm television accompanied by a sign "U-ri Ttang Toktosarang (Love of Our Land Dokdo)" provides a live streaming video of the islets, as if to suggest a right to surveille that is premised on ownership (Fig. 4.15). These artifacts and visual stimuli, in the aggregate, enthymatically "prove" Korean ownership of the territory across time.

So what does all of this have to do with scale? I earlier described my reasons for avoiding politicized references to the islets as Dokdo, Takeshima, or even Liancourt Rocks. Another reason is to emphasize

Fig. 4.14   Diorama at Dokdo Museum

Fig. 4.15   Live streaming video at Dokdo Museum

the reality that they are indeed islets, rather than *islands* as they are commonly labelled, suggesting a greater geographic size. By emphasizing the point that they are islets, I wish to signal the aggrandizing tendencies of alternate geographic labels while simultaneously emphasizing that their representationality hinges on scalar practices that are inevitably ideological. Certainly, it is not controversial to note that certain landmarks, whether national landmarks or not, by the very conditions of their size, must be re-presented and, crucially, rescaled. A large mountain or even a comparatively modest hill, for instance, cannot possibly be re-presented to scale but must be scaled in order to be re-presented. Such objects therefore can only ever be re-presented through an unordinary locus – reminiscent of Michel de Certeau's (1984) ruminations on observing New York City from a privileged vantage point from the top of the (former) World Trade Center – which in turn phenomenalizes the scale of social space otherwise imperceptible through the act of traversing the same space on a quotidian basis. Understood from this perspective, scaling – as a practice of re-presentation – is a privileged praxis subject to the ideological priorities and commitments of the scaling agent. The representational praxis of the islets, in particular, is reflective of what Carr and Lempert (2016) have referred to as "predatory scaling" (p. 16), or the deceptive prioritization or deprioritization of aspects of a phenomenon through scalar work.

One of the most interesting details about the islets is the fact that their total surface area is only 0.19 km^2. As a point of comparison, the city of Seoul alone expands across 605 km^2 and Tokyo spans 2,188 km^2. However, the problem facing the scaling of the islets is not the general problem of re-presenting large objects always already to a smaller scale. The fact that the total surface area of the islets is a mere 0.19 km^2 means that on any map that is to accurate scale, the islets become virtually unrepresentable. For instance, if one were to use Google Maps, it is not until the map has been zoomed to 2.7:10,000 scale that one is able to even see the islets (see Fig. 4.16 and Fig. 4.17). Put differently, in order for the islets to be presented as the size of two sesame seeds, the Korean peninsula would need to be rendered the size of a dining table that comfortably seats eight people. In the case of the islets, the issue is not only that they must be scaled as a result of their diminutive size relative to their interscalar object of the Korean peninsula; it is that they must *always be* scaled not only ideologically but hyperbolically. This scalar work that entails an exaggeration of the size and geographic features of the islets is evident in a variety of depictions of the islets across various institutional spaces of national memory across Korea. They are inaccurately scaled at the Independence Hall of Korea (Fig. 4.18) and at the Korean War Memorial (Fig. 4.19). In fact, they are even rescaled in places such as textbooks for schoolchildren, sometimes at up to 100 times larger than they would be on an accurately scaled map (see Jerry Won Lee, 2019).

Fig. 4.16   Google Maps image at 2.7:1,000 scale

Fig. 4.17   Google Maps image at 2.7:10,000 scale

Fig. 4.18 Depiction of the islets at the Independence Hall of Korea

In an age when satellite images of the world are readily accessible through applications and services such as Google Maps, it is easy to forget how maps have historically been used to serve political purposes. J. B. Harley (1988) notes that maps are reflective of a particular cartographer's interpretation of the world. Further, cartographic distortion can be instrumental to the advancement of colonialist agendas (Wainwright & Bryan, 2009). For instance, the placement of a particular country at the center of a map could be reflective of an assumption of that country's supposed ontological centrality, and thus, ostensibly, cultural superiority, whereas the placement of other countries on the peripheries of the map might represent their marginal status in the eyes of the cartographer. Scaling too is another indication of how geographic representations are subject to a high degree of ideological distortion. I acknowledge the fact that museums and other historical sites are notorious for promoting distorted reflections of reality (c.f., Richard R. Flores, 2009; Lepawsky, 2008; Phillips & Phillips, 2009). I also acknowledge that the exaggeration of geographical features is a common practice in maps that are used for illustrative purposes. In the United States, for instance, it is fairly common to provide a map of the 48 contiguous states with two separate maps for Hawaii and Alaska with each larger and smaller than

Fig. 4.19 Depiction of the islets at the Korean War Memorial

scale, respectively. And of course, with the exception of the empire described in Borges's "On Exactitude in Science," a map can never be expected to be at the scale of the territory it intends to represent. It could therefore perhaps be argued that the hyperbolic geography of the islets is not a result of ideologically manipulative rescaling but rather a pragmatic consideration for the sake of mere representational convenience. Nonetheless, this particular act of caricatural scaling, even if not strictly predatory, warrants suspicion insofar as it hyperbolizes the geographic magnitude and thus cultural value of an ideological investment in a territory that is in dispute. Beyond being merely misrepresentative and misleading, such practices are – through *scaling* – a means of *escalating* the historical and national significance of the islets, if not outright endowing the islets with a significance that is incommensurate with their geographic size. The islets are unrepresentable through accurate cartographic scaling but must be re-presented, through predatory scaling, if they are to be rendered legible and relevant to individuals that constitute the Korean national imaginary.

It is this scalar contingency that invites us to explore questions of geographic territory operating at the rupture between Korea as an ontological entity and a representational entity (i.e., what Korea actually is versus what Korea is believed to be at the moment of semiotic representation). More specifically, the islets – as I argue, because of their scalar contingency – function as something more than an object of international dispute. Earlier I referred to the islets as a global phenomenon with respect to the global spread of the discourse of the islets. However, perhaps it is appropriate to say that the discourse of the islets is not merely a byproduct of "global Korea" but also reflective of the very possibility of "Korea" in tandem with the "global." What I mean by this is that the islets are an important example of the very semiotic conditions by which the national can be rendered visible in the context of the global: in the same way that the islets can only ever be caricaturally scaled (or perhaps predatorially scaled), the same might be said of any metonymic image of the nation. Therefore, it is not merely a matter of problematizing the outcomes of such scalar work but about reconsidering the range of images that have come to be established as having a naturalized relationship to the nation while also acknowledging the inevitability of scalar work to the representability of the nation as a culturally discrete entity.

4.6   CONCLUSION: IS IT POSSIBLE TO SEE THE NATION?

Is it possible to see the nation?[12] Beyond symbols of the nation such as national flags, which are visible almost anywhere, I have tried to show

---

[12]   I thank Webb Keane for posing this question to me, and for offering me lots more to think about, in his role as a discussant on our panel on "Performative Images"

that the mechanics of seeing the nation can be made sense of through the work of scale. In short, it is through the work of scale that we can "see" the nation and as a result of such seeing, begin to understand what semiotic traits have been in circulation across global contexts and have come to be naturalized as representative of the nation as a discrete entity transposable to other national imaginaries. In the previous sections, I have tried to make this point through a discussion of three kinds of semiotic scaling: chromatic scaling (via the color red), chronotopic scaling (via the trope of the Koryo dynasty), and cartographic scaling (via the islets, Dokdo/Takeshima/Liancourt Rocks, disputed between Korea and Japan). What these case studies collectively point to is how the notion of Korea as a representable entity is contingent on scalar work. From this vantage point, I would like to suggest that we are put in a position to not only revisit the various ways in which we semiotically encounter the nation but also reconsider the extent to which seeing images of the nation is different from seeing the nation itself. On the one hand, one is almost always seeing a nation – for instance while driving on an ordinary road in a town that is part of a given nation – but such encounters will rarely ever register as emblematic of the nation. And since driving on an ordinary road cannot be what renders one national experience distinct from that of another, we can start paying closer attention to the various emblems that are deployed as representative of a given nation and exploring how distinctive such emblems are, which can in turn tell us how distinctive their respective national imaginaries are.

at the 2019 Annual Meeting of the American Anthropological Association / Canadian Anthropology Society.

5   Semiotic Excess: Tracing Culture

5.1 *COOL STORY, HANGUK*

Among the most enduring and influential scenes from the 2001 US American film *Zoolander* is actually one in which nothing really happens. Hansel, the hopelessly self-centered model who lacks any sense of social awareness or consciousness, recounts an incident of drug-induced hallucination to the film's eponymous Derek Zoolander, another model who shares similar traits with Hansel though he is, at least compared to Hansel, endearingly naïve:

HANSEL: So, I'm rappelling down Mount Vesuvius when suddenly I slip, and I start to fall. Just falling, ahh ahh, I'll never forget the terror. When suddenly I realize "Holy shit, Hansel, haven't you been smoking Peyote for six straight days, and couldn't some of this maybe be in your head?"

ZOOLANDER: And?

HANSEL: And it was. I was totally fine. I've never even been to Mount Vesuvius.

After telling the story, one of Hansel's friends, Olaf, who is not the immediate audience but is in the same room and within audible range, replies with an enthusiastic "Cool story, Hansel!," to which Hansel replies "Thanks, Olaf!" It is unclear whether Olaf genuinely feels that Hansel's story was in fact "cool," or whether he was just sarcastically performing interest in Hansel's story. What is clear is that the story being told was undoubtedly uninteresting. Meanwhile, the expression "cool story, Hansel" came to be popularized in the years following the film as a way of delivering a stinging dismissal toward someone who has told a story that was either uninspiring or otherwise has no obvious point. It can be frequently found online on Twitter in responses to tweets that are deemed by other users to fall into the category of a "cool story," as was the case in one such exchange in 2018:

USER 1: Ugh. Think I need to move out of NYC. Told June we were taking her to the zoo today, and she says she wants to go to Duane Reade instead.
USER 2: I went on a third date to the zoo once, about six years ago.
USER 3: Cool story Hansel

The expression "Cool story, Hansel" is an apt version of what Agha (2007) describes as a semiotic activity that reveals a socially routinized metapragmatic construct, typifying a given utterance (see Silverstein [1993] on metapragmatics). Indeed, it represents a specific kind of metapragmatic activity that aims to typify the interaction through an explicit orientation to a speech act (whether to the content or the delivery of the story) in situ and as such has potential to shape the nature of the subsequently unfolding interaction (e.g., please try to do a better job with the next story you tell).[1]

"Cool story, Hansel" is in many ways a reminder of the adage that "stories only happen to those who know how to tell them." What this means is that while interesting things happen to everybody, they don't really count as an interesting story unless you are able to tell it in a manner that is interesting: narrating at an appropriate pace, highlighting relevant details while selectively disregarding unimportant ones, and of course, being able to convey the *point*, or the "so what?" Sometimes, however, the outcome of the story being unworthwhile falls not on the audience who "doesn't get it," or even on the teller who has narrated it ungracefully. Sometimes, the outcome falls on the teller who made the assumption that there was a story worth telling in the first place. And this brings me to my two interrelated points in referencing the metapragmatic device of "Cool story, Hansel."

The first is to draw a connection to the fact that the word "story" is coincidentally readily visible in the linguistic/semiotic landscape of global Korea. I have encountered, for instance, a hair salon called Hair Story and a nail salon called Nail Story, both in Los Angeles, and an eatery named Rice Story in Seoul (Fig. 5.1), among countless other occurrences. The usage of story in these instances is of course not derivative of "Cool story, Hansel." However, they are curious in many

---

[1] In fact, a derivative expression, "Cool story, bro!" itself became a popular metapragmatic device, specifically as an embodiment of toxic, hypermasculine "bro" culture, in which camaraderie is frequently performed through "friendly" acts of ridicule rather than through displays of genuine affection or appreciation.

Fig. 5.1   Rice Story (Myeongdong)

ways because it is not a matter of formal equivalence in translation from Korean (e.g., the functionally equivalent translation of the Korean expression "필름이 끊겼다 [pil-leum-i kkeun-kyeot-da]" into English would be "to black out [from drinking too much]" while its literal translation would be "the film got cut."). Meanwhile, the Korean word for story, or 이야기 [i-ya-gi], would not typically be used in the way it is for Hair Story (머리이야기 [meo-ri-i-ya-gi]), Rice Story (밥 이야기 [bab-i-ya-gi]),[2] and the like. It might seem like the use of "story" in this manner is somewhat akin to the phenomenon of weird language that I described in Chapter 3. However, I would like to suggest that "story" introduces an additional layer of complexity in that it serves as an example of a recurring token of Koreanness that has, at first glance, nothing to do with Koreanness.[3]

[2] Rice can be translated as either 밥 [bab] or 쌀 [ssal]. The former can be used to indicate rice itself or simply food, perhaps because Korean meals frequently include rice. The latter is typically only used to refer to uncooked rice and as such is likely not the best Korean language equivalent to be used for "Rice Story."
[3] To be sure, "story" is a reminder that cataloguing artifacts of the linguistic/semiotic landscape of global Korea according to language as code cannot allow us to understand the full complexities of language in such contexts. In fact, while

The second reason for mentioning "Cool story, Hansel" is to point out that looking for culture in global space is sometimes a matter of appraising significance in the unexpected, particularly with respect to the seemingly insignificant details. "Stories only happen to those who know how to tell them" means that an effective storyteller will offer important, relevant, and interesting details – whether subtly or explicitly – nevertheless in a way that their audience can readily piece together and arrive at an understanding of the overall point of the story. Relatedly, the recurrence of "story" in the linguistic/semiotic landscape of global Korea is a reminder that looking for indexicals of Korea is sometimes a matter of knowing where to look and what to look for. I am not referring to a secret, subscribers-only, ethnic-heritage-insider-club knowledge of what is "truly" Korean. Instead, I am simply referring to the fact that sometimes these tokens operate at the excess of signification: that which would typically be overlooked or disregarded as inconsequential or insignificant. I refer to these as the traces of culture, and the phenomenon of encountering culture via these traces is what I refer to as tracing culture. In the pages that follow, I explore what this looks like in the case of tracing global Korea.

5.2 UNEXPECTEDNESS AND THE TRACES OF CULTURE

In our attempt to delineate a relationship between the trace and the unexpected, what we will come to see is that encounters with unexpected traces of culture across global space frequently put us in a position where we are tasked with conceptualizing culture not directly or conclusively but in ways that not fully comprehensible or immediate. Such encounters happen "at a distance," as it were. In this regard, while a description of tracing and the trace could begin in many places, for our purposes it might be productive to begin with Walter Benjamin's ([1955]1968) notion of the aura. As Benjamin argues, it is an artistic work's "aura" – its unique essence, which must remain at a distance and inaccessible – that has historically afforded art its aesthetic value. Benjamin draws a parallel to the perception of nature: "If, while resting on a summer afternoon, you follow with your eyes a mountain range on the horizon or a branch which casts its shadow over you, you experience the aura of those

"story" is for all intents and purposes "English," I would argue that, in such moments of encounters, it is indeed more "Korean" than "English."

mountains, of that branch" (pp. 222–223). Both experiences, whether it is to view a mountain range or to have a tree branch's shadow cast upon oneself, represent a degree of separation from the *original*. Certainly, Benjamin's primary concern is not to examine the aesthetic potential of nature but rather the shifting perceptions of the aesthetic value of art in the age of its mechanical reproducibility, a moment which signals, for Benjamin, challenges in efforts to evaluate the aesthetic. According to Benjamin, the aesthetic aura of art ceases to be once it becomes readily accessible for it is the very distance between the viewer and the art from which the aura can emerge and exist in the first place. But perhaps what is most useful from Benjamin's critique is not the concept of the aura as an aesthetic phenomenon but instead as a valence through which to make sense of the representational logics of culture in spaces of semiotic precarity.

More specifically, it is not what is immediately visible or accessible but rather that which can be sensed indirectly in a manner that is, in spite of its indirectness, nonetheless compelling in the same way that the aesthetic value of art can be indisputably known through its aura. While the aura of a work of art can be said to be a characteristic of art, it is simultaneously difficult to reduce to a specific detail. The notion of the aura is thus a productive way to begin thinking about the possibility of how to approach culture not only through definitively characteristic traits (which, as we saw in Chapter 4, are flexible as well), but also through traits, or traces, that are difficult to pinpoint. In this sense, a productive parallel could be drawn to Roland Barthes's (1985) notion of the "third meaning," which occurs "in excess" (p. 44). For Barthes, the first level of meaning is merely "informational" and operates at the level of "communication," while the second level, or the "symbolic," involves "referential symbolism" (pp. 41–42). The third meaning, however, is "erratic yet evident and persistent" (p. 42) and therefore also referred to by Barthes as an "obtuse" meaning in that it operates not at the level of signification, but merely at that of "signifying [*signifiance*]," what might be called a moment of incomplete signification (p. 43). The third meaning is characterized by "representation that cannot be represented" (p. 58).

Any description of trace and tracing is perhaps expected to make at least an attributional detour to the work of Jacques Derrida, who wrote extensively on the notion of the trace. For Derrida ([1967]1974), the act of textual signification can only ever be achieved tentatively, never definitively, via traces within and surrounding the signifier. Of course, at first glance, given the stated attempt not only in this chapter but more generally in this book to delineate a particular logic of signification (the conditions by which a culture comes to be semiotically salient), it may seem somewhat paradoxical to invoke the work of Derrida, which has tended to prioritize the ways in which signification comes to be unraveled when accounting for the traces of a given signifier. Nevertheless, perhaps the Derridian approach to the trace is at least a useful entry point in exploring the question of cultural distinctiveness according to its traces and through the practice of tracing. For one, it could invite us to attend critically to the significance of the trace as something of an intertextual residue (i.e., an inadvertent indexicality resulting from the inherent instability of a signifier, as in the indexically polysemous functions of the color red described in the previous chapter). But more pertinent to the focal point of this chapter, it allows us to take seriously the possibility of culture becoming semiotically encountered via the trace. The trace, for our purposes, can be defined as that which has the capacity to index unexpected cultural–etymological connections, which in turn provides new opportunities to understand the culture in question that is being semiotically represented. I therefore refer to tracing in multiple senses. First, I refer to tracing in terms of outlining the contours of a given culture, as in the practice of tracing a picture or drawing as one would using semi-translucent tracing paper. I also refer to tracing in terms of following general paths of signification across time and space, as in the practice of tracing the origins of a given thing (when something comes from, or where something comes from). Finally, trace can be treated in its noun form, as in an indexical residue of something that is no longer physically present, at least in an obviously perceivable way.

The notion of trace as residue can be useful in many arenas, and it has had a minor influence in the practice of identifying counterfeit art through what is known as the "Morelli method." Named after art historian Giovanni Morelli, the method proposes that

> one should abandon the convention of concentrating on the most obvious characteristics of the paintings, for these could most easily be imitated ... Instead one should concentrate on minor details, especially those least significant in the style typical of the painter's own school: earlobes, fingernails, shapes of fingers and toes. (Ginzburg, [1979]1980, p. 7)

According to Carlo Ginzburg, Morelli's theory, which would go on to inspire the thinking of Sigmund Freud and the fictional detective Sherlock Holmes in the writings of Sir Arthur Conan Doyle, was guided by the premise that "tiny details provide the key to a deeper reality, inaccessible by other methods" (p. 11). The Morelli method parallels the practice of locating unintended traces in penmanship in efforts to determine textual or stylistic forgery in the realm of forensic linguistics (see Brault & Plamondon, 1993). Of course, as noted by Ginzburg, the Morelli method would come to be criticized for a variety of reasons, including the assumption "that personality should be found where personal effort is weakest" (Wind, 1963, p. 40, cited in Ginzburg, [1979]1980, p. 9). The Morelli method likewise raises an immediate question: If that which distinguishes an authentic piece of art from a counterfeit is a detail that could be overlooked by an amateur counterfeiter but noticed by another more discriminating critic, what prevents another more discriminating counterfeiter from simply replicating said detail to reproduce the authentic? Ackbar Abbas (2008) raises a point that is relevant to the discussion at hand, specifically in relation to fake designer watches, which are sometimes made of internal movement components identical to those used in authentic watches:

> When one's product can be reproduced almost to perfection and sold for often less than 10 percent of one's own price, one may have to reexamine the product and the design process. Products that are content to repeat themselves become so much more easy to copy. (p. 262)

Following this consideration, if the distinguishing feature that differentiates the authentic and the counterfeit is in fact something so minor that could be overlooked by so many, there might be reason to reexamine what makes the authentic so special. In the end, of course, my point is not to rationalize the production of counterfeit art but to signal the importance of attending to unexpected details not only in the pursuit of authentication, but also in semiotic meaning making more broadly.

In this regard, given that our focus is on the unexpected semiosis of cultural distinctiveness across global space, it becomes productive to address the question of unexpectedness as it has been addressed in the context of the sociolinguistics of globalization. Of most immediate note is Monica Heller's (2007) observation of how it has become increasingly expected to encounter language in unexpected places:

> As soon as we start looking closely at real people in real places, we see movement. We see languages turning up in unexpected places, and

not turning up where we expect them to be. We also see them taking unexpected forms. (p. 343)

Blommaert (2010) similarly notes how semiosis has come to be increasingly unpredictable in what he terms a "messy new market-place" (p. 28). Pennycook (2012) takes up this issue in order to call into question the criteria by which we delineate differences between the expected and the unexpected: "this is not so much about being light on one's feet, ready for the new, as it is a question of asking why the unexpected is unexpected" (p. 36). My purpose in describing the unexpectedness of the mobile ways in which people and linguistic and semiotic resources move and migrate is not so much about foregrounding how to treat unexpectedness as the norm, or about revisiting our assumptions about where certain resources can be expected to be encountered. Instead, I propose that, if we are to take seriously such premises, we need to more thoroughly entertain the possibility of how semiosis can occur in unexpected ways. In part, I am referring to unexpectedness in terms of semiotic encoun-ters *with the unexpected*, as in, for instance, peoples with uncommon transnational life trajectories or linguistic repertoires, such as the Senegalese man residing in France who speaks a northern Ontario variety of Canadian French described in Heller's (2011) work. However, I am additionally referring to unexpectedness in terms of semiotic encounters that occur in unexpected ways, including, as I will discuss, ways that can be made sense of through the semiotic work of the *trace*.

To that end, attending to the role of the trace in the act of cultural signification across global space may be understood through what we might call "carnivalesque" semiosis, which results in the upending of the semiotic logic of iconization. As Mikhail Bakhtin ([1965]1968) notes, in the European Middle Ages, the "carnival celebrated tempor-ary liberation from the prevailing truth and from the established order; it marked the suspension of all hierarchical rank, privileges, norms and prohibitions" (p. 10). In Francois Rabelais's *Gargantua and Pantagruel* – which is emblematic of the carnivalesque for Bakhtin – the King, appropriately named Anarchus, is defeated, made to dress in a "strange clownish costume" and sent to be "a vendor of greensauce, the lowest step in the social hierarchy" (p. 199). Bakhtin celebrates the liberatory potential of the trope of the carnivalesque: it "frees human consciousness, thought, and imagination for new potentialities" (p. 49). The carnivalesque, importantly, is a *temporary* moment in which the established order is upended. This being said, it is within this limited moment that established or "permanent" realities can be overturned as well, in turn leading to new social arrangements.

The carnivalesque, I propose, is also a way to approach the possibility of alternative semiotic arrangements, specifically in terms of new potentialities in the realm of cultural semiosis. Specifically, it invites a temporary liberation from the established semiotic order: that which is salient is no longer consequential but also that which is seemingly inconsequential. In having no indexical or iconic capacity, it can be viewed anew while also affording a new understanding of that which is being indexed. In short, the carnivalesque invites us to follow paths of signification that both take us to unexpected places while also exposing us to unexpected kinds of signification. Sites of semiotic precarity are apt spaces in which to find such semiotic traces.

5.3 KOREATOWN™

My first set of examples of tracing global Korea focuses on the establishment of cultural distinctiveness in spite of or otherwise contrary to "official" brandings and designations of the given space as a Koreatown akin to "trademarking" a space as such. One such official designation exists in Toronto's Koreatown, whose Korean-owned businesses – and thus semiotically salient markers of Koreanness in the linguistic/semiotic landscape – are concentrated on Bloor Street in Seaton Village of the downtown area. In the neighborhood, Koreatown signage, accompanied by the Tae-geuk-gi, is visible above the official street signage (Fig. 5.2). In the New York Koreatown in Midtown Manhattan, one can see "Korea Way" signage around 32nd Street. The "old" Koreatown of Dallas, Texas, is designated by signage for "Asian Trade District," on which the panethnic label "Asian" is complemented by Korea-specific Tae-geuk icons (Fig. 5.3). Of all the Koreatowns in the world, perhaps the one in Los Angeles features the most prominent municipally endorsed official signage. This Koreatown was officially designated as such by the City of Los Angeles in 1980 following years of lobbying by Korean American developers (Kyeyoung Park & Jessica Kim, 2008). In addition to an official "Koreatown" sign bearing the seal of the City of Los Angeles, there is a wide range of semiotic artifacts and monuments, including one that commemorates the accomplishments of "Korean American Heroes" (Fig. 5.4). However, what compelled me to acknowledge the potential disconnect between official designations of Koreanness relative to rates of semiotically perceivable Koreanness

Fig. 5.2   Koreatown Toronto

Fig. 5.3   Asian Trade District (Dallas, TX)

Fig. 5.4   Korean American Heroes signage (Los Angeles)

beyond such designations was my first visit to the Koreatown of Chicago. While the Koreatown has historically been concentrated on Lawrence Street, as indicated by "Honorary Seoul Drive" signage (Fig. 5.5), what was evident that the official designations of Koreanness were not reflective of where Korean people and Korean establishments were concentrated. Indeed, what I had come to discover was that, as a result of a decades-long pattern of suburban outmigration, conceptualizing Chicago's Koreanness was complicated by the fact that it was not saturated to a specific location as I had expected. This is not to say that there is not a large and thriving Korean community in Chicago and the surrounding suburbs. Instead, the explicit markers of Koreanness (e.g., "Honorary Seoul Drive") are but traces of a Korean community that is not so much diluted but dispersed.

Indeed, sometimes official and even seemingly conspicuous designations of Koreanness do not really index Koreanness at all. Take, for instance, the Koreatown of Osaka, which features a clear "entrance" in the form of two gates in succession that one must traverse, each just meters apart from one another (Fig. 5.6). Within the neighborhood itself, the proximity of the establishments, the narrowness of one of

Fig. 5.5   Honorary Seoul Drive (Chicago)

Fig. 5.6   Koreatown entry gates (Osaka)

the main streets, Miyuki Street, along with the official landmarks –
which encourage the use of two main entrances, rather than the side
streets and alleys – produces a hermetically sealed space. It is known
that Osaka was the site of Japan's earliest ethnic Korean ghetto dating
to the early 1900s (Lie, 2008). As John Lie (2008) notes, the Koreatown
of Osaka has remained largely "invisible," exemplified by its description by Zainichi poet Kim Sijong: "Everyone knows / But it's not on the
map / Because it's not on the map / It's not Japan" (quoted in Lie, 2008,
p. 17). The compressed space of Miyuki Street is a relic of the Korean
community's historical isolation and alienation from the rest of
Osaka. The contained space of Osaka's Koreatown is especially evident
when juxtaposed with other Koreatowns in East Asia, such as those in
Beijing, Shanghai, and even in Tokyo, where there are no official
designations to be found, and any indication of it being a Koreatown
is the wealth of establishments featuring Korean language signs. To
return to the aforementioned gates themselves, the first gate does
feature two sam-saeg-ui-Tae-geuk, or three-colored Tae-geuk, an alternative version of the more common two-colored Tae-geuk of the South
Korean flag. However, the semiotic salience of Koreanness on both
gates is minimalized as well. Significantly, "KOREA TOWN" is
repeated on both gates in English, rather than in Korean. Most interestingly, the non-English script that appears on these gates, "百済門"
and "御幸通中央," both allude to the area's Japanese – not Korean –
history. "百済門," or "Baekje Gate," is named after the ancient kingdom of Paekche. According to the Osaka Convention & Tourism
Bureau's English-language website, "it is said that Miyuki-dori is
named after Miyuki-no-mori Shrine, which was established around
the 5th century on the site where the Emperor Nintoku took a rest
when he visited the area to inspect people who had come from
Paekche to live there (in the woods formerly located at the west end
of where the street now stands)." "御幸通中央," or "Miyuki Street
Center," refers simply to the street's Japanese name. As Lie (2008)
argues, Japanese–Korean hybridity, unlike categories such as
"Korean American" or "Korean Canadian," is not feasible because of
the "essentialist mind-set" that prioritizes ethnically homogeneous
national imaginaries of both Japan and Korea (p. 85). However, as
Jackie Jia Lou (2016) notes, transnational community neighborhoods
need to be understood as "ritual places," constructed not only through
"planning discourse" and "material construction" but also in terms of
"celebratory events and tourist spatial practices" (p. 130). With respect
to the example at hand, the gates of Osaka's Koreatown create
a unique experience of producing a designated space of Koreanness,

especially through the practice of traversing the gates to enter and leave the space. This being noted, the gates of Osaka's Koreatown are "official" Japanese discourses (established and endorsed by the city of Osaka). The fact that they are "official" Osaka discursive artifacts is not what disqualifies the surrounding space as Korean. However, the gates do indeed constitute tourist spatial practices in which readers of Japanese are the primary audience, and through the practice of tracing, it becomes difficult to interpret such space as discretely "Korean."

As noted in previous chapters, "invention" is central to what we accept as seemingly "natural" facts about the nation. The idea of invention is perhaps most explicitly addressed in Hobsbawm's (1983) work on the instrumentalist theory of nationalism, in which national heritage is viewed as a construct of "invented traditions," defined as "a set of practices, normally governed by overtly or tacitly accepted rules and of a ritual or symbolic nature, which seek to inculcate certain values and norms of behavior by repetition, which automatically implies continuity with the past" (p. 1). The famous example provided by Hobsbawm is the nineteenth-century reconstruction of the British Parliament building in Gothic style; the choice was not simply an anachronistic architectural choice but a deliberate attempt to engineer and manage a temporal link to the distant past. What is evident in the case of global Korea is that traditions are not merely invented once but continually reinvented, a phenomenon apparent in the architecture of "national" monuments around the world. In the case of the British Parliament building, tradition has been blatantly invented; in spaces of semiotic Korea in which Korea can be encountered, there are instances of a continual reinvention of tradition, and understanding the logics of such reinvention offer an important lesson in tracing. Consider the Gwanghwamun, the main gate to the Gyeongbokgung Palace in the heart of Seoul, which is a popular tourist attraction today (Fig. 5.7). As noted on an informational panel at the Gyeongbokgung Palace, the Gwanghwamun, originally constructed in 1395 during the Joseon dynasty, was destroyed during the 1592 Japanese invasion of the Korean peninsula, only to be rebuilt in 1867. In 1926, during the Japanese colonial occupation, the gate was deconstructed and relocated in order to accommodate the Japanese Government-General Building at the center of Seoul. It was destroyed once again during the Korean War (1950–1953) and partially rebuilt in 1963. While the 1963 restoration was not faithful to the original design – for instance, having been built with a disproportionate amount of concrete rather than wood – it was again rebuilt. This time, it was

Fig. 5.7   Gwanghwamun (Seoul)

moved back to its original location in front of Gyeongbokgung Palace and unveiled on August 10. 2010, on Gwangbokjeol, a national holiday commemorating Korea's independence from Japan.

Lee Myung Bak (2010), then president of Korea, begins his commemorative Gwangbokjeol speech by drawing his audience's attention to Gwanghwamun: "We can now see Gwanghwamun standing tall here once again, restored to its past glory." He adds the following statement just moments later: "A century ago, we lost our country. Gwanghwamun was blocked and neglected, and the flow of our national spirit was choked off. Though we were deprived of our national sovereignty, we continued to persist as Koreans." On the occasion of Gwangbokjeol, the fact that Gwanghwamun had been, most recently, destroyed as a result of the Korean War is deliberately neglected in favor of emphasizing the role of Japanese colonial officials in the removal of the national monument. In fact, the gate was originally scheduled for destruction by Japanese officials, but it was a Japanese intellectual, Yanagi Muneyoshi, who ensured its preservation (Ch'oe, 2008). In 1922 Yanagi wrote an open letter as a plea to the colonial government declaring the following: "Politics must not be insensible to art. One must refrain from infringing on art in the exercise of power" (Ch'oe, 2008, p. 553). The moving letter stirred enough public unrest that the Japanese government decided to deconstruct and relocate the gate to a peripheral location instead of destroying it. As Ch'oe (2008, p. 552) writes, "Yanagi's case is a reminder that in the midst of strong authoritarian, ultranationalist, and imperialist trends, there were independent voices among Japanese scholars and writers who spoke for cultural values that should be defended and preserved from both Western and Japanese hegemonism." In 2010, the choice by Korean officials to have the Gwanghwamun restored and unveiled on the occasion of Korea's independence from Japanese rule functioned enthymematically, causing most Koreans to infer that it is primarily – if not solely – the Japanese who are responsible for Gwanghwamun's destruction. One is reminded again of Renan's ([1882]1990) famous declaration: "Forgetting, I would even go so far as to say historical error, is a crucial factor in the creation of a nation, which is why progress in historical studies often constitutes a danger for [the principle of] nationality" (p. 11; see Chapter 1). The distinction in the narrative of Gwanghwamun is that the crassness of the historiography is not a result of careless historical inquiry but a deliberate neglect of key details in the historical narrative. This willful neglect enables a reinvention of tradition in a strategic manner.

The Gwanghwamun is a conspicuous relic of "tradition" in a city like Seoul, which, like many other affluent Asian cities, is comprised largely of high-rise corporate and residential buildings with features such as cooler tones – silvers, greys, and blues – and mirrored windows that reflect (quite literally) their modernity. Such buildings, which evoke a modern Western architectural aesthetic, produce an unusual temporal and cultural juxtaposition with the Gyeongbokgung Palace, as it is merely a few meters of asphalt that separate the pace from the rest of the city. Gwanghwamun, for one, is the ideal chronotopic centerpiece for Seoul precisely because, in addition to its dubious historical significance, its grandiose presence forcefully demands a recognition to establish a temporal tie to a premodern past. In fact, throughout the day, national history is performed repeatedly in an elaborate spectacle of the changing of the royal guards. Of note is the fact that on the gate itself, Gwanghwamun is presented not in the Korean alphabet (광화문) but in Han-ja (門化光). As suggested in Chapter 2, the very presence of Han-ja, which predates the modern Korean alphabet, reminds us yet again of Renan's dictum on the importance of "forgetting." The usage of Han-ja, in an attempt to conjure a premodern national imaginary, simultaneously asks us to forget that the development of Korea's own alphabet, Han-geul, distinct from Han-ja, was crucial to the establishment of a uniquely modern "Korean" national identity. It is not so much that contemporary understandings of Koreanness could not have been realized without the development of its own alphabet; rather, it is that the contemporary state-sponsored metadiscourse of Han-geul frames it as such. It follows therefore that any rendering of traditional Koreanness in the form of Han-ja is a paradoxical indexing of something decidedly non-Korean. However, while Gwanghwamun was constructed in 1395, if we recall from the previous chapter, Han-geul was not invented until 1443. In other words, the case of Gwanghwamun and its surrounding discourse is compromised in the attempt to locate Korea through a historical relic representative of its cultural essence. We find ourselves having gone too far back in time and in troubled semiotic grounds wherein the distinctiveness of Korea is called into question.

5.4   X-MODERNITY

Encountering Korea in the linguistic/semiotic landscape sometimes requires a detour through Europe. I am referring to the fact that, across the linguistic/semiotic landscape of global Korea, there are frequent encounters with tokens of Frenchness and to some extent even Italianness. Regarding the latter, such cases seem to appear only in the Koreatown of Los Angeles (as far as I have seen) and seem to limit themselves to the word "Italy" itself, as in "이태리양복점 [i-tae-ri-yang-bok-jeom] or Italy Tailor" (Fig. 5.8). Tokens of Frenchness, on the other hand, are considerably more abundant. Examples range from Chic Hair Design in Oakland (Fig. 5.9), Hair Atelier in Fort Lee (Fig. 5.10), Le Matin de Paris in Annandale (Fig. 5.11), and Haute in Los Angeles (Fig. 5.12), to provide just a small sampling. Sociolinguists have commented on the fact that English for Koreans is frequently associated with cosmopolitanism and Western modernity (see Chapter 2). Meanwhile, there has not been much commentary on what it means for transnational Koreans to appropriate and deploy European semiosis in their communicative efforts on public signage. At first glance, there might be a temptation to understand the frequency of European semiotic allusions in the context of the long-standing association as the barometer of social and cultural progress. This presumption, of course, has been forcefully problematized, for instance, in Edward Said's (1979) thesis of Orientalism, which

Fig. 5.8   Italy Tailor (Los Angeles)

Fig. 5.9   Chic Hair Design (Oakland, CA)

Fig. 5.10   Hair Atelier (Fort Lee, NJ)

Fig. 5.11   Le Matin de Paris (Annandale, VA)

foregrounds how the invention of the "Orient" by Europeans was oper-
ationalized in a manner that reaffirmed Europe as culturally and ideologically normative. No doubt, some tokens of Europeanness are likely

Fig. 5.12 Haute (Los Angeles)

the result of individuals' internalized belief in Europe as culturally sophisticated in the areas of fashion and cuisine. However, in this section, I am not aiming to merely "problematize" the seeming obsession among some Koreans with the idea of Europe. I indicated previously that I am not interested in questions of "code choice" in the linguistic/semiotic landscape; here, I am not interested in what might be called "culture choice." Instead, I wish to show how the use and circulation of such tokens point to unexpected ways in which cultural entities become not only salient but subdued and effaced. In other words, it is not simply a matter of Europeanness unexpectedly indexing Koreanness, but about how traces of Koreanness can be found through European semiosis, and what such tracing reveals about the assumption that culture X must be indexed through tokens of culture X.

Therefore, perhaps it could be said that the tracing of Korea that occurs via European semiosis that I describe in this section is not a matter of indexing "modernity" but of producing what might be called X-modernity. The phenomenon of X-modernity that I describe here draws inspiration from the idea of X-urbanism described by Mario Gandelsonas (1999). Post-WWII urban development in the United States saw a gradual rise in the suburban city: a central downtown metropolitan area with a range of surrounding suburbs composed predominantly of single-family homes. By the 1980s, there was a gradual movement toward developmentally blending the city and residential suburbs, exemplified, for instance, by the growth of "office campuses" across the country (p. 36). The X-urban city blends the workplace and the residential space through a blurring of the distinction between the urban and the suburban. Importantly, as noted by Abbas (2008), the X-urban city "does not supplement the suburban city, but supplants it, changing it from the inside out" (p. 247).

I would like to suggest that the outcomes of the practice of adopting European tokens in the linguistic/semiotic landscape might be conceptualized via the notion of X-modernity in that it is analogous to the multistep process of blending of distinctions between the urban and the suburban and the eventual supplanting of the urban with the X-urban as described in the phenomenon of X-urbanism. More specifically, while the indexing of modernity might very well have been a factor in the original calculus of choosing a European token over, say, a Korean or a "placeless" one, what these signs show is not only how the traces of Korea will frequently be present after various attempts at subduing them but also how the capacity for an originally Korean entity to do semiotic work through icons of a different cultural imaginary illuminate something about what Korea is, and how such understandings can be ascertained via semiotic traces.

To illustrate my point, I focus on the case of the Korean-originated bakery chain known as Paris Baguette. As recently as the mid- to late-2000s, one could typically only find Paris Baguette locations in Korea, a Koreatown, and in other areas with a high concentration of transnational Koreans. Within a few years, the bakery chain's popularity warranted expansion into other "non-Korean" areas as well, including – of all places – Paris. The opening of a Paris Baguette in Paris was indeed a most interesting development, and it was covered in a 2014 article in *The Guardian*, with a headline utilizing ellipticals to perform the verbal pause it would give most readers: "Korea's Paris Baguette chain expands to … Paris." What made the opening of a Paris Baguette in Paris of interest was not only the fact that there is not a well-known and well-established consolidated Korean community in Paris (which is not to say there are not Koreans in Paris) but also, and perhaps quite obviously, the fact that baguettes are not only iconically French but also among the most recognizable tokens of Frenchness. Kim Willsher (2014), the author of the *Guardian* article, refers to the opening as a "perfect coals-to-Newcastle move," a UK idiom designed to underscore the seeming illogicality of transporting something to a place where the object in question is plentiful, deriving from the history of coal mining from Newcastle Upon Tyne. However, Willsher's analogy, as she herself implies, is of course not entirely applicable: Paris Baguette does indeed serve baguettes, but that is by no means the bakery's main attraction and certainly not what has made it the famous global brand that it is today.

The very idea of Paris Baguette is a most interesting case study in the legibility of the national in relation to the global. Consider a comparison of Paris Baguette to other Korean global brands, including appliance and consumer electronics giants Samsung and LG, and automotive brands Hyundai and Kia. What Hyundai and Samsung have in common is that their names "look" and "sound" very much Korean, though the argument could be made that Samsung does perhaps less so (maybe "Samsung" looks like "Sam" as in the name and "sung" as in the past participle of "sing."). Kia, on the other hand, does not "look" and "sound" unmistakably Korean, though maybe approximately Asian. LG, meanwhile, at least in its current branding strategy, has no evidence of Koreanness. LG itself dates to the 1983 merger between Lucky Chemical and Goldstar, resulting in a new brand Lucky Goldstar Group. Lucky Goldstar would adapt its name to the simplified LG in 1995.[4] The new tagline of "Life's Good," in addition to leading many consumers to presume that LG is an acronym for the slogan, is what enables LG to remain ambiguous in terms of its national origins. As such, it might be said that LG has come to be almost fully enregistered as a culturally "neutral" or "placeless" entity (see Introduction).

Paris Baguette, though, is quite different. While for LG there is at least a trace of Korean genealogy in its name, in the case of Paris Baguette, its name, along with its iconic logo, represents a constellation of the metropolitan city, food item, and national landmark that many would immediately envision as associated with Frenchness: Paris, baguette, and the Eiffel Tower, respectively.[5] Of course, since baguettes are by no means central to Paris Baguette's business model, its incorporation into the brand name is purely for symbolic purposes. Not surprisingly, the use of tokens of Frenchness is a prominent feature of Paris Baguette's branding strategy: in almost any location, there is certainly a concerted effort in the interior design to provide a consolidated representation of Paris, with imagery of Parisian streets, furniture resembling what one might find in a Parisian café, and employees uniformed as if they were French *boulangers*. And while the Korean origins of LG could be ascertained via a relatively quick online

---

[4] See www.lgcorp.com/about/history/1.
[5] See Chapter 3 for Blommaert's (2010) description of semiotically conveying "Frenchness."

search, it is notable that Paris Baguette's online presence has been subject to continual neutralization. For instance, the "About Us" description on the company's current website, www.parisbaguette .com, indicates the following:

> Born from a love of bread and a passion for quality, we are an international bakery founded in 1988, specializing in French-inspired goods. In addition to chef-inspired cakes, pastries, sandwiches, salads, and signature coffee and tea, we offer a unique experience to thousands of guests daily. Today we have over 4,000 locations worldwide, satisfying cravings and taste buds of all ages and backgrounds.

Noteworthy is the fact that there is no mention of Paris Baguette's Korean origins. Perhaps the closest hint is the self-identification as an "international bakery," which could be an allusion to its non-French origins but also to the thousands of locations worldwide referenced in the third sentence. The only other possible hint in the About Us description is the reference to "French-inspired goods," which seems to disclose the fact that products are not necessarily "authentically" French but merely *inspired* by French items, as in a film that is "inspired by true events," which in effect means that the entire thing might as well have been made up. Paris Baguette's minimalization of its Korean origins becomes even more striking when compared to the online discourse of the brand Tous Les Jours, perhaps Paris Baguette's largest competitor. Of course, the current version of the English language website for Tous Les Jours, http://tljus.com, makes no effort to invoke its Korean origins, though it explicitly notes its Asian inspiration: "Since its launch in the United States in 2004, TOUS les JOURS has developed into a reputable bakery & café franchise, specializing in French-Asian inspired baked goods, passionately made from the finest ingredients." This is especially intriguing given the fact that earlier editions of the website, http://touslesjoursusa .com, make clear that it is in fact a Korean-originated brand: "'Tous les Jours' brand was launched in Korea in 1996 to give customers a totally satisfying bakery experience."

An additional point of interest in the case of Paris Baguette surrounding its culturally "neutral" website is the URL itself. While the current URL for the English-language website is www.parisbaguette.com, according to Internet archives, the previous URL was www .parisbaguetteusa.com, and prior to that, it was http://eng.paris.co.kr/.[6]

---

[6] See the Internet Archive, also known as the Wayback Machine, a database of previously cached websites, which can be accessed at https://archive.org.

In the earliest version of the website, the "kr" country code in the top-level domain would have been a clear indication that it was a Korean site, and the "eng" subdomain would have been an indicator that it was an English version of the Korean site. The second iteration of the domain name, www.parisbaguetteusa.com, was indeed less Korean in that it did not rely on the Korean top-level domain or the translational subdomain. However, the "usa" in the domain name itself could lead users to come to one of two conclusions: that this was the US version of Paris Baguette's website, or that Paris Baguette was a US American brand. It is likely that the very decision to use USA in the domain name was a branding oversight: the speaking of English does not necessarily presume one is US American, and if the brand were truly international in its aspirations, it would need to frame its digital presence in a less nationalistically confined manner, which is indeed reflected in the current URL. The evolution of the Paris Baguette domain name, along with the company's current branding strategy, shows that locating Koreanness is becoming increasingly complicated, especially when its legibility circulates through the (manufactured) semiotic repertoire of another national imaginary such as Frenchness.

The phenomenon of European semiosis in the linguistic/semiotic landscape of global Korea, irrespective of whether we are talking specifically about the case of Paris Baguette, offers a lesson in the unexpected layers of complexity in the effort to encounter Korea in global space, especially if what we are looking for does not look very Korean at all. What I am describing is in many ways akin to the phenomenon of "nonnationality" described by music critic Young Dae Kim (2020, p. 10), reflective of the inherently transnational composition and production process of contemporary K-pop, which benefits from the artistic expertise of producers, songwriters, and choreographers from all around the world.[7] However, it is not entirely analogous in that what I have described in this section is both distinct from the practices described in the previous chapter (culture X via scalar representations of X) and from nonnationality (culture X via an amalgamation of culture Y, Z, etc. without obvious evidence of Y, Z, etc.). The semiotics of X-modernity is more a matter of culture X (Korea) via tokens of culture Y (e.g., Paris) in a manner that puts

---

[7] John Lie (2012) also asks a prudent question: "What is the K in K-pop?" In other words, Lie asks us to be mindful of the fact that the popularity of K-pop is the result of the "export-oriented South Korean government since the 1960s" and as such has very little to do with "traditional Confucian, Korean culture" (pp. 361–362).

into crisis a range of assumptions about culture X and Y and their semiotic representability: not only can culture X be appropriately represented through tokens of culture X, but can culture X indeed be represented through tokens of culture Y? And what does it mean that, while culture Y has conventionally been regarded as more "modern" than culture X, culture X has found a way to appropriate and redefine culture Y in the realm of semiosis? And finally, what does the variety of ways in which culture X can be traced via semiotic tokens of culture Y say about culture X? In other words, who is to say that baguettes can't be Korean, especially since Paris Baguette was never about baguettes to begin with? And conversely, who is to say that Korea can't be about baguettes?

5.5   GLOBAL KOREA AS TOILETSCAPE

I have been to over 20 Koreatowns around the world, and many of them have a Paris Baguette, and in some cases, as noted in the previous section, multiple locations in one city. However, arguably a more reliable indicator of Koreanness can be found not on storefront signage but on signage in an establishment's restroom. Specifically, I am referring to notes in restrooms of restaurants and other establishments advising patrons not to flush paper down the toilet (Fig. 5.13). These notes can range from gentle advisement to frighteningly aggressive threats, written likely in a moment of sheer frustration or exasperation. These signs are reflective of the fear that many Koreans have

Fig. 5.13   Do not flush paper signage

that the flushing of toilet paper is the root cause of toilet clogging. Encountering such signage is no doubt a strange experience for those who are accustomed to disposing of used toilet paper in the toilet and not in a bin, as it implies, even if it does not always offer such explicit guidance on an alternative disposal site. I analyze the meaning of such signage as an especially significant trace of Koreanness because, not only is this for the most part a uniquely Korean preoccupation but also because – as I will attempt to show – attending to the social and historical factors that are encoded in such signage offers an important lesson in how the discourse of the universal human experience of relieving oneself can operate as a semiotic trace of a preoccupation of a particular culture.

I admit that the public toilet and its surrounding discourse might appear to be something of an unusual object of sociolinguistic inquiry. This being noted, other scholars have offered productive analyses of the semiotics of such spaces. As Jocelyn Amevuvor and Greg Hafer (2019) note, graffiti in public restrooms are important sites of communication occurring at the nexus of the private and the public. These are spaces not only to relay hateful sentiment but also to display feminist solidarity. Rafael de Vasconcelos Barboza and Rodrigo Borba's (2018) analysis of graffiti in public restrooms at a university in Rio de Janeiro shows that, in spite of the circulation of homophobic discourses, the graffiti in such spaces can also "destabilize what is often taken as a very rigid structure such as cisheteronormativity" and invite us to consider "different ways of being in space and of spatializing our being" (p. 273). In short, the toilet and the discourse in the space around the toilet are not simply about immature humor or inane observations; they also represent opportunities for meaningful social commentary and inquiry into the nuances of how ideological factors shape our relation to and experience in such spaces. And since my present inquiry centers on signage next to toilets of the Korean linguistic/semiotic landscape, it is important to note that a majority of linguistic/semiotic landscape research has tended to focus on external signage, largely overlooking the semiotic potential of what kinds of discourses and meaning making practices circulate within establishments (Pennycook & Otsuji, 2019; Sharma, 2019).

For my purposes, there are varied reasons for focusing on the toilet. For one, the focus of this chapter is on the excess of semiosis, and the toilet is by its nature a space of excess: the toilet is where one goes to dispose of excreta, or feces and urine, which both represent what the body decides to expel after it has extracted what it needs from any food or liquids that have been consumed: what it deems worthy of waste. Further, the toilet – in particular the public toilet – provides a unique opportunity to explore the semiotic dynamics of the trace. Indeed, toilets are generally associated with a particular kind of smell: likely unpleasant, and understandably so. Such a smell – whether pleasant or unpleasant – is itself a trace of a physical object. This association with smell provides an opportunity to make productive inroads to other theorizations of smell in relation to space. Yi-Fu Tuan (1977) argues that "odors lend character to objects and places, making them distinctive, easier to identify and remember" (p. 11). Martyna Śliwa and Kathleen Riach (2012) have shown how residents of the city of Krakow, Poland, tended to associate the smell of disinfectant with the nation's pre-1989 communist past and certain brands of perfume with the capitalist transition. Alex Rhys-Taylor's (2013) study of London's Ridley Road marketplace points to the "mundane" intermingling of odors from different foods as representative of a convivial "urban multiculture" (p. 394). And of course, to return to the case of Korea, Robert Ji-Song Ku (2014) has commented on the unpleasant smell associated with kimchi, which has in turn prompted various manufacturers (not all Korean) to develop recipes that are not so malodorous. However, one probably need not conduct a scientific study to conclude that people, regardless of their cultural background, will find the odors associated with the toilet unpleasant. I mention this because the toilet, as a general category of sensory experience, reflects something somewhat universal, while the semiotic act of prohibiting the flushing of paper down the toilet represents, at least potentially, something unique to a particular culture.

This having been noted, it is important to stress that this discussion is not about smellscapes (Pennycook & Otsuji, 2015a; Śliwa & Riach, 2012) or smells but about traces and tracing: what is it about the Korean public toilet, as a space in which the traces of human activity, in particular the consumption of food and drink, that can be ascertained, and as a space in which one can trace uniquely Korean sociocultural history in semiotic practices. The Korean discourse of the toilet and toilet paper can be traced to the 1988 Summer Olympics, which was hosted in Seoul. In an attempt to make the nation appear more "modern" or "Westernized" to its foreign visitors, numerous Western-style toilets were installed throughout the city and the surrounding areas (Ra, 2017). Prior to this, a vast majority of restrooms in urban areas had squat toilets and many rural areas relied on a 똥뚜깐 [ddong-ddu-kkan], or a community pit latrine. Many residences in such areas did not have a restroom with a toilet and would instead rely on a designated bowl left in the house, preferably made of a non-porous material, which could be used to collect excreta and then emptied into the nearby pit latrine. The existence of flush toilets has been cited as an index of Korea's modernity, as in Lie's (1998) *Han Unbound: The Political Economy of South Korea*, in which Lie, born in Korea in 1959 but raised in Japan, recalls as a child regretting Korea's "non-flush toilets without toilet paper" (p. 1).

Toilet paper did exist in Korea prior to the mass installation of Western-style toilets, as early as 1971 (Kim So Dam, 2017). However, around the same time, the practice of using other cheaper and more readily available paper products, including newspaper, presented challenges for the emptying of pit latrines, which initiated the practice of relying on adjacent trash bins for the disposal of used papers (Kim So Dam, 2017). For the Olympics themselves, the demand of toilet paper outpaced its supply, leading people to rely on likely alternatives: newspaper and other products not designed to be flushed (Ra, 2017). Of course, it is perhaps important to note that, given the widespread use of other kinds of toilets, including pit latrines, toilet paper in Korea at that time did not need to be manufactured in a way to be rapidly dissolvable. But in either case, it would have been comparatively more appropriate to dispose of objects like napkins and newspapers in something like a pit latrine, but not in something like a Western-style toilet. This led to the widespread clogging of toilets throughout the city (Ra, 2017). In short, for most Koreans, their first exposure to these kinds of toilets was associated with clogging, and the flushing of foreign objects, toilet paper included, became isolated as the necessary culprit.

However, the story does not end there. The collective memory, to borrow Maurice Halbwachs's (1992) expression, of Korea's embrace of the Western toilet in the late 1980s and its immediate obstructionary aftermath continues to shape public discussion of, attitudes about, and in fact policy around latrinal disposal practices. Various reasons have been explored as to why toilets used by Koreans seem to be more susceptible to clogging. There is no notable difference in the construction and design of toilets used in Korea and elsewhere. It has therefore been suggested that the typical Korean diet, which contains a high amount of vegetables, leads to the production of excrement with a high dietary fiber content that is purportedly able to pass through the body but not through septic plumbing (Kim So Dam, 2017). However, while this might momentarily explain the preoccupation with clogging in a toilet in a Korean restaurant outside of Korea, it does not account for the slew of other cultures with high-vegetable or even exclusively vegetarian diets who do not have the same concerns with clogging. The alternative of placing bins next to toilets has raised serious sanitary concerns, leading the Ministry of Government Administration and Home Affairs to pass a law, effective January 1, 2018, prohibiting the placement of trash bins in public bathroom stalls (Lee Sung In, 2017). Initial reports, based on records from the Seoul Metropolitan Subway, noted that abiding by these guidelines did not cause an increase in the number of clogged toilets in a given day (Yoo, 2018). The same report indicated a series of items that are common causes of clogged toilets other than toilet paper: credit cards, straws, feces, miscellaneous plastics, and coffee lids. It is therefore indeed possible that Koreans' obsession with the clogged toilet might appear to have been based on an invalidated misunderstanding of how Western toilets work.

So what is the takeaway from all of this? Most immediately, signs asking users not to flush paper down the toilet are an important trace of Koreanness. Indeed, I am almost tempted to claim that, if the Morelli method can be a potentially reliable means of determining whether a work of art is genuine or counterfeit (see Section 5.2), the presence/absence of prohibitory latrinal signage can be a means of determining whether a Korean restaurant is "authentic" or not. But this being noted, I am of course not trying to suggest that the problem of a clogged toilet is by any means a uniquely Korean issue. A recent report from the Ryerson Urban Water research group from Ryerson University in Canada, based on a study of 101 frequently flushed paper products, found that none – including those that are marketed and sold as "flushable" – dissolve as readily as advertised, leading to clogs in septic piping.[8] An extreme lesson in the dangers of flushing too much unnatural substance down the toilet was the discovery of the massive 130-ton "fatberg" in London's sewer in 2017.[9] It is called a fatberg because its base is cooking fat washed down the sink, combined with items that should not be flushed down the toilet, including diapers, syringes, and of course – ironically enough – "flushable" wipes.

However, while the disdain for a clogged toilet might not be particular to a given national imaginary or its respective culinary practices, it has come to be enregistered as a semiotic token of Koreanness through the acts of individuals producing and placing such prohibitory signage. Something as simple as an unusual sign, through its emplacement (Scollon & Scollon, 2003) within the bathroom, has the remarkable capacity to in turn transform an ordinary restroom into a decidedly "Korean" one. And while such a point might seem

[8] See Khan, Orr, and Joksimovic (2019).   [9] See Slotkin (2017).

implausible to some, it is critical to note that Korea was the only nation to be tasked with the (voluntary) imperative to rapidly "modernize" via a large-scale toilet installation initiative though with a quite different understanding of what a toilet of this kind could or could not do. Having to deal with a clogged toilet is an experience that can be frustrating, embarrassing, and potentially traumatizing. And this range of negative associations with the toilet has been difficult to shake for many Koreans. There is, in other words, on every such sign next to a toilet, whether in the form of a plea, demand, or even threat, a trace of Korea's not entirely successful attempt to appear "cultured" in the eyes of the world in the most unexpected of places: the restroom. And today the signage is the encoded legacy of that experiment in latrinal modernity, which can in turn be found in the most unexpected of ways.

5.6 CONCLUSION: KOREA AS TRACE

This chapter was an attempt to take seriously the role of the trace in the phenomenon of cultural signification, to consider how that which has been ignored, effaced, or even discarded can play an important – even if unexpected – role in the production of culture as a discrete entity across global space. The trace, as I have noted, is not always easy to pinpoint or conceptualize (and hence it is akin to what Walter Benjamin describes as the "aura"), but it can be made sense of when approached in a manner that allows a disruption of an ordered and predictable method of semiosis: if we try to see significance in the insignificant, or, as Pennycook suggests, expect the unexpected. By looking at "official" discourses of Koreanness, whether in the form of municipal designations of Koreatowns or the Gwanghwamun in Seoul, I have tried to show that sometimes that which seems authentically or unmistakably Korean is not necessarily so. In the case of the Gwanghwamun, despite being a key tourist destination and an important relic of Korean heritage, its history and its surrounding contemporary discourse point to a more complicated reality. Indeed, questions of what "Korea" is are coming to be increasingly complicated elsewhere as well. By looking at tokens of European semiosis across the linguistic/semiotic landscape of global Korea, we encounter unusual exceptions to the very notion of representation via the framework of the nation: the national need not be represented via tokens of the national, as we see in the case of Paris Baguette. This case, however, is not simply a matter of Frenchness coming to be hybridized with Koreanness but of Frenchness being reinvented and resemiotized via Koreanness, which in turn raises a series of questions about Koreanness itself. And finally, the toilet. Why is it that Koreans have a particular disdain for the clogged toilet? Much of it has to do with the history of Korea's encounter with the Western toilet but, as I have tried to show in the previous section, that is not the whole story. In fact, insofar as "stories only happen to those who know how to tell them," not all semiotic features or spatial elements have a story behind them, and sometimes their stories can take us down unexpected paths and allow us to view the very idea of Korea anew. In sum, this chapter, through a series of unusual examples of Koreanness, has tried to show how we can approach the trace, even the most unexpected of traces – or perhaps especially the most expected of traces – as something worthy of our collective attention.

Conclusion: More Locations of Culture

In the opening pages of this book, I mentioned how the bird enjoys both immense privileges (of seeing the world from above) but also extraordinary challenges (of never being sure whether something is safe to eat or not, as in the case of the caterpillar that looks like a snake). In the pages that followed, I tried to show that humans are in many ways bound to face many similar challenges: we think we know what culture looks like but we don't actually ever know what it looks like or how it can be encountered. Of course, the encounter with the wrong version of culture is hardly ever as high stakes as what the bird faces. We might mistakenly assume that a certain custom is associated with culture X when it is in fact associated with culture Y. Or not being familiar enough with culture X can render one susceptible to other kinds of misrecognition, like maybe becoming a victim of a scam designed to lure unsuspecting tourists, such as buying an "authentic" relic that is in fact a meaningless, mass-produced trinket that one can also purchase at the airport. But in either case, the misrecognition of culture is typically not a life-or-death matter for humans as it is for the bird.

But approaching culture from the perspective of the bird gives us the unique opportunity to view culture anew. I have tried to show that by adopting such a global view of culture, in my case through the linguistic/semiotic landscape of global Korea, we can revisit and reassess what the very notion of culture is by grappling with the ways in which it is semiotically mediated and thus rendered legible. I have made this case by focusing on spaces characterized by what I term semiotic precarity: those where the authenticity or the ontological certitude of culture is not presumed and wherein such certitude can be momentarily represented via semiosis. Significantly, in such spaces the question of whether it is the "original" version of culture or merely the "derivative" version of culture becomes largely irrelevant. Because of this, it is important to reiterate that this has not been an attempt to chronicle and certify what is truly or "authentically" Korean and to scorn, ridicule, or dismiss that which is the commercialized and inauthentic version of Korea. As noted in the Introduction, at least for the bird, their "irrational fear" drives them not to put too much stock into trying to decide whether the caterpillar is really a caterpillar or not. Likewise, tourists who visit the Gwanghwamun probably do not need to concern themselves too much with the fact that the relic they eagerly pose for photos in front of is a reconstructed version. After all, it still looks quite neat. And the point of the matter is that the very fact that notions of what "actually" is culture versus what a mere "representation" of culture is are so readily blurred provides an opportunity to rethink the kinds of traits we envision as standing in as representative of a given culture, and how their associations with a given culture have come to be naturalized over time. As I have attempted to illustrate, the experience of viewing culture anew can be thought through in terms of translingual inversion: when we try to make sense of the traits of a culture as they can be seen in moments of semiotic precarity, things don't always make sense, in part because in many instances the naturalized associations between a given culture and its distinguishing semiotic traits are anything but natural. And I believe this applies not only to the case of Korea, but potentially to a wider range of cultural entities as well.

C.1   MODULAR IMAGINARIES; OR, CITIZEN SOCIOLINGUISTICS AS A HUMAN RIGHT

As I noted earlier, I have written this book not as a scholar of Korean studies per se, or as a "Koreanist," as some might self-identify, but as a scholar interested in the notion of "culture" as it is encountered via language and semiosis within the context of globalization. And while what I have offered is a sustained study of the linguistic/semiotic landscape of global Korea, I hope that the general approach could be of use to scholars interested in language and globalization even without a stated interest in "Korea" per se. Indeed, I hope that what I have offered throughout these pages might inspire other scholars to explore similar questions regarding the iterability of other cultural imaginaries. I, for one, believe that there is still much work to do to understand what the idea of culture looks like not only in the context of globalization (how culture changes) but *through* globalization (as a lens): how the perspective of the global allows us to see culture anew. It is my great hope that my work will inspire others interested in language and globalization to pursue studies of other global imaginaries, particularly those that are known for their worldwide presence: Little Arabias, Chinatowns, Little Ethiopias, Finnish Quarters, Frenchtowns, Germantowns, Greektowns, Little Indias, Little Italies, Little Manilas, Little Moscows, Little Persias, Little Saigons, or Little Tokyos, to name a few examples. And perhaps this analytical approach could lead to interesting discoveries for imaginaries that do not have a notable diaspora presence as well. Such inquiries would not only be in and of themselves interesting but are warranted in that they can help us to collectively arrive at better understandings of what it means to belong to a given culture in the twenty-first century.

And while the heuristic I have outlined in this book professes to be modular in that it can be applied to investigations of other cultural entities as they are rendered legible in their own sites of semiotic precarity, it does not do so following an endorsement of a "modular" theory of culture generally and of national culture specifically. As noted in Chapter 1, assumptions of modularity can have the unintended effect of privileging certain kinds of epistemological vantage points while dismissing the possibility of different kinds of knowledge making and community building (see also Chapter 2 on my epistemological vantage point in pursuing this project). The presumption of a modular, uniform kind of framework for culture, in other words, would seem counterproductive and counterintuitive to the aims of understanding cultural difference. Therefore, my project should not be construed as one that presupposes a singular, uniform notion of culture as such. This disclaimer is especially urgent for inquiries into national imaginaries as a discrete subset of cultural entities. Nonetheless, there is certainly some value in approaching national imaginaries in accordance with a (tentatively) generalizable series of traits. But such traits should always be treated as mere starting points from which sustained inquiry can be pursued, rather than as immutable features and certainly not as the end goal of research. After all, what is the point of *research* if you have determined what will be found before you even begin searching for it?

In order to facilitate such inquiries, it is imperative to find ways of democratizing research, following Arjun Appadurai's (2013) call to reimagine research "as a human right." The objects of analysis in this book are on the one hand reflective of "research data" that is publicly available: it is not premised on the study of inaccessible archives held by elite and exclusive institutions that are inherently and are indeed – by definition – exclusionary. In addition, the study of linguistic/semiotic landscapes in many ways blurs the boundaries between scholarly thought and "nonspecialist" inquiry insofar as we are always already studying linguistic/semiotic landscapes. It is common practice in many parts of the world, especially in urban, developed regions, to make use of signage and other semiotic landmarks of the built environment to navigate such spaces. In this sense, any kind of linguistic/semiotic landscape analysis can be treated as a project within the paradigm of what has been described as citizen sociolinguistics (Rymes, 2020; Svendsen, 2018). Betsy Rymes (2020) defines citizen sociolinguistics as "the study of world of language and communication by the people who use it and, as such, have devised ways to understand it that may be more relevant than the way professional sociolinguists have developed" (p. 5). At first glance, citizen sociolinguistics would appear similar to other frameworks used to conceptualize language phenomena, including what Dennis Preston (1993, 2011) terms folk linguistics, or everyday individuals' linguistic metacommentary. However, as Rymes (2020) clarifies, whereas the research program of folk linguistics ultimately serves the interest of professional linguists, citizen sociolinguists "are everyday people and linguistics may be among them – but their primary audience is each other, not a professional community of research scholars" (p. 59). Most importantly, then, citizen sociolinguistics entails a redistribution of expertise and the aspiration of a culture of knowledge exchange that takes seriously the privileges not only of formal scholarly credentials but rights to citizenship: in this scenario of intellectual exchange, an individual "won't be reprimanded, or worse, sent across the border and far from home, for saying what they believe in" (p. 52). In order to realize such a paradigm, it perhaps goes without saying that research "data" needs to be readily accessible, whether it be everyday speech practices or everyday public language artifacts. With respect to the "data" for my project, like the materials for any linguistic/semiotic landscape project, it falls within the category of that which is publicly accessible. That being said, I of course do not mean to discount the reality that the research itself, especially given the sheer number of sites visited, was made feasible through considerable institutional support and resources over several years of time. Nonetheless, local linguistic/semiotic landscapes are more accessible than many other kinds of research data, and, perhaps a point could be made that for any researcher, given the abundance of digital resources available online such as Google Maps through the Street View function, there are increasingly more opportunities to access sites remotely. In fact, scholars such as Xiaofang Yao (2021) have already demonstrated how linguistic/semiotic landscape research can be conducted via digitally available materials combined with ethnographic methods.

This is related to the next point, which is that the democratization of language research will inevitably require a flexibilization of research methods. As Eve Darian-Smith and Philip McCarthy (2017) note, "global" inquiries such as the one I am presenting need to be mindful of the reality that a majority of extant research methods are products of Western epistemology. For instance, even sampling logic, which aims to offer a representative portrait of a larger population or context, "developed in the nineteenth and twentieth centuries alongside the growing modern bureaucracies of nation-states, and as a mode of statistical calculation that is very much part of defining national citizens, public policies, and nationalist agendas" (p. 104; see also Vertovec, 2007). In any project that purports to be "global," while also aiming to problematize the representational logics of the cultural difference, it will be necessary to adopt an approach that is not grounded in the bureaucratic epistemology of the nation-state, akin to what Ulrich Beck and Johannes Willms (2004) have described as "methodological nationalism." In the context of language-oriented research, it is especially urgent that we attend to the affordances of alternative research epistemologies. As Finex Ndhlovu (2018) puts it:

> How realistic is it for new philosophies of language to claim they are pushing scholarship forward in a new direction when their theoretical suppositions are supported by data generated through conventional research methods? How do we do ethnographic social science research in ways that allow us to capture the complex relations between society and communication resources? In other words, can we really claim to be theorising in unconventional ways when our methodologies remain conventional? (p. 3)

This is of course not to suggest that all research methods that are "conventional" are inherently flawed. However, if we abide by Ndhlovu's point, then the "validity" or "reliability" of the research design might be considered as secondary to the aims of the research to begin with.

One way forward is to consider the usefulness of intermittent ethnography, as suggested in the work of Bob Jeffrey and Geoff Troman (2004). Of course, this is not to dismiss the value of "deep ethnographic immersion" advocated by Blommaert (2013, p. xi). Instead, I am referring specifically to the conventional premise of ethnography as necessitating extended and uninterrupted fieldwork. This premise, rather than viewed as universal dogma, can be adapted in relation to the object of inquiry and the goals of the field research. For instance, many scholars of new media and digital phenomena have relied on alternative ethnographies such as "netnography" (Dovchin, 2015; Kozinets, 1998), "virtual ethnography" (Hine, 2000), or "discourse-centred online ethnography" (Androutsopoulos, 2008). While the flexible, intermittent approach described by Jeffrey and Troman has primarily been adopted in organizational ethnography contexts, an added benefit to such an approach is the ability to engage in continual analytical and indeed comparative reflection of findings across multiple sites over an extended period of time.

It is especially crucial to emphasize that the call for the democratization of research should not be confused for a call for the repudiation or disavowal of scholarly expertise. The democratization of knowledge in my view does not mean that anybody's opinions are as valid as an expert's. If the COVID-19 pandemic taught us one thing, it's that it is actually quite dangerous to allow any and all opinions to matter. I am referring, in particular, to how many in the United States simply refused to acknowledge the research-based scientific evidence on the spread of the virus, along with the research-based recommendations provided by medical and public health experts on protocols for reducing its spread. Expertise is not something to be taken lightly and certainly not something to be gained by reading a blog, listening to a podcast, or watching a video on YouTube. These can be starting points, of course. But expertise is something that is gained first and foremost by sustained and systematic inquiry: the methods can be unconventional, and the findings can be unexpected, but they need to be pursued in a manner that views expert knowledge not as an irrefutable and sacred dogma but at the very least as something that warrants serious acknowledgment and consideration. There is no substitute for expertise, though there is value in continuing to reconceive of ways to facilitate its pursuit and to accommodate different kinds of expertise. In short, we need to collectively imagine ways to facilitate sustained inquiry "as a human right."

C.2   *DEPARTING THOUGHTS*

It is hard to say definitively what the future of transnational Korean communities will look like into the future. As I've noted earlier, establishing tight-knit communities with individuals and families of shared Korean heritage has proven to be either politically expedient or otherwise important for the purposes of maintaining a sense of belonging in a foreign country. It is clear that the improvement or even availability of transportation technologies has enabled transnational Koreans to view a Koreatown not only as a space of residence but as a space of sojourn. Even when I was growing up in Los Angeles in the 1980s and 1990s, my family did not live in its Koreatown proper but we spent quite a bit of time there and it always felt very familiar to me. In other words, we didn't need to live in Koreatown to enjoy the full affordances of having a Koreatown nearby, and no doubt the same thing might be said by countless others of Korean heritage. Another factor that undoubtedly poses a threat to the viability of Koreatowns and other transnational communities is the expansion of online commerce in the last couple of decades. The trip to Koreatown has in many ways been about getting a certain item that you could only get in Korea or in Koreatown because it wouldn't be available at other non-Korean markets or stores (books, cosmetics, utensils, and the like). But now many of these same items can be readily purchased online and, in some cases – because of the growth of popularity of Korean culture thanks in large part to the influence of "K-pop" and "K-beauty" – accessible at non-Korean establishments as well. This is to say that all Koreatowns, in spite of what they represent for local communities in terms of offering an important space of heritage maintenance, can expect to undergo change over time. The Los Angeles's Koreatown that I knew growing up is different from the Koreatown that someone even a decade older than me or younger than me experienced growing up. And even in the past few years in the Korean district of Garden Grove I have noticed that many of the smaller stores and restaurants have closed down, and all that remains is a "For Lease" sign. If the study of linguistic/semiotic landscapes, as initiated by the work of Landry and Bourhis (1997), was to trace a community's ethnolinguistic vitality, one would be right to be concerned for Korean cultural vitality in certain spaces. Yet, people at the level of both the individual and the community have always found ways to redefine what it means to belong to a given cultural entity. And maybe that means viewing Koreanness not as a means unto itself but as an entity that is meant to be redefined, needs to be redefined, and has always already been redefined across space and time.

In my time traveling around the world looking for different transnational iterations of Koreanness, what I ended up finding was Korea itself. In other words, my travels have reshaped my understanding of what "Korea" as a culture looks like and therefore is, and I'm not sure I could have reached such conclusions by looking at Korea only as it exists and as it is represented in Korea proper. Of course, I am not saying I have it all figured out, and in many senses I now have more questions than answers. But perhaps that is what it means to know what a culture is: to acknowledge that it can both be a thing but also a thing that really isn't, except for in moments where it becomes imperative and even possible to differentiate it from another thing. It is likely that a similar phenomenon could be experienced by an examination of the global iterations of other cultural imaginaries, and I look forward to learning about what others might find.

References

Abbas, Ackbar. (2008). Faking globalization. In Andreas Huyssen (ed.), *Other cities, other worlds: Urban imaginaries in a globalizing age* (pp. 243–264). Durham, NC: Duke University Press.

Abelmann, Nancy, and Lie, John. (1995). *Blue dreams: Korean Americans and the Los Angeles riots*. Cambridge, MA: Harvard University Press.

Acosta, Abraham. (2014). *Thresholds of illiteracy: Theory, Latin America, and the crisis of resistance*. New York: Fordham University Press.

Agha, Asif. (2007). *Language and social relations*. Cambridge: Cambridge University Press.

Ahn, Hyejeong. (2017). English as a discursive and social communication resource for contemporary South Koreans. In Christopher J. Jenks and Jerry Won Lee (eds.), *Korean Englishes in transnational contexts* (pp. 157–179). Basingstoke: Palgrave Macmillan.

Amevuvor, Jocelyn, and Hafer, Greg. (2019). Communities in the stalls: A study of latrinalia linguistic landscapes. *Critical Inquiry in Language Studies*, 16(2), 90–106.

Anderson, Benedict. (1983). *Imagined communities: Reflections on the origin and spread of nationalism*. London: Verso.

(1991). *Imagined communities: Reflections on the origin and spread of nationalism* (2nd ed.). London: Verso.

(1998). *The spectre of comparisons*. London: Verso.

(2002). 상상의 공동체: 민족주의의 기원과 전파에 대한 성찰 [*Sang-sang-ui Gong-dong-chei: Min-jok-ju-ui-ui gi-won-gwa jeon-pa-ei dae-han seong-chal / Imagined communities: Reflections on the origin and spread of nationalism*] (trans. Yoon Hyung Suk). Seoul: Nanam. (Original work published 1991.)

Anderson, Perry. (1974). *Lineages of the absolutist state*. London: Verso.

Androutsopoulos, Jannis. (2008) Potentials and limitations of discourse-centred online ethnography. *Language@Internet*, 5, n.p.

Aneesh, A. (2015). *Neutral accent: How language, labor, and life become global*. Durham, NC: Duke University Press.

Appadurai, Arjun. (1996). *Modernity at large: The cultural dimensions of globalization*. Minneapolis, MN: University of Minnesota Press.

(2001). Grassroots globalization and the research imagination. In Arjun Appadurai (ed.), *Globalization* (pp. 1–21). Durham, NC: Duke University Press.

(2013). *The future as cultural fact: Essays on the global condition*. London: Verso.

Appiah, Kwame Anthony. (2006). *Cosmopolitanism: Ethics in a world of strangers*. New York: Norton.

Apter, Emily. (2013). *Against world literature: On the politics of untranslatability*. London: Verso.

Backhaus, Peter. (2006). Multilingualism in Tokyo: A look into the linguistic landscape. *International Journal of Multilingualism*, 3(1), 52–66.

Bakhtin, Mikhail. (1968). *Rabelais and his world* (trans. Helene Iswolsky). Cambridge, MA: MIT Press. (Original work published 1965.)

(1981). *The dialogic imagination : Four essays* (trans. Caryl Emerson and Michael Holquist). Austin, TX: University of Texas Press. (Original work published 1975.)

Balibar, Étienne. 1990. The nation form: History and ideology. In Étienne Balibar and Immanuel Wallerstein (eds.), *Race, nation, class: Ambiguous identities* (pp. 86–106). London: Verso.

Banda, Felix, and Jimaima, Hambaba. (2015). The semiotic ecology of linguistic landscapes in rural Zambia. *Journal of Sociolinguistics*, 19(5), 643–670.

Barthes, Roland. (1985). *The responsibility of forms: Critical essays on music, art, and representation* (trans. Richard Howard). Berkeley, CA: University of California Press. (Original work published 1970.)

Baudrillard, Jean. (1994). *Simulacra and simulation* (trans. Sheila Faria Glaser). Ann Arbor, MI: University of Michigan Press. (Original work published 1981.)

Bauman, Richard, and Briggs, Charles L. (2003). *Voices of modernity: Language ideologies and the politics of inequality*. Cambridge: Cambridge University Press.

Beck, Ulrich, and Willms, Johannes. (2004). *Conversations with Ulrich Beck*. Cambridge: Polity Press.

Ben-Rafael, Eliezer, Shohamy, Elana, Amara, Muhammad Hasan, and Trumper-Hecht, Nira. (2006). Linguistic landscape as symbolic construction of the public space: The case of Israel. *International Journal of Multilingualism*, 3(1), 7–30.

Benjamin, Walter. (1968). *Illuminations: Essays and reflections* (trans. Harry Zohn). New York: Schocken Books. (Original work published 1955.)

Berthele, Raphael. (2000). Translating African-American vernacular English into German: The problem of 'Jim' in Mark Twain's Huckleberry Finn. *Journal of Sociolinguistics*, 4(4), 588–614.

Bhabha, Homi (ed.). (1990). *Nation and narration*. London: Routledge.

(1994). *The location of culture*. London: Routledge.

Billig, Michael. (1995). *Banal nationalism*. London: Sage.

Blommaert, Jan. (2010). *The sociolinguistics of globalization*. Cambridge: Cambridge University Press.

(2013). *Ethnography, superdiversity and linguistic landscapes: Chronicles of complexity*. Bristol: Multilingual Matters.

(2019). Formatting online actions: #justsaying on Twitter. *International Journal of Multilingualism*, 16(2), 112–126.

Blommaert, Jan, and Backhus, Ad. (2011). Repertoires revisited: "Knowing language" in superdiversity. *Working Papers in Urban Language and Literacies*, 67, 2–26.

Bolander, Brook, and Sultana, Shaila. (2019). Ordinary English amongst Muslim communities in South and Central Asia. *International Journal of Multilingualism*, 16(2), 162–174.

Bonfiglio, Thomas Paul. (2010). *Mother tongues and nations: Inventing the native speaker*. Berlin: Mouton de Gruyter.

Bong, Youngshik D. (2013). Built to last: The Dokdo territorial controversy. The baseline conditions in domestic politics and international security of Japan and South Korea. *Memory Studies*, 6(2), 191–203.

Bourdieu, Pierre. (1984). *Distinction* (trans. Richard Nice). London: Routledge. (Original work published 1979.)

(1991). *Language and symbolic power*. (trans. Gino Raymond). Cambridge, MA: Harvard University Press. (Original work published 1982.)

Brass, Paul R. (1991). *Ethnicity and nationalism: Theory and comparison*. London: Sage.

Brault, Jean-Jules, and Plamondon, Réjean. (1993). A complexity measure of handwritten curves: Modeling of dynamic signature forgery. *IEEE Transactions on Systems, Man, and Cybernetics*, 23(2), 400–413.

Butler, Judith. (1997). *Excitable speech: The political promise of the performative*. London: Routledge.

Calhoun, Craig. (1997). *Nationalism*. Minneapolis: University of Minnesota Press.

(2007). *Nations matter: Culture, history, and the cosmopolitan dream*. London: Routledge.

Cameron, Deborah. (2012). *Verbal hygiene* (2nd ed.). London: Routledge.

Canagarajah, Suresh. (2013). *Translingual practice: Global Englishes and cosmopolitan relations*. London: Routledge.

(2018). Translingual practice as spatial repertoires: Expanding the paradigm beyond structuralist orientations. *Applied Linguistics*, 39(1), 31–54.

Canagarajah, Suresh, and Dovchin, Sender. (2019). The everyday politics of translingualism as a resistant practice. *International Journal of Multilingualism*, 16(2), 127–144.

Carr, E. Summerson, and Lempert, Michael (eds.). (2016). *Scale: Discourse and the dimensions of social life*. Berkeley: University of California Press.

Castellano, Sergio, and Cermelli, Paolo. (2015). Preys' exploitation of predators' fear: When the caterpillar plays the Gruffalo. *Proceedings of the Royal Society B: Biological Sciences*, 282(1820), 20151786.

Cenoz, Jasone, and Gorter, Durk. (2011). Focus on multilingualism: A study of trilingual writing. *Modern Language Journal, 95*(3), 356–369.

Certeau, Michel de. (1984). *The practice of everyday life* (trans. Steven Rendall). Berkeley, CA: University of California Press. (Original work published 1980.)

Ch'ien, Evelyn Nien-Ming. (2004). *Weird English.* Cambridge, MA: Harvard University Press.

Chatterjee, Partha. (1986). *Nationalist thought and the colonial world: A derivative discourse?* Minneapolis, MN: University of Minnesota Press.

(1993). *The nation and its fragments: Colonial and postcolonial histories.* Princeton, NJ: Princeton University Press.

Ch'oe, Yong-ho. (2008). Yanagi Muneyoshi and the Kwanghwa Gate in Seoul, Korea. In William Theodore De Bary (ed.), *Sources of East Asian tradition*, Vol. 2 (pp. 551–553). New York: Columbia University Press.

Choi Jang Gun. (2012). 독도의 「가치.명칭.실효적 관리」 대한 편견 연구- 無人孤島라는 독도의 특징적 관점을 중심으로 [Dok-do-ui (ga-chi.myeong-ching.sil-hyo-jeok gwal-li) dae-han pyeon-gyeon yeon-gu – mu-in-do-la-neun Dok-do-ui teuk-jing-jeok gwan-jeom-eul jung-sim-ui-ro/Research about the prejudice (value.name.management) of Dokdo territorial rights problems]. 일본근대학연구 [*Il-bon-geun-dae-hak-yeon-gu/Journal of the Japanese Modern Association of Korea*], 38, 131–152.

Choi Ji-Man. (2007). 광복이후 한국 축구 국가대표 유니폼의 변천사 [*Kwang-bok-i-hu han-guk chuk-ku guk-ga-dae-pyo yu-ni-pom-ui byeon-cheon-sa/The changes of Korean National Football Team's uniform after Independence*]. Unpublished master's thesis. Jung-Ang University.

Choi, Jinny K. (2015). Identity and language: Korean speaking Korean, Korean-American speaking Korean and English? *Language and Intercultural Communication, 15*(2), 240–266.

Choi, Sung-jae. (2005). The politics of the Dokdo issue. *Journal of East Asian Studies, 5*(3), 465–494.

Choi, Yeomi. (2020). Running for Korea : Rethinking of sport migration and in/flexible citizenship. *International Review for the Sociology of Sport, 55*(3), 361–379.

Choi Yong-gi. (2010). 세종의 문자 정책과 한글 진흥 정책의 미래 [Sejong-ui mun-ja jeong-chaek-gwa han-geul jin-heung jeong-chaek-ui mi-rae/ The alphabet policy of the Great King Sejong and the measures for the promotion of the Hangeul]. 국어문학 [*Guk-eo-mun-hak/Korean Language and Literature*], 49, 39–64.

Chow, Rey. (2002). *The protestant ethnic and the spirit of capitalism.* New York: Columbia University Press.

(2014). *Not like a native speaker: On languaging as a postcolonial experience.* New York: Columbia University Press.

Connor, Walker. (1990). When is a nation? *Ethnic and Racial Studies, 13*(1), 92–103.

(1994). *Ethnonationalism: The quest for understanding.* Princeton, NJ: Princeton University Press.

Cosgrove, Denis. (2003). *Apollo's eye: A cartographic genealogy of the Earth in the Western imagination.* Baltimore, MD: Johns Hopkins University Press.

Crutzen, Paul J., and Stoermer, Eugene F. (2000). The "anthropocene." *Global Change Newsletter*, *41*, 17–18.

Curtin, Melissa. (2015). Creativity in polyscriptal typographies in the linguistic landscape of Taipei. *Social Semiotics*, *25*(2), 236–243.

Darian-Smith, Eve, and McCarthy, Philip. (2017). *The global turn: Theories, research designs, and methods for global studies.* Berkeley: University of California Press.

De Costa, Peter. (2014). Cosmopolitanism and English as a lingua franca: Learning English in a Singapore school. *Research in the Teaching of English*, *49*, 9–30.

Derrida, Jacques. (1974). *Of grammatology* (trans. Gayatri Chakravorty Spivak). Baltimore, MD: Johns Hopkins University Press. (Original work published 1967.)

(1998). *Monolingualism of the Other; Or, the prosthesis of origin* (trans. Patrick Mensah). Stanford, CA: Stanford University Press. (Original work published 1996.)

Do, Youngah, Ito, Chiyuki, and Kenstowicz, Michael. (2014). Accent classes in South Kyengsang Korean: Lexical drift, novel words and loanwords. *Lingua*, *148*, 147–182.

Dovchin, Sender. (2015). Language, multiple authenticities and social media: The online language practices of university students in Mongolia. *Journal of Sociolinguistics*, *19*(4), 437–459.

(2017). Translocal English in the linguascape of Mongolian popular music. *World Englishes*, *36*(1), 2–19.

(2018). *Language, media and globalization in the periphery: The linguascapes of popular music in Mongolia.* London: Routledge.

(2020). The psychological damages of linguistic racism and international students in Australia. *International Journal of Bilingual Education and Bilingualism*, *23*(7), 804–818.

Dovchin, Sender, and Lee, Jerry Won (eds.). (2019). *Translinguistics: Negotiating innovation and ordinariness.* London: Routledge.

Dovchin, Sender, Pennycook, Alastair, and Sultana, Shaila. (2018). *Popular culture, voice and linguistic diversity: Young adults on- and offline.* Basingstoke: Palgrave Macmillan.

Dovchin, Sender, Sultana, Shaila, and Pennycook, Alastair. (2016). Unequal translingual Englishes in the Asian peripheries. *Asian Englishes*, *18*(2), 1–17.

Du, Qian, Lee, Jerry Won, and Sok, Sarah Y. (2020). Using China English: Creating translingual space. *World Englishes*, *39*(2), 275–285.

Duchêne, Alexandre, and Heller, Monica (eds.). (2012). *Language in late capitalism: Pride and profit.* London: Routledge.

Eckert, Penelope. (2008). Variation and the indexical field. *Journal of Sociolinguistics*, *12*(4), 453–476.

(2018). *Meaning and linguistic variation: The third wave in sociolinguistics.* Cambridge: Cambridge University Press.

Fahim, Kareem. (2009, March 20). On city's plastic bags, an old and distant dispute. *New York Times.* www.nytimes.com/2009/03/21/nyregion/21islands.html

Fairclough, Norman. (2003). *Analysing discourse: Textual analysis for social research.* London: Routledge.

Faist, Thomas. (2013). The mobility turn: A new paradigm for the social sciences? *Ethnic and Racial Studies*, *36*(11), 1637–1646.

Flores, Nelson, and Rosa, Jonathan. (2015). Undoing appropriateness: Raciolinguistic ideologies and language diversity in education. *Harvard Educational Review*, *85*(2), 149–171.

Flores, Richard R. (2009). The Alamo: myth, public history, and the politics of inclusion. In Daniel J. Walkowitz and Lisa Maya Knauer (eds.), *Contested histories in public space: Memory, race, and nation* (pp. 122–135). Durham, NC: Duke University Press.

Gandelsonas, Mario. (1999). *X-Urbanism: Architecture and the American city.* Princeton, NJ: Princeton Architectural Press.

García, Ofelia. (2009). *Bilingual education in the 21st century: A global perspective.* Oxford: Wiley-Blackwell.

Geertz, Clifford. (1973). *The interpretation of cultures.* New York: Basic Books.

Gellner, Ernest. (1983). *Nations and nationalism.* Ithaca, NY: Cornell University Press.

Ginzburg, Carlo. (1980). Morelli, Freud, and Sherlock Holmes: Clues and scientific method (trans. Anna Davin). *History Workshop*, *9*, 5–36. (Original work published 1979.)

Glissant, Édouard. (1997). *Poetics of relation* (trans. Betsy Wing). Ann Arbor: University of Michigan Press. (Original work published 1990.)

González, Roseann Dueñas, and Melis, Ildikó (eds.). (2000). *Language ideologies: Critical perspectives on the Official English movement.* Carbondale, IL: National Council of Teachers of English.

Gorter, Durk (ed.). (2006). *Linguistic landscape: A new approach to multilingualism.* Bristol: Multilingual Matters.

Gorter, Durk, and Cenoz, Jasone. (2015). Translanguaging and linguistic landscapes. *Linguistic Landscape*, *1*(1/2), 54–74.

Gramling, David. (2016). *The invention of monolingualism.* London: Bloomsbury.

Guissemo, Manuel. (2019). Orders of (in)visibility: Colonial and postcolonial chronotopes in the linguistic landscapes of memorization in Maputo. In Amiena Peck, Christopher Stroud, and Quentin Williams (eds.), *Making sense of people and place in linguistic landscapes* (pp. 29–48). London: Bloomsbury.

Hall, Stuart. (1996). Who needs "identity"? In Stuart Hall and Paul Du Gay (eds.), *Questions of cultural identity* (pp. 1–17). London: Sage.

Halbwachs, Maurice. (1992). *On collective memory* (trans. Lewis A. Coser). Chicago: University of Chicago Press. (Original work published 1952.)

Halliday, M. A. K. (1978). *Language as social semiotic*. London: Edward Arnold.

Han, Enze. (2013). *Contestation and adaptation: The politics of national identity in China*. Oxford: Oxford University Press.

Han, Kyung-Koo. (2007). The archaeology of the ethnically homogeneous nation-state and multiculturalism in Korea. *Korea Journal*, 47(4), 8–31.

Hangeul Society. (2020). 인사말 [*In-sa-mal / Introduction*]. 한글학회 [Hangeul-Hak-hui/Hangeul Society. https://hangeul.or.kr/인사말

Harley, J. B. (1988). Maps, knowledge, and power. In Denis Cosgrove and Stephen Daniels (eds.), *The iconography of landscape: Essays on the symbolic representation, design and use of environments* (pp. 277–312). Cambridge: Cambridge University Press.

Harvey, David. (1989). *The condition of postmodernity: An enquiry into the origins of cultural change*. Oxford: Blackwell.

He, Agnes. (2010). The heart of heritage: Sociocultural dimensions of heritage language learning. *Annual Review of Applied Linguistics*, 30, 66–82.

Heater, Derek. (1998). *The theory of nationhood: A platonic symposium*. Basingstoke: Palgrave Macmillan.

Heller, Monica. (1999). *Linguistic minorities and modernity: A sociolinguistic ethnography*. London: Pearson Longman.

(2007). The future of "bilingualism"? In Monica Heller (ed.), *Bilingualism: A social approach* (pp. 340–345). Basingstoke: Palgrave Macmillan.

(2011). *Paths to post-nationalism: A critical ethnography of language and identity*. Oxford: Oxford University Press.

Hendershot, Steve. (2017). *Undisputed street fighter: A 30th anniversary retrospective*. Mt. Laurel, NJ: Dynamite Entertainment.

Heo, Uk, and Roehrig, Terence. (2014). *South Korea's rise: Economic development, power, and foreign relations*. Cambridge: Cambridge University Press.

Herder, Johann Gottfried. (1967). Idee zum ersten patriotischen Institute für den Allgemeingeist Deutschlands [Ideas for the First Patriotic Institute for the common spirit of Germany]. In Bernard Suphan (ed.), *Sämtliche Werke* (pp. 600–616), Vol. 16. New York: Georg Olms. (Original speech delivered 1788.)

Heyd, Theresa. (2014). Folk-linguistic landscapes: The visual semiotics of digital enregisterment. *Language in Society*, 43(5), 489–514.

Hine, Christine. (2000). *Virtual ethnography*. London: Sage.

Hinton, Kip. (2016). Call it what it is: Monolingual education in US schools. *Critical Inquiry in Language Studies*, 13(1), 20–45.

Hobsbawm, Eric J. (1983). Introduction: Inventing traditions. In Eric Hobsbawm and Terence Ranger (eds.), *The invention of tradition* (pp. 1–14). Cambridge: Cambridge University Press.

(1990). *Nations and nationalism since 1780: Programme, myth, reality*. Cambridge: Cambridge University Press.

Holquist, Michael. (2014). What would Bakhtin do? *Critical Multilingualism Studies*, 2(1), 6–19.

Hong Hyun-bo. (2007). 개화기 나랏글 제정과 "한글"의 발전 과정 연구 [Gae-hwa-gi na-rat-geul je-jeong-gwa "Han-geul"-ui bal-jeon gwa-jeong yeon-gu/On the exclusive use of "Hangeul" during the Enlightenment Period]. 한글 [*Han-geul/Korean Language*], 277, 217–243.

Hong Sunae. (2009). 근대계몽기 단군신화 담론의 서사적 재현 : 박은식을 중심으로 [Geun-dae-gye-mong-gi Dan-gun-sin-hwa dam-non-ui seo-sa-jeok jae-hyun: Bak Eun Sik-eul jung-sim-eu-ro/Narrative representation of discourses on Dangun mythology during the Modern-Enlightenment Period: The case of Park Eun-Sik]. 한민족문화연구 [*Han-min-jong-mun-hwa-yeon-gu/Journal of Korean Cultural Studies*], 28, 197–225.

Hossie, Thomas John, and Sherratt, Thomas N. (2014). Does defensive posture increase mimetic fidelity of caterpillars with eyespots to their putative snake models? *Current Zoology*, 60(1), 76–89.

Hossie, Thomas John, Sherratt, Thomas N., Janzen, Daniel H., and Hallwachs, Winnie. (2013). An eyespot that "blinks": An open and shut case of eye mimicry in *Eumorpha* caterpillars (Lepidoptera: Sphingidae). *Journal of Natural History*, 47(45–46), 2915–2926.

Huebner, Thomas. (2006). Bangkok's linguistic landscapes: Environmental print, codemixing and language change. *International Journal of Multilingualism*, 3(1), 31–51.

Hymes, Dell. (1985). Preface. In N. Wolfson and J. Manes (eds.), *Language of inequality* (pp. v–xi). Berlin: Walter de Gruyter.

Iedema, Rick. (2003). Multimodality, resemiotization: Extending the analysis of discourse as multi-semiotic practice. *Visual Communication*, 2(1), 29–57.

Im Chong-Myong. (2007). 脱식민지 시기(1945~1950 년) 남한의 국토 민족주의와 그 내재적 모순 [Tal-shing-min-ji si-gi(1945~1950nyeon) nam-han-ui guk-to min-jok-ju-ui-wa geu nae-jae-jeok mo-sun/The soil nationalisms and their contradictions in post-colonial South Korea (1945~1950)]. 역사학보 [*Yeok-sa-hak-bo/Korean Historical Review*], 193, 77–121.

Inoue, Miyako. (2004). What does language remember?: Indexical inversion and the naturalized history of Japanese women. *Journal of Linguistic Anthropology*, 14(1), 39–56.

Irvine, Judith, and Gal, Susan. (2000). Language ideology and linguistic differentiation. In Paul V. Kroskrity (ed.), *Regimes of language: Ideologies, polities, and identities* (pp. 35–84). Santa Fe, NM: School of American Research Press.

Jacquemet, Marco. (2005). Transidiomatic practices: Language and power in the age of globalization. *Language and Communication*, 25(3), 257–277.

Jameson, Frederic. (1998). *The cultural turn: Selected writings on the postmodern, 1983–1998*. London: Verso.

Jang Young-gil. (2008). 한글의 문자학적 우수성 [Han-geul-ui mun-ja-hak-jeok u-su-seong / On the Korean alphabet Hangeul]. 국제언어문학 [*Guk-jei-eon-eo-mun-hak / International Language and Literature*], 17, 79–99.

Janzen, Daniel H., Hallwachs, Winnie, and Burns, John M. (2010). A tropical horde of counterfeit predator eyes. *Proceedings of the National Academic of Sciences of the United States of America*, 107(26), 11659–11665.

Jaworski, Adam, and Thurlow, Crispin (eds.). (2010). *Semiotic landscapes: Language, image, space*. London: Continuum.

Jeffrey, Bob, and Troman, Geoff. (2004). Time for ethnography. *British Educational Research Journal*, 30(4), 535–548.

Jenks, Christopher J. (2017). *Race and ethnicity in English language teaching: Korea in focus*. Bristol: Multilingual Matters.

(2018). Meat, guns, and God: Expressions of nationalism in rural America. *Linguistic Landscape*, 4(1), 53–71.

Jenks, Christopher J., and Lee, Jerry Won (eds.). (2017). *Korean Englishes in transnational contexts*. Basingstoke: Palgrave Macmillan.

Jeon, Mihyon. (2010). Korean language and ethnicity in the United States: Views from within and across. *Modern Language Journal*, 94(1), 43–55.

Jeong Hui Chang. (2015). 외래어 순화의 내용과 앞으로의 방향 [Oe-rae-eo sun-hwa-ui nae-yong-gwa ap-eu-lo-ui bang-hyang/Lessons from the purification policy of the Korean language]. 한국어학 [*Han-guk-eo-hak / Korean Linguistics*], 67, 89–104.

Jo Hyeon Seol. (2006). 근대계몽기 단군 신화의 탈신화화와 재신화화 [Geun-dae-gye-mong-gi Dan-gun sin-hwa-ui tal-sin-hwa-hwa-wa jae-sin-hwa-hwa/Demythologization and remythologization of the Dangun mythology in the Modern Enlightenment Period]. 민족문학사연구 [*Min-jok-mun-hak-sa-yeon-gu / Studies in Korean Literary History*], 32, 10–32.

Joo, Rachael Miyung. (2012). *Transnational sport: Gender, media, and global Korea*. Durham, NC: Duke University Press.

Jørgensen, J. Normann. (2008). Polylingual languaging around and among children and adolescents. *International Journal of Multilingualism*, 5(3), 161–176.

Jørgensen, J. Normann, and Møller, J. S. (2014). Polylingualism and languaging. In Constant Leung and Brian V. Street (eds.), *The Routledge companion to English studies* (pp. 67–83). London: Routledge.

Jung Jae-hwan. (2012). 해방 후 우리말 도로 찾기 운동의 내용과 성과 [Hae-bang hu u-ri-mal do-ro chak-gi un-dong-ui nae-yong-gwa seong-gwa / Recovery campaign of mother tongue and its result after Korean liberation]. 한글 [*Han-geul / Korean Language*], 296, 151–196.

Jung Yong Wook. (2004). 19 세기 말 20 세기 초 외국문헌에 나타난 우리나라 국호 영문 표기 [19 sei-gi mal 20 sei-gi cho wei-guk-mun-heon-ei na-ta-nan u-ri-na-ra guk-ho yeong-mun-pyo-gi / References to the spelling of

Korea in late nineteenth and early twentieth century foreign literature]. 국제한국학연기구 [*Guk-jei-han-guk-hak-yeon-gi-gu/Journal of International Korean Studies*], *2*, 199–215.

Kaier, Jieun. (2014). *The history of Korean loanwords in Korean*. Munich: LINCOM.

Kang, Hyun-Sook. (2013). Korean American college students' language practices and identity positioning: "Not Korean, but not American." *Journal of Language, Identity & Education*, *12*(4), 248–261.

Kerr, William. (2019). The descent of nations: Social evolutionary theory, modernism and ethno-symbolism. *Nations and Nationalism*, *25*(1), 104–123.

Khan, Anum, Orr, Barry, and Joksimovic, Darko. (2019). Defining "flushability" for sewer use. Research report, Ryerson Urban Water, Ryerson University.

Khubchandani, Lachman M. (1997). *Revisualizing boundaries: A plurilingual ethos*. London: Sage.

Kim, Eun-Young Julia. (2012). Creative adoption: Trends in Anglicisms in Korea. *English Today*, *28*, 15–17.

Kim, Kyung Hyun, and Choe, Youngmin (eds.). (2014). *The Korean popular culture reader*. Durham, NC: Duke University Press.

Kim, Miso. (2017). The centripetal and centrifugal forces of Englishes in South Korea. In Christopher J. Jenks and Jerry Won Lee (eds.), *Korean Englishes in transnational contexts* (pp. 137–156). Basingstoke: Palgrave Macmillan.

Kim, Myung Mi. (1991). *Under flag*. Berkeley, CA: Kelsey St. Press.

Kim, Nadia. (2008). *Imperial citizens: Koreans and race from Seoul to LA*. Stanford, CA: Stanford University Press.

Kim, Nora Hui-Jung. (2012). Multiculturalism and the politics of belonging: The puzzle of multiculturalism in South Korea. *Citizenship Studies*, *16*(1), 103–117.

Kim, Richard S. (2011). *The quest for statehood: Korean immigrant nationalism and US sovereignty, 1905–1945*. Oxford: Oxford University Press.

Kim So Dam. (2017, April 9). " 왜 한국만 변기에 휴지 못넣나" 4 대 의문 추적 해보니 ["Wae han-guk-man byeon-gi-e hyu-ji mon-neon-na" 4dae ui-mun chu-jeok-hae-bo-ni/"Why is putting tissue in the toilet prohibited only in Korea?" Exploring four possibilities]. *Chosun Ilbo*. www.chosun.com/site/data/html_dir/2017/04/09/2017040900510.html

Kim Sun Chul. (2009). 국어 순화의 개념과 방향 설정에 대하여 [Guk-eo sun-hwa-ui gae-nyeom-gwa bang-hyang seol-jeong-e dae-ha-yeo/On the concept and new direction of Gugeo Sunhwa]. 사회언어학 [*Sa-hwe-eon-eo-hak/Sociolinguistic Journal of Korea*], *17*(2), 1–23.

Kim, Young Dae. (2020). *The pursuit of modernity: The evolution of Korean popular music in the age of globalization*. Unpublished doctoral dissertation, University of Washington.

Kim Yung-Myung. (2013). 한글 창제의 목적과 정치적 의미 [Han-geul chang-je-ui mok-jeok-gwa jeong-chi-jeok ui-mi / The purpose of the creation of Hangeul and its political meaning]. 한국동양정치사상사연구 [*Han-guk-dong-yang-jeong-chi-sa-sang-sa-yeon-gu/Review of Korean and Asian Political Thoughts*], *12*(1), 63–86.

Kotze, Chrismi-Rinda. (2010). The linguistic landscape of rural South Africa after 1994: A case study of Philippolis. Doctoral dissertation, University of the Free State.

Kozinets, Robert V. (1998). On netnography: Initial reflections on consumer research investigations of cyberculture. *Advances in Consumer Research*, *25*, 366–371.

Kramsch, Claire. (2018). Trans-spatial utopias. *Applied Linguistics*, *39*(1), 108–115.

Krompák, Edina, and Meyer, Stephan. (2018). Translanguaging and the negotiation of meaning: Multilingual signage in a Swiss linguistic landscape. In Gerardo Mazzaferro (ed.), *Translanguaging as everyday practice* (pp. 235–255). Cham, Switzerland: Springer.

Ku, Robert Ji-Song. (2014). *Dubious gastronomy: The cultural politics of eating Asian in the USA*. Honolulu: University of Hawai'i Press.

Kubota, Ryuko. (2016). The multi/plural turn, postcolonial theory, and neoliberal multiculturalism: Complicities and implications for applied linguistics. *Applied Linguistics*, *37*(4), 474–494.

Labov, William. (1972). *Language in the inner city: Studies in the Black English vernacular*. Philadelphia, PA: University of Pennsylvania Press.

Landry, Rodrigue, and Bourhis, Richard Y. (1997). Linguistic landscape and ethnolinguistic vitality: An empirical study. *Journal of Language and Social Psychology*, *16*(1), 23–49.

Lawrence, C. Bruce. (2012). The Korean English linguistic landscape. *World Englishes*, *31*(1), 70–92.

Lee, Chungjae, and Lee, Jerry Won. (2021). Show me the monolingualism: Korean hip-hop, translation, and the discourse of difference. *Inter-Asia Cultural Studies*, *22*(1), 1–15.

(2022). Translational nation: Politics and re-presentation at the Independence Hall of Korea. *positions: asia critique*, *30*(1), 85–110.

Lee, Claire Seungeun. (2017). Narratives of "mixed race" youth in South Korea: Racial order and in-betweenness. *Asian Ethnicity*, *18*(4), 522–542.

Lee, Erika. (2007). The "yellow peril" and Asian exclusion in the Americas. *Pacific Historical Review*, *76*(4), 537–562.

Lee, Eunjeong, and Alvarez, Sara P. (2020). World Englishes, translingualism, and racialization in the US college composition classroom. *World Englishes*, *39*(2), 263–274.

Lee, Jamie Shinhee. (2004). Linguistic hybridization in K-Pop: Discourse of self-assertion and resistance. *World Englishes*, *23*(3), 429–450.

(2006). Linguistic constructions of modernity: English mixing in Korean television commercials. *Language in Society*, *35*(1), 59–91.

(2014). English on Korean television. *World Englishes*, *33*(1), 33–49.

(2016). "Everywhere you go, you see English!": Elderly women's perspectives on globalization and English. *Critical Inquiry in Language Studies*, *31*(4), 319–350.

Lee, Jenny, and Rice, Charles. (2007). Welcome to America? International student perceptions of discrimination. *Higher Education*, *53*, 381–409.

Lee, Jerry Won. (2014). Transnational linguistic landscapes and the transgression of metadiscursive regimes of language. *Critical Inquiry in Language Studies*, *11*(1), 50–74.

(2017). Semioscapes, unbanality, and the reinvention of nationness: Global Korea as nation-space. *Verge: Studies in Global Asias*, *3*(1), 107–136.

(2018). *The politics of translingualism: After Englishes*. London: Routledge.

(2019). Translingualism as resistance against what and for whom? In Tyler Andrew Barrett and Sender Dovchin (eds.), *Critical inquiries in the sociolinguistics of globalization* (pp. 102–118). Bristol: Multilingual Matters.

Lee, Jerry Won, and Canagarajah, Suresh. (2021). Translingualism and world Englishes. In Theresa Heyd and Britta Schneider (eds.), *Bloomsbury world Englishes. Vol. 1: Paradigms* (pp. 99–112). London: Bloomsbury.

Lee, Jerry Won, and Lou, Jackie Jia. (2019). The ordinary semiotic landscape of an unordinary place: Spatiotemporal disjunctures in Incheon's Chinatown. *International Journal of Multilingualism*, *16*(2), 187–203.

Lee, Jung Woo. (2020). A thin line between a sport mega-event and a mega-construction project: The 2018 Winter Olympic Games in Pyeongchang and its event-led development. *Managing Sport and Leisure*, *26*(5), 395–412.

Lee, Mary. (2008). Mixed race peoples in the Korean national imaginary and family. *Korean Studies*, *32*, 65–71.

Lee, Mun Woo. (2016). "Gangnam style" English ideologies: Neoliberalism, class and the parents of early study-abroad students. *International Journal of Bilingual Education and Bilingualism*, *19*(1), 35–50.

Lee Myung Bak. (2010, August 15). Marching together toward a greater Republic of Korea (Address by President Lee Myung Bak on the 65th anniversary of national liberation). Address at Gyeongbokgung Palace, Seoul, Republic of Korea.

Lee Sang-hyeok. (2008). 훈민정음과 한글의 언어문화사적 접근 [Hun-min-jeong-eum-gwa han-geul-ui eon-eo-mun-hwa-sa-jeok jeop-geun/An approach to Hunminjeongeum and Hangeul through a cultural history of language]. 한국어학 [*Han-guk-eo-hak/Korean Linguistics*], *41*, 61–81.

Lee Sang Tae. (2009). 고지도가 증명하는 독도의 영유권 [Go-ji-do-ga jeung-myeong-ha-neun Dok-do-ui yeong-yu-gwan/Territorial dispute over

Dokdo as verified through old maps. 한국지도학회지 [*Han-guk-ji-do-hak -hoe-ji* / *Journal of the Korean Cartographic Association*], 9(2), 33–58.

Lee Sung In. (2017). 공중화장실 휴지통, 이 헤어질 시간 [Gong-jung-hwa-jang-shil hyu-ji-tong, i-jen he-eo-jil si-gan/It's about time to say goodbye to toilet-adjacent trash bins]. *News Way.* http://news .newsway.co.kr/news/view?tp=1&ud=2017051215324941416

Lefebvre, Henri. (1991). *The production of space* (trans. Donald Nicholson-Smith). Oxford: Blackwell Publishing. (Original work published 1974.)

Lemrow, Erin Moira. (2016). Creolization and the new cosmopolitanism: Examining twenty-first-century student identities and literacy practices for transcultural understanding. *Journal of Multilingual and Multicultural Development*, 38(5), 1–15.

Lepawsky, Joshua. (2008). A museum, the city, and a nation. *Cultural Geographies*, 15, 119–142.

Li, Tian. (2019). "Bang bang bang" – Nonsense or an alternative language?: The lingualscape in the Chinese remake of *I Am a Singer. China Perspectives*, 3, 37–45.

Li, Wei. (2011). Moment analysis and translanguaging space: Discursive construction of identities by multilingual Chinese youth in Britain. *Journal of Pragmatics*, 43(5), 1222–1235.

(2018). Translanguaging as a practical theory of language. *Applied Linguistics*, 39(1), 9–30.

Li, Wei, and Zhu Hua. (2013). Translanguaging identities and ideologies: Creating transnational space through flexible multilingual practices amongst Chinese university students in the UK. *Applied Linguistics*, 34(5), 516–535.

(2019). Tranßcripting: Playful subversion with Chinese characters. *International Journal of Multilingualism*, 16(2), 145–161.

Lie, John. (1998). *Han unbound: The political economy of South Korea*. Stanford, CA: Stanford University Press.

(2008). *Zainichi: Diasporic nationalism and postcolonial identity*. Berkeley, CA: University of California Press.

(2012). What is the K in K-pop?: South Korean popular music, the culture industry, and national identity. *Korea Observer*, 43(3), 339–363.

Lim, Timothy. (2009). Who is Korean? Migration, immigration, and the challenge of multiculturalism in homogeneous societies. *Asia-Pacific Journal*, 7(30), 1–21.

(2010). Rethinking belongingness in Korea: Transnational migration, "migrant marriages" and the politics of multiculturalism. *Pacific Affairs*, 83(1), 51–71.

Lindemann, Stephanie, and Moran, Katherine. (2017). The role of descriptor "broken English" in ideologies about nonnative speech. *Language in Society*, 46(5), 649–669.

Lippi-Green, Rosina. (2012). *English with an accent: Language, ideology and discrimination in the United States* (2nd ed.). London: Routledge.

Lo, Adrienne, and Kim, Jenna. (2011). Manufacturing citizenship: Metapragmatic framings of language competencies in media images of mixed race men in South Korea. *Discourse & Society, 22*(4), 440–457.

Lorente, Beatriz, and Tupas, Ruanni. (2013). Emancipatory hybridity: Selling English in an unequal world. In Rani Rubdy and Lubna Alsagoff (eds.), *The global–local interface and hybridity: Exploring language and identity* (pp. 66–82). Bristol: Multilingual Matters.

Lou, Jackie Jia. (2016). *The linguistic landscape of Chinatown: A sociolinguistic ethnography*. Clevedon: Multilingual Matters.

Lu, Song, Li, Guanghui, and Xu, Ming. (2020). The linguistic landscape in rural destinations: A case study of Hongcun Village in China. *Tourism Management, 77*, 104005.

Magdalinski, Tara, and Nauright, John. (2004). Commercialisation of the modern Olympics. In Trevor Slack (ed.), *The commercialisation of sport* (pp. 185–205). London: Routledge.

Maher, John C. (2005). Metroethnicity, language, and the principle of cool. *International Journal of the Sociology of Language, 175/176*, 83–102.

(2010). Metroethnicities and metrolanguages. In Nicholas Coupland (ed.), *The handbook of language and globalization* (pp. 575–591). Oxford: Wiley-Blackwell.

Makoni, Sinfree. (1998). African languages as European scripts: The shaping of communal memory. In Sarah Nuttall and Carli Coetzee (eds.), *Negotiating the past: The making of memory in South Africa* (pp. 242–248). Oxford: Oxford University Press.

(2002). From misinvention to disinvention: An approach to multilingualism. In Sinfree Makoni, Geneva Smitherman, Arnetha F. Ball, and Arthur K. Spears (eds.), *Black linguistics: Language, society, and politics in Africa and the Americas* (pp. 132–153). London: Routledge.

Makoni, Sinfree, and Pennycook, Alastair. (2005). Disinventing and (re) constituting languages. *Critical Inquiry in Language Studies, 2*(3), 137–156.

Malinowski, David. (2008). Authorship in the linguistic landscape: A multimodal-performative view. In Elana Shohamy and Durk Gorter (eds.), *Linguistic landscape: Expanding the scenery* (pp. 107–125). London: Routledge.

Masahiro, Miyoshi. (2014). 竹島問題と クリティカル　デート [Takeshima mondai to kuritikaru deto/The critical date of the Takeshima dispute]. 島嶼研究ジャーナル [Tosho Kenkyu Journal/Island Research Journal], 3(2), 28–49.

Massey, Doreen. (1995). *Spatial divisions of labour : Social structures and the geography of production* (2nd ed.). Basingstoke: Macmillan Press.

Matsuda, Paul K. (2006). The myth of linguistic homogeneity in US college composition. *College English, 68*(6), 637–651.

Mazak, Catherine M., and Carroll, Kevin S (eds.). (2017). *Translanguaging in higher education: Beyond monolingual ideologies*. Bristol: Multilingual Matters.

Mbembe, Achille. (2003). Necropolitics. *Public Culture*, *15*(1), 11–40.

MBN. (2016, July 7). 독립기념관 관람하면 "보너스휴가"... 하루 평균 군인 관람객 100 명 안팎 [Dok-nip-gi-nyeom-gwan gwan-nam-ha-myeon "bo-neo-seu-hyu-ga"... ha-ru pyeong-gyun gun-in gwan-nam-gaek 100-myeong-an-pak/Bonus vacation for attending the Independence Hall ... For the first 100 military attendees). *MBN News*. http://mbn.mk.co.kr/pages/news/newsView.php?category=mbn00009&news_seq_no=2941026.

Medzini, Arnon. (2017). The role of geographic maps in territorial disputes between Japan and Korea. *European Journal of Geography*, *8*, 44–60.

Mendoza-Denton, Norma. (2008). *Homegirls: Language and cultural practice among Latina youth gangs*. Oxford: Blackwell Publishing.

Ministry of Foreign Affairs (MOFA). (2013). Why Dokdo is Korean territory. https://dokdo.mofa.go.kr/eng/dokdo/reason.jsp

(2019). Overseas Koreans definition and status. www.mofa.go.kr/www/wpge/m_21509/contents.do

Møller, Janus Spindler. (2008). Polylingual performance among Turkish-Danes in late-modern Copenhagen. *International Journal of Multilingualism*, *5*(3), 217–236.

Moriarty, Máiréad. (2019). Regimes of voice and visibility in the refugees-cape: A semiotic landscape approach. *Linguistic Landscape*, *5*(2), 142–159.

Mufti, Aamir. (2018). *Forget English!: Orientalisms and world literatures*. Cambridge, MA: Harvard University Press.

Mukerji, Chandra. (2012). Space and political pedagogy at the Gardens of Versailles. *Public Culture*, *24*(3), 509–534.

Nakassis, Constantine. (2016). Scaling red and the horror of trademark. In E. Summerson Carr and Michael Lempert (eds.), *Scale: Discourse and the dimensions of social life* (pp. 159–184). Berkeley, CA: University of California Press.

Ndhlovu, Finex. (2018). Omphile and his soccer ball: Colonialism, methodology, translanguaging research. *Multilingual Margins*, *5*(2), 2–19.

Ngũgĩ wa Thiong'o. (2012). *Globalectics: Theory and the politics of knowing*. New York: Columbia University Press.

Nilsson, Leonard Jägerskiöld. (2018). *World football club crests: The design, meaning and symbolism of world football's most famous club badges*. London: Bloomsbury.

Nora, Pierre. (1989). Between memory and history: Les lieux de mémoire (trans. Marc Roudebush). *Representations*, *26*, 7–24. (Original work published 1984.)

Oh Gangwon. 2014. 고려~조선시대 단군 전승의 변형과 확대, 그리고 역사화 과정 [Go-ryeo~Jo-seon-si-dae Dan-gun jeon-seung-ui byeon-hyeon-gwa hawk-dae, geu-ri-go yeok-sa-hwa gwa-jeong/The transformation, expansion, and historicization process of the Dangun Myth during the Goryeo and Joseon periods]. 한국사학보 [*Han-guk-sa-hak-bo/Journal for the Study of Korean History*], 56, 33–64.

Olson, Kevin. (2016). *Imagined sovereignties: The power of the people and other myths of the modern age*. Cambridge: Cambridge University Press.

Ong, Aihwa. (1999). *Flexible citizenship: The cultural logics of transnationality*. Durham, NC: Duke University Press.

Paek, Seunghan. (2016). Asian city as affective space: Commercial signs and mood in the paintings of Manoel Pillard. *Verge: Studies in Global Asias*, 2(1), 222–249.

Paik, Nak-Chung. (1996). Habermas on national unification in Germany and Korea. *New Left Review*, 219, 14–21.

Paris, Django, and Alim, H. Samy (eds.). (2017). *Culturally sustaining pedagogies: Teaching and learning for justice in a changing world*. New York: Teachers College Press.

Park Jae-young. (2013). 다문화적 관점에서 본 한글과 동아시아문자와의 관련성 [Da-mun-hwa-jeok gwan-jeom-e-seo bon han-geul-gwa dong-a-si-mun-wa-ui gwan-ryeon-seong/Hangeul and the East Asian relations from a multicultural perspective. 경주사학 [*Kyung-ju-sa-hak/Kyungju History*], 37, 101–127.

Park, Jonghyun. (2016). Rap as Korean rhyme: Local enregisterment of the foreign. *Journal of Linguistic Anthropology*, 26(3), 278–293.

Park, Joseph Sung-Yul. (2009). *The local construction of a global language: Ideologies of English in South Korea*. Berlin: Walter de Gruyter.

Park, Kyeyoung, and Kim, Jessica. (2008). The contested nexus of Los Angeles Koreatown: Capital restructuring, gentrification, and displacement. *Amerasia Journal*, 34(3), 126–150.

Park, Kyung-Ja. (2009). Characteristics of Korea English as a glocalized variety. In Kumiko Murata and Jennifer Jenkins (eds.), *Global Englishes in Asian contexts* (pp. 94–107). Basingstoke: Palgrave Macmillan.

Park, So Jin, and Abelmann, Nancy. (2004). Class and cosmopolitan striving: Mothers' management of English education in South Korea. *Anthropological Quarterly*, 77(4), 645–672.

Pennycook, Alastair. (2008). English as a language always in translation. *European Journal of English Studies*, 12(1), 33–47.

(2010a). *Language as a local practice*. London: Routledge.

(2010b). Spatial narrations: Graffscapes and city souls. In Adam Jaworski and Crispin Thurlow (eds.), *Semiotic landscapes: Language, image, space* (pp. 137–150). London: Continuum.

(2012). *Language and mobility: Unexpected places*. Clevedon: Multilingual Matters.

(2017). Translanguaging and semiotic assemblages. *International Journal of Multilingualism*, 14(3), 269–282.

(2018). *Posthumanist applied linguistics*. London: Routledge.

(2019). From translanguaging to translingual activism. In Donaldo Macedo (ed.), *Decolonizing foreign language education: The mis-teaching of English and other colonial languages* (pp. 169–185). London: Routledge.

(2020). Translingual entanglements of English. *World Englishes*, *39*(2), 222–235.

Pennycook, Alastair, and Otsuji, Emi. (2015a). Making scents of the landscape. *Linguistic Landscape*, *1*(3), 191–212.

(2015b). *Metrolingualism: Language in the city*. London: Routledge.

(2017). Fish, phone cards and semiotic assemblages in two Bangladeshi shops in Sydney and Tokyo. *Social Semiotics*, *27*(4), 434–450.

(2019). Mundane metrolingualism. *International Journal of Multilingualism*, *16*(2), 175–186.

Phillips, Ruth B., and Phillips, Mark S. (2009). Contesting time, place, and nation in the First Peoples' Hall of the Canadian Museum of Civilization. In Daniel J. Walkowitz and Lisa Maya Knauer (eds.), *Contested histories in public space: Memory, race, and nation* (pp. 49–70). Durham, NC: Duke University Press.

Piller, Ingrid. (2016). *Linguistic diversity and social justice: An introduction to applied sociolinguistics*. Oxford: Oxford University Press.

Piller, Ingrid, and Cho, Jinhyun. (2013). Neoliberalism as language policy. *Language in Society*, *42*(1), 23–44.

Pratt, Mary Louise. (1987). Linguistic utopias. In Nigel Fabb, Derek Altridge, Alan Durant, and Colin MacCabe (eds.), *The linguistics of writing: Arguments between language and literature* (pp. 48–66). Manchester: Manchester University Press.

(1991). Arts of the contact zone. *Profession*, 33–40.

(2012). "If English was good enough for Jesus ..." Monolinguismo y mala fe. *Critical Multilingualism Studies*, *1*(1), 12–30.

Preston, Dennis. (1993). The uses of folk linguistics. *International Journal of Applied Linguistics*, *3*(2), 181–259.

(2011). Methods in (applied) folk linguistics: Getting into the minds of the folk. *AILA Review*, *24*(1), 15–39.

Queen, Robin. (2004). "Du hast jar keene Ahnung": African American English dubbed into German. *Journal of Sociolinguistics*, *8*(4), 515–537.

Ra Ye Jin. (2017, October 24). 화장실 휴지, 이제 변기에 양보하세요 [Hwa-jang-shil hyu-ji, i-je byeon-gi-e yang-bo-ha-se-yo/Toilet paper, let it go in the toilet now]. *JoongAng Ilbo*. https://news.joins.com/article/22041947

Radcliffe, Shawn. (2020, May 14). Here's why COVID-19 is much worse than the flu. *Healthline*. www.healthline.com/health-news/why-covid-19-isnt-the-flu

Radhakrishnan, R. (1996). *Diasporic mediations: Between home and location*. Minneapolis, MN: University of Minnesota Press.

Radtke, Oliver Lutz. (2007). *Chinglish: Found in translation*. Layton, UT: Gibbs Smith.

Renan, Ernest. (1990) What is a nation? (trans. Martin Thom). In Homi K. Bhabha (ed.), *Nation and narration* (pp. 8–22). London: Routledge. (Original work published 1882.)

Rhys-Taylor, Alex. (2013). The essences of multiculture: A sensory exploration of an inner-city street market. *Identities*, *20*(4), 393–406.

Rosch, Eleanor H. (1973). Natural categories. *Cognitive Psychology*, *4*, 328–350.

Rubdy, Rani, and Alsagoff, Lubna. (2014). The cultural dynamics of globalization: Problematizing hybridity. In Rani Rubdy and Lubna Alsagoff (eds.), *The global–local interface and hybridity* (pp. 1–16). Bristol: Multilingual Matters.

Rüdiger, Sofia. (2017). Spoken English in Korea: An expanding circle English revisited. In Christopher J. Jenks and Jerry Won Lee (eds.), *Korean Englishes in transnational contexts* (pp. 75–92). Basingstoke: Palgrave Macmillan.

(2019). *Morpho-syntactic patterns in spoken Korean English*. Amsterdam: John Benjamins.

(2021). Like in Korean English speech. *World Englishes*, *40*(4), 548–561.

Rymes, Betsy. (2020). *How we talk about language: Exploring citizen sociolinguistics*. Cambridge: Cambridge University Press.

Said, Edward. (1979). *Orientalism*. New York: Vintage Books.

Sakai, Naoki. (1997). *Translation and subjectivity: On "Japan" and cultural nationalism*. Minneapolis, MN: University of Minnesota Press.

Sampson, Geoffrey. (1985). *Writing systems: A linguistic introduction*. Palo Alto, CA: Stanford University Press.

Scollon, Ron, and Scollon, Suzie Wong. (2003). *Discourses in place: Language in the material world*. London: Routledge.

Seol, Dong-Hoon. (2012). The citizenship of foreign workers in South Korea. *Citizenship Studies*, *16*(1), 119–133.

Sharma, Bal Krishna. (2019). The scarf, language, and other semiotic assemblages in the formation of a new Chinatown. *Applied Linguistics Review*, *12*(1), 65–91.

Shifman, Limor. (2014). The cultural logic of photo-based meme genres. *Journal of Visual Culture*, *13*(3), 340–358.

Shin, Gi-Wook. (2006). *Ethnic nationalism in Korea: Genealogy, politics, and legacy*. Stanford, CA: Stanford University Press.

Shin, NaRi, Park, DooJae, and Peachey, Jon Welty. (2020). Taegeuk warriors with blue eyes: A media discourse analysis of the South Korean Men's Olympic Ice Hockey Team and its naturalized athletes. *Communication & Sport*. Advance online publication.

Shohamy, Elana, Ben-Rafael, Eliezer, and Barni, Monica (eds.). (2010). *Linguistic landscape in the city*. Bristol: Multilingual Matters.

Silva, Daniel N. (2020). Enregistering the nation: Bolsonaro's populist branding of Brazil. In Irene Tjhodoropoulou and Johanna Tovar (eds.), *Research companion to language and country branding* (pp. 37–56). London: Routledge.

Silverstein, Michael. (1993). Metapragmatic discourse and metapragmatic function. In John A. Lucy (ed.), *Reflexive language: Reported speech and metapragmatics* (pp. 33–57). Cambridge: Cambridge University Press.

(1996). Indexical order and the dialectics of sociolinguistic life. *SALSA*, 3, 266–295.

(2003). Indexical order and the dialectics of sociolinguistic life. *Language & Communication*, 23, 193–229.

(2013). Discourse and the no-thing-ness of culture. *Signs and Society*, 1(2), 327–366.

Śliwa, Martyna, and Riach, Kathleen. (2012). Making scents of the transition: Smellscapes and the everyday in "old" and "new" urban Poland. *Urban Studies*, 49(1), 23–41.

Slotkin, Jason. (2017, September 12). Behold the fatberg: London's 130-ton "rock-solid" sewer blockage. *NPR*. www.npr.org/sections/thetwo-way /2017/09/12/550465000/behold-the-fatberg-london-s-130-ton-rock-solid-sewer-blockage

Smith, Anthony D. (1986). *The ethnic origins of nations*. Oxford: Blackwell Publishing.

(1991). *National identity*. Reno: University of Nevada Press.

(1995). *Nations and nationalism in a global era*. Cambridge: Polity Press.

(1999). *Myths and memories of the nation*. Oxford: Oxford University Press.

(2008). *The cultural foundations of nations: Hierarchy, covenant, and republic*. Oxford: Blackwell Publishing.

Son Hwan and Choi Ji-Man. (2009). 광복이후 한국축구대표팀 유니폼의 변천사 [Kwang-bok-i-hu han-guk-chuk-ku-dae-pyo-tim yu-ni-pom-ui byeon-cheon-sa/The changes of Korean National Football Team's uniform after independence]. 한국체육사학회지 [*Han-guk-chei-sa-hak-hui-ji/Korean Journal of History for Physical Education, Sport and Dance*], 14(1), 135–144.

Song, Rayoung. (2019). Invisible and ubiquitous: Translinguistic practices in metapragmatic discussions in an online English learning community. In Jerry Won Lee and Sender Dovchin (eds.), *Translinguistics: Negotiating innovation and ordinariness* (pp. 217–227). London: Routledge.

Spivak, Gayatri Chakravorty. (1999). *A critique of postcolonial reason : Toward a history of the vanishing present*. Cambridge, MA: Harvard University Press.

(2010). *Nationalism and the imagination*. New Delhi: Seagull Books.

Subtirelu, Nicholas Close. (2013). "English ... it's part of our blood": Ideologies of language and nation in United States Congressional discourse. *Journal of Sociolinguistics*, 17(1), 37–65.

Sugiharto, Setiono. (2015). The multilingual turn in applied linguistics? A perspective from the periphery. *International Journal of Applied Linguistics*, 25(3), 414–421.

Suh, Serk-Bae. (2013). *Treacherous translation: Culture, nationalism, and colonialism in Korea and Japan from the 1910s to the 1960s*. Berkeley, CA: University of California Press.

Sultana, Shaila, Dovchin, Sender, and Pennycook, Alastair. (2015). Transglossic language practices of young adults in Bangladesh and Mongolia. *International Journal of Multilingualism*, 12(1), 93–108.

Svendson, Bente Ailin. (2018). The dynamics of citizen sociolinguistics. *Journal of Sociolinguistics*, 22(2), 137–160.

Szabo, Liz. (2020, January 24). Something far deadlier than the Wuhan coronavirus lurks near you, right here in America. *USA Today*. www .usatoday.com/story/news/health/2020/01/24/coronavirus-versus-flu-influenza-deadlier-than-wuhan-china-disease/4564133002/

Tchen, John Kuo, and Yeats, Dylan (eds.). (2014). *Yellow peril! An archive of Anti-Asian fear*. London: Verso.

Thurlow, Crispin, and Aiello, Georgia. (2007). National pride, global capital: A social semiotic analysis of transnational visual branding in the airline industry. *Visual Communication*, 6(3), 305–344.

Tuan, Yi-Fu. (1977). *Space and place: The perspective of experience*. Minneapolis, MN: University of Minnesota Press.

Tupas, Ruanni (ed.). (2015). *Unequal Englishes: The politics of Englishes today*. Basingstoke: Palgrave Macmillan.

    (2020). Decentering language: Displacing English from the study of Englishes. *Critical Inquiry in Language Studies*, 17(3), 228–245.

Van Dyke, Jon M. (2007). Legal issues related to sovereignty over Dokdo and its maritime boundary. *Ocean Development and International Law*, 38 (1–2), 157–224.

Van Leeuwen, Theo. (2005). *Introducing social semiotics*. London: Routledge.

Vasconcelos Barboza, Rafael de, and Borba, Rodrigo. (2018). Linguistic landscapes as pornoheterotopias: (De)regulating gender and sexuality in the public toilet. *Linguistic Landscape*, 4(3), 257–277.

Venuti, Lawrence. (2008). *The translator's invisibility* (2nd ed.). London: Routledge.

Vergano, Dan. (2020, January 28). Don't worry about the coronavirus. Worry about the flu. *BuzzFeed News*. www.buzzfeednews.com/article/ danvergano/coronavirus-cases-deaths-flu

Vertovec, Steven. (2007). Super-diversity and its implications. *Ethnic and Racial Studies*, 30(6), 1024–1054.

Wainwright, Joel, and Bryan, Joe. Cartography, territory, property: Postcolonial reflections on indigenous counter-mapping in Nicaragua and Belize. *Cultural Geographies*, 16, 153–178.

Watson, Iain. (2010). Multiculturalism in South Korea: A critical assessment. *Journal of Contemporary Asia*, 40(2), 337–346.

Wierzbicka, Anna. (1992). *Semantics, culture, and cognition: Universal human concepts in culture-specific configurations*. Oxford: Oxford University Press.

Willsher, Kim. (2014, August 12). Korea's Paris Baguette chain expands to … Paris. *Guardian*. www.theguardian.com/world/2014/aug/12/korea-paris-baguette-chain-expands-french-bakery

Wittgenstein, Ludwig. (1953). *Philosophical investigations* (trans. G. E. M. Anscombe). New York: Pearson. (Original work published 1953.)

Yao, Xiaofang. (2021). Metrolingualism in online linguistic landscapes. *International Journal of Multilingualism*. Advance online publication.

Yoo Kyung Sun. (2018, March 30). "휴지통 없는 화장실"이 변기막힘 주범?… 답은 "시민의식" ["Hyu-ji-tong eob-neun hwa-jang-sil"-i byeon-gi-mak-him ju-beom?… dab-eun "si-min-ui-sik"/"A bathroom that does not have a trash bin" Who's guilty of clogging this toilet? The answer is "global citizens"]. *News 1 Korea*. www.news1.kr/articles/?3275468

You, Xiaoye (2016). *Cosmopolitan English and transliteracy*. Carbondale, IL: Southern Illinois University Press.

Zabrodskaja, Anastassia, and Milani, Tommaso M. (2014). Signs in context: Multilingual and multimodal texts in semiotic space. *International Journal of the Sociology of Language*, *228*, 1–6.

Zhang, Hong, and Chan, Brian Hok-Shing. (2015). Translanguaging in multimodal Macao posters: Flexible versus separate multilingualism. *International Journal of Bilingualism*, *21*(1), 34–56.

Zhou, Xiaojing. (2006). *The ethics and poetics of alterity in Asian American poetry*. Iowa City, IA: University of Iowa Press.

LEGAL CASES

Sugawara v. *Pepsico*, E.D. Calif. No. 08–01335, 2009.

Index